KNOXVILLE, TENNESSEE

by

Andrew Morrison

1891

THE ENGELHARDT SERIES: AMERICAN CITIES VOLUME 25

A reproduction of a book originally
published in 1891, from a copy owned
and generously provided by Robert McGinnis.

This version by Charles A. Reeves, Jr.
November, 2002

©2002
CHARLES A. REEVES, JR.

Charles A. Reeves, Jr.
Technical Illustration & Publishing
Specializing in Cartography and Genealogy

10812 Dineen Drive　　　　　　(865) 966-5768
Knoxville, Tennessee 37934-1809
e-mail: reevesca@tds.net
Home Page: http://www.ReevesMaps.com

ISBN 978-0-9800984-1-9

How this booklet was produced: Robert McGinnis' original copy was scanned at 300 dpi and the images edited in Adobe Photoshop to remove artifacts. The pages were then created in Adobe Illustrator and saved as PDF for printing. The original was approximately 6" wide by 8-1/2" tall. This version was enlarged to fill an 8-1/2" x 11" page.

Table of Contents

Knoxville Briefly Described   3

The Valley of East Tennessee   3
A Region of Matchless Resources   3
The Panorama from Knoxville   6
Progress Invades Even Cloudland   6
Speed the Windlass, Speed the Plow   7
A Wilder Prospect Unfolded   8
Transportation Facilities   9
Knoxville as a Center of Trade   9
Signs of the City's Progress   11
A Center Also of Institutions   12
Social Considerations   12

Three Knoxvilles; In Reality However, But One   14

Municipal Characteristics   14
The Mayor and the Council   14
Finances of Knoxville Proper   15
Public Health, Fire Service, Police   15
Public Improvements   17
Old Knoxvilles' Minor Sisters   18
Street Lights, Rapid Transit, Resorts   19
Hotels of the City   22
Education and Aesthetics   24
The Press of Knoxville   29
Letters, Art, Song and Drama   29

Real Estate and Betterments   31

Prosperous Conditions   31
Architectural Improvements   31
Enhanced Values and Prices   32
Rents and other Considerations   32
The Subject in General   33
Country Lands   33
Leading Dealers in Real Estate   33
Lawyers of Knoxville   40
The Builders' Trade   43
Architects and Builders   44

Knoxville The Trade Center - Its Railroad, Banking, Distinctive and Jobbing Business and Manufacturers   49

The Favor Shown to Railroads   49
The East Tennessee, Virginia & Georgia   50
The Marietta & North Georgia Railway   52
The Knoxville, Cumberland Gap and Louisville Railroad   54
Railroads Proposed   56
The Tennessee River   56
Miscellaneous Concerns   56

Knoxville as a Financial Center   58

Notes on the Knoxville Banks   58
Underwriting Business of Knoxville   59
Insurance and Kindred Business Men   60

Characteristic Trade   65

The Marble Men of Knoxville   65
Knoxville's Coal Trade   70
Leading Coal Concern   71
Lumber and Building Material   75
Representative Concerns   75

Knoxville's Jobbing Trade   77

Commercial Enterprise   77
Ten Years' Gain in Trade   77
Sales in Various Lines   77
Some Local Estimates   77
Credit of the Community   78
Leading Grocery Houses Described   78
Wholesale Liquor Dealers   82
Brokerage and Commissions   82
Knoxville's Drug Houses   83
Wholesale Hardware   84
Allied Lines   87
Carriages, Harness, Iron Companies   90
Stables; Horse Stock   90
Dry Goods, Notions, Millinery, etc.   91

Knoxville as a Manufacturing Place   100

Some Large Concerns   100
Special Industries of the City   100
The Cotton and Woolen Mills   100
Estimated Totals   100
Manufacturing Opportunities   101
A Digression as to Leather   101
Labor, Transportation, etc.   101
Coal and Incidentals   101
Iron Works of the City   102

State of Tennessee   115

Other Characteristics   115
Past and Present Contrasted   115
The Change Through War   116
The State Re-Established   116
The Story of Tennessee   117
An Array Simply of Fact   117
Tennessee Farm Products   118
Mineral Wealth of the State   119
Other Manufacurers   119
Various Matters   120
Resources of East Tennessee   120
Coal in the Valley   121
Metaliferous Wealth   122
Tennessee Marble   123
The Timber Supply   123
The County of Knox   124

General Index   125-127

Index, Tennessee Topics   128

Illustrations

Residence of Harvey Abrams, Building Contractor	47
Ante-Bellum Residence Type, Tennessee	123
Bayless, King & Cruze, Stoves, Tinware, etc.	112
Residence of Ex Gov. Blount	6
Residence of the Late Parson Brownlow	6
J. P. Carpenter's Coal and Brick Yards, Knoxville	72
Offices of the Central Guarantee Life Association, Knoxville	62
Coal Chute of the Coal Creek Coal Company, at Coal Creek, Anderson County, Tenn.	72
Confederate Monument, Knoxville Made by Geo. W. Callahan & Bros.	69
Court House of Knox County, Knoxville - By Courtesy of the Stephenson & Getaz Manufacturing Co., of Knoxville	18
Offices of the Covenant Building and Loan Association	35
Residence of J. D. Cowan, of Cowan, M'Clung & Co. Wholesale Dry Goods	20
Cullen & Newman, Wholesale Crockery	95
Daniel & Bostwick, Dry Goods	92
Davis Sewing Machine Works, at Dayton, Ohio J. E. Martin, Agent at Knoxville	99
Deaf & Dumb Asylum	7
Dempster's Machine Shop	104
Entrance to the Mines of the East Tennessee Coal Company, Near Jellico, Tenn.	71
Works of the East Tennessee Stone and Marble Company	70
A Mountain Grade - On the Line of the East Tennessee, Virginia & Georgia Railroad	52
Tennessee Scenery - On the Line of the East Tennessee, Virginia & Georgia Railway	53
Scenery, East Tennessee, Virginia & Georgia Railroad The Sphinx, Emory River	48
Station and General Offices of the East Tennessee, Virginia & Georgia Railroad, Knoxville	51
Residence of Mrs. D.J. Eggleston Geo. F. Barber & Co., Architects.	39
First Baptist Church, Knoxville - Bauman Bros., Architects	44
Fountain Head Hotel, Suburb of Knoxville	21
Interior of the Knoxville Central Station, East Tennessee Telephone Company	19
Galyon & Selden Co.'s Mill and Lumber Yard	47
Gay Street, Looking West	11
Girls' High School - Bauman Bros., Architects	13
Auction Sale of Marble by T.S. Godfrey	66
S. W. Graves' Carpet and Furniture House	99
The Greer Machinery Company's Warehouse	85
"Greystone," The Residence of E. C. Camp, of the Coal Creek Coal Co. Cost $125,000.	8
"The Hermitage," Near Nashville, Tenn. - Showing Jackson's original cabin home, and on the right his tomb.	118
Hooker, Littlefield & Steere, Manufacturing Confectioners	108
Scenery of the Holston and French Broad	8
The Hotel Knox	23
Hotel Vendome	22
Insane Asylum	7
Statue of Jackson - Capitol Grounds, Nashville, Tenn.	120
Thomas Kane & Co.'s Factory, at Chicago Beech Bros. & Co. Agents, Knoxville	88
Peter Kern's Wholesale Confectionery	108
Knoxville in Gala Attire - Reunion of the Blue and Gray, October 7th, 1889	41
Knoxville Brewery	110
Knoxville Business College	28
Knoxville Car Wheel Works	103
Knoxville College (Colored)	25
Offices of the Knoxville Fire Insurance Company	61
Knoxville Savings Bank	17
The Knoxville Stock Yards	81
Knoxville Supply Co.'s Warehouse and Yards	89
W. B. Lockett & Co, Wholesale Grocers	80
Gen. Longstreet's Headquarters during the Siege of Knoxville, Nov. 1863	9
Market Square, East Side	10
Interior and Exterior of the McArthur Music House	97
Residence of F. E. McArthur, of the McArthur Music House Geo. F. Barber & Co., Architects	45
McCrary & Branson, Photographers' Supplies	98
M'Callum Block, Occupied in part by Young's College of Shorthand	29
M'Ghee Public Library Building	17
Marble Works of W.H. Evans & Son	68
First Train Load of Marble Shipped from Knoxville - John M. Ross, Shipper	67
Mester, Newcomer & Paulus, Dry Goods House	92
Moccasin Bend, Tennessee River, from Lookout Mountain, Near Chattanooga	116
National Cemetery, Knoxville, Tenn.	121
The National Garmet Cutter Company's Establishment	113
National Manufacturing Company's Offices	114
H. O. Nelsen's Iron Fence Factory	105
S. B. Newman & Co.'s Printing House	112
Palace Hotel	23
Home and Tomb of President Polk, Nashville, Tenn.	119
Post Office and Government Building	12
Powers, Little & Co., Wholesale Clothing	94
Residence of Mrs. Lou. M. Rogers - R. Z. Gill, Architect	46
The Ross Flats - R. Z. Gill, Architect	35
First Train Load of Marble Shipped from Knoxville - John M. Ross, Shipper	67
Knoxville in Gala Attire - Reunion of the Blue and Gray, October 7th, 1889	41
Second Baptist Church, West Knoxville	24
Shepard & Manning, Plumbers' Supplies	87
Shetterly & Tipton's Place	86
Office of the Southern Building and Loan Association of Knoxville	36
Scenery, East Tennessee, Virginia & Georgia Railroad The Sphinx, Emory River	48
The State House of Tennessee, Nashville	117
C. C. Sullins' Flats - R.Z. Gill, Architect	46
Sunset Rock, Lookout Mountain - Line of the Nashville, Chattanooga & St. Louis Railway	122
Swan Bros., City Bakery	109
Tipple House at the Mines of the Tennessee Coal Mining Company, Briceville, Tenn.	73
Tennessee Medical College	25
Scene on the Tennessee River	30
Knoxville Offices of the Sun Life Insurance Company of Louisville - L.P. Knoke, Agent	63
University of Tennessee	29
View from the Grounds of the University of Tennessee	26
University School of Knoxville - Baker & Himel, Principals	27
"Westwood," Kingston Pike, Knoxville - Residence of J. E. Lutz, dealer in boots and shooshes, hats, etc.	16
W. W. Woodruff & Co., Wholesale Hardware	84
Y.M.C.A. or Borches Building	29

The Engelhardt Series: American Cities.

VOLUME XXV.

Knoxville, Tennessee.

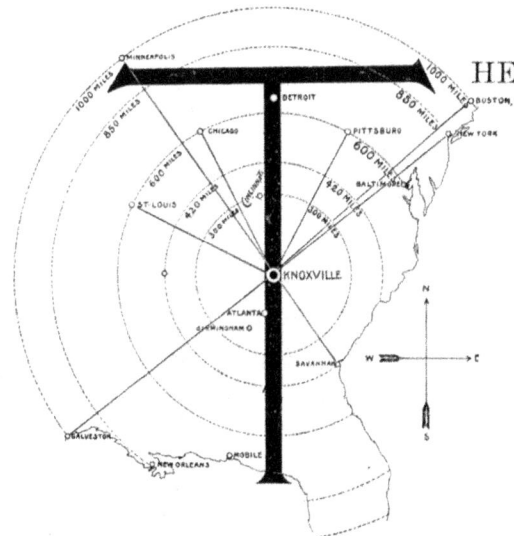

THE South still continues to quicken, as it has for these ten years back, with that marvelous industrial ripening of which its lesser cities are the blossom, and its greater cities the flower. Richmond, Norfolk, Charleston, Savannah, Atlanta, Augusta, Chattanooga, Nashville, Memphis, Birmingham, New Orleans, Galveston, Houston, San Antonio, Dallas, Fort Worth, and a score of minor places, are unfolding, expanding, blooming, flourishing, gloriously and spontaneously, like the roses and jasmins, the oleanders and magnolias of their efflorescent zone. And along with these, KNOXVILLE, the Lily of the Valley of East Tennessee.

But to abandon metaphor for a moment, and descend to hard cold fact, Knoxville is one of those Southern cities, which, departing somewhat from the ancestral way, have developed, lately, aspirings to metropolitan ascendancy, of the genuine exuberant Occidental sort. It has grown prodigiously since the new currents of thought and aim, taking the direction largely of industrial purpose and achievement, have swept the South. And it is especially true of this bustling and thrifty city of Tennessee, that it owes much, indeed, most, of its progress in recent years, to its own native spirit of emulation and forward desire.

That progress proceeds directly from development of the country surrounding it, a region richer in the diversity and abundance, both, of its mineral deposits—though not perhaps of the precious kinds—than that over which the splendid city of Denver presides.

The manifestations of the enterprise of Knoxville that might be instanced, in this connection, are many and various; for the present, however, a few illustrations thereof, will suffice.

It has carved out for itself a trade territory embracing Southwest Virginia, Eastern Kentucky and Tennessee, the western parts of the Carolinas, and the northern parts of Georgia and Alabama; and it boldly crosses sword and lance with competitors of larger growth than itself, for the title to tributaries remoter even than these. It has embarked a million, at least, of its capital, in the operation of coal mines in its vicinity, and it owns or controls other ledges of the "black diamonds" of commerce of inestimable value and extent, near by besides. In the production and finish of fine marbles it is, so to speak, the Carrara of the West. And the tall stacks of its cotton mill, its woolen mill, its rail mill and furnace, its railroad shops, its foundries and forges, its flouring mills, planing mills, furniture factories, marble works, and other concerns of the first order of mechanical importance, are the milestones of its march toward that industrial eminence, for the honor of which all the Southern cities bravely contend.

First and last, it has contributed, in aid of railroads, to solidify it in trade, $700,000. It was the first of the Tennessee cities to prepare for its part in the Chicago World's Fair by a liberal appropriation of funds. It begins the current year with an expenditure of $500,000 for street improvements, and for a comprehensive sewerage system; and an equal sum will likely be spent for a similar purpose, in its outlying parts this year.

Travelers agree, with singular unanimity, that it is the best-built city of its size in the South. It is modern in its architecture and in its aspects everywhere; in the precincts of its homes as well as in those of its trade; in its schools, churches, theatres, places of suburban resort, electric street lights and electric street railways— in all its characteristics, truly a City of To-day.

A city existing in the present, and unmindful, if not oblivious, to the dead and buried past. And yet with something of a story—a hundred years old this year. But while there was proposed for its founder's day a centenary observance, the event passed by, in February last, unhonored, and scarcely as much as remarked.

It has, to be sure, its local pride, and its sense of its share of historic renown, as the home of Sevier, that pioneer of pioneers, of Andrew Johnson and "Parson" Brownlow, and as a city that was thrice besieged in war-time. So the Old may be still a cherished remembrance, though dead ideal, to Knoxville; while the New is at once, its hope and its pledge of further advancement.

KNOXVILLE BRIEFLY DESCRIBED.

THE Appalachian chain of mountains—the breastbone of the Continent, framing, though scantily enough, a womb of Old Mother Earth beneath, pregnant with untold mineral wealth — extends southwestward through Pennsylvania, and then, as nearly everyone knows, through the two Virginias, the Carolinas, Kentucky and Tennessee, until it reaches, at length, in Georgia and Alabama, the very bowels of the South. Below the old median line of Mason and Dixon, this great continental sternum is a broken, disjointed, fractured mass, in parts bulkier than the parent stem; still preserving, however, with all this confusion, a show of order and arrangement; vaguely resembling, in its parallel branchings, the ribs of the globe that mountains are figuratively said to be; and pursuing, as a whole, a course toward the Mexican Gulf of the same general southwestward inclination and trend.

THE VALLEY OF EAST TENNESSEE.

Two of these Southern, rib-like ranges, which are approximately parallel in the direction they take toward the Southwest, enclose the Valley of East Tennessee. This great vale stretches from Bristol, at the Virginia line on the north, very nearly to Chattanooga, not far off from the boundary of Georgia to the south. Its length is 240 miles; its average breadth 60. It has, therefore, an area of almost 15,000 square miles, and it comprises something like a third of the State. It is, in fact, larger than Maryland, and is nearly as big as the country of the Swiss.

A REGION OF MATCHLESS RESOURCES.

ON the one hand—to the east and southeast, we may say—this valley is walled in by the range that partitions North Carolina from Tennessee, the range variously known, throughout its length, as the Unicoi, Great Smoky and Unaka mountains; and on the other—to the west—by the Cumberland range; on all sides bounded by the most prolific of ore-bearing sierras, scarcely concealing, under so thin an earthy cuticle that the veins may be frequently traced on the surface for miles, their wealth of iron and coal, copper, zinc, manganese, mica, marble and soapstone, and even of gems and gold; sierras, crowned, too, with a sylvan glory of virgin forests of valuable woods. A storehouse here, the hoard of ages, a magazine *par excellence*, of natural resource, the key to which, comparatively speaking, has but just been found. For utilization of it all is only begun.

And almost precisely in the center of this treasury valley, KNOXVILLE, high treasurer of all it contains, has its seat. Its station is a thousand feet or so above sea level, and is a few miles, only, from the marriage bed of the Holston and the French Broad, plebeian and rather inglorious channels themselves, but wedded, however, the parents of the nobler stream of the Tennessee; a broad, a picturesque, and useful river, renowned in the ballads of slavery days, and familiar, by name, through the action of war, when its tide more than once ran red.

THE PANORAMA FROM KNOXVILLE.

KNOXVILLE rises, compact and sightly, from the high banks of this river, and upon rolling

RESIDENCE OF THE LATE PARSON BROWNLOW

ground. Its surroundings are scenic. The valley is one of sweet waters and green pastures; the rivers meander through, reflecting, for more than half the year, the aquarelle blue of untroubled skies; and the city is confronted, at no great distance, by the mountains known as the American Alps, rugged, serried, hoary, majestic, symbols of the Everlasting—Atlases and Olympuses, Pelions and Ossas, Pisgahs and Mont Blancs in solid phalanx. As a whole, a prospect, which, from any of the heights of the city, and from its "Summit Hill" especially, is a revelation at once of the delectable and superb.

An even-measured space from Knoxville the two great ranges seem apart. The Cumberland range, the western and southwestern rim of the valley, lies to the north of the city; and to the south are the "Great Smoky mountains" of Miss Murfree's romance, presenting to the dwellers of the plain, an imposing array of acclivities in all a hundred miles long. Foothills and spurs of these main ranges, stationed, some of them, like marshals of the grand column, break at intervals the continuity of the valley.

There are a dozen mountains, peaks and "domes," among the Smokies, that are over a mile high. One of the most conspicuous altitudes from Knoxville is "Castle Colton," grand warder of the Chilhowie range, which extends down into Georgia. This peak is south of the city, twenty-five or thirty miles.

From the southern side of the river, and from any of the taller buildings of the city, "Montvale," one of the numerous spas in this highland region, which is situated at the base of old Colton, can easily be descried.

PROGRESS INVADES EVEN CLOUDLAND.

HIGHLANDERS, distinctively in their traits and manner of existence, as any of the wild clansmen of old Scotland, are the denizens of these Alpine fastnesses; rude, unlettered, hardy, punctiliously observant of the *lex talionis*. Desperate family feuds prevail among them, and the "moonshiner" thrives despite the indefatigable efforts of the Revenue police to abate him. During the war these people were sympathetically loyal; but they are of the mettle that spurns the curb of regular military discipline, and their patriotism had vent chiefly in the free and untrammeled occupation of the bushwhacker, evenhandedly foraging, friend, neutral and foe.

Progress, nevertheless, bestriding the iron horse of the moderns, is fast surmounting these

RESIDENCE OF EX GOV. BLOUNT

very ranges; civilization boldly invades the strongholds of the fierce mountaineer. Settlements, thriving towns, cities even—like Lenoir,

Harriman, Middlesboro, Bristol, and all paying their tribute of trade to Knoxville—are springing up with the development of the lumbering, sheltered; it is copiously watered and generously wooded; and it is, in very large measure, fertile, particularly so along the rivers, and in

DEAF & DUMB ASYLUM

mining and other industries of this region; and the bone and sinew utilized for these enterprises as fast as they originate, is largely native, of this same independent, wildish, but vigorous upland stock.

SPEED THE WINDLASS, SPEED THE PLOW.

LIKE the eagles that nest in their cloudland these people of the mountains. But the inhabitants of the valley, peacefully subsisting, for the most part, upon the fruits of the soil, are of a milder temper and a gentler disposition. This province of East Tennessee, embraced as it is by the frowning mountains, is thoroughly the "coves" of the protruding spurs of the ranges. A half, at least, of its area, is considered cultivable, and of the remainder, most is luxuriantly carpeted with native grasses, and is the finest of pasture land. It responds readily to intelligent husbandry where it is tillable; the grains grow thriftily; and the small fruits reach, with little more than ordinary attention, the superlative degree of perfection. And exceptionally favorable conditions for dairying and fine stock-breeding here, are beginning to receive recognition.

A great impetus indeed, has been given to the agriculture of the valley by the evolution of these mining and lumbering industries, which

INSANE ASYLUM

consume so extensively the farming staples; by the rise of new markets on the lines of new railroads in this part of the country. Mining and farming, in fact, are Siam twins in this favored valley; a living bond in trade connects them; and the valley—mark well that point—is as much a repository of mineral wealth as the mountains are themselves. The marbles of Knox county buttress the very foundation stones of Knoxville, and outcroppings of iron are plainly revealed in the ballast that paves its streets.

SCENERY OF THE HOLSTON AND FRENCH BROAD.

A WIDER PROSPECT UNFOLDED.

GEOGRAPHICALLY speaking, Knoxville is remarkably central with reference to all of the country east of the Mississippi river; and its railroad connections render it readily accessible from all prominent Eastern, Southern, and mid-Western points. An "X" roughly described on the map from New York to New Orleans one way, and from Chicago to Savannah the other, would intersect it almost exactly; and radii projected from it as a common center, in any direction, would bisect, not one, but several of the most notable places of the land.

The diagram initial on page 3 of this work is intended to exhibit this peculiar centrality of the city's position. By rail, the distances from it to some of these larger places, are as follows:

Of points in its trade field, or comparatively near it, Chattanooga is 110 miles; Bristol (one-half of which is in Virginia and the other in Tennessee,) 180 miles; Atlanta, 210; Birmingham, 250; Louisville, 260; and Cincinnati, 300 or thereabouts.

Memphis, at the other extreme of its own State, is 420 miles; the National Capital, 475; St. Louis, Chicago, Baltimore and Pittsburgh, all four, 600; New York and New Orleans, 850 each; and Galveston, Minneapolis and Boston, equi-distant a thousand miles.

Of Southern seaports, Norfolk is 540 miles northeast; Brunswick, 500 southeast; Savannah, 420 southeast; Wilmington, 400 east; Charleston, 390 southeast; Mobile, 375 southwest. To Port Royal, in an air line nearest of all ports to it, it has not yet a through rail

"GREYSTONE," THE RESIDENCE OF E. C. CAMP, OF THE COAL CREEK COAL CO.
Cost $125,000.

route, but one is proposed, and projected in part.

TRANSPORTATION FACILITIES.

IN the three railroads for which it is the focus, and the river that runs by, Knoxville has four broad and unobstructed avenues by which to reach the great world of trade that lies beyond its own immediate pale.

The East Tennessee, Virginia & Georgia Railway, which has headquarters in the city, affords it a through line to Washington, Baltimore, Philadelphia, New York and Boston, by its connection in Virginia with the Richmond Terminal System.

To sea on the Southern coasts, it has the East Tennessee, Virginia & Georgia's connection with the Norfolk & Western road, the latter extending from Bristol to Norfolk and Newport News, on opposite sides of the harbor of Hampton Roads; the East Tennessee's indirect connection with the Richmond and Danville lines to Charleston; the Marietta & North Georgia's connection with the Central Railroad of Georgia *via* Atlanta to Savannah; the East Tennessee, Virginia & Georgia direct to Brunswick, and the same road, also, direct to Mobile.

To the central west and northwest, it has the Knoxville, Cumberland Gap & Louisville's "L. & N." connection, which is a direct route to Louisville, Cincinnati, Chicago and St. Louis, and to Evansville, Indianapolis, and other places between it and these.

To Birmingham and the Alabama mineral region, Memphis and all the Lower Mississippi valley (and thence to the great Southwest) it has the lines of the East Tennessee, Virginia & Georgia direct.

And last, but not least, perhaps, in serviceability, it has the river Tennessee; bending in circuitous traverse of East Tennessee, North Alabama, West Tennessee and Southwest Kentucky, past Chattanooga, Decatur, Florence, Sheffield, and, at length, Paducah, to its junction with the Ohio; a highway, in all, affording 700 miles' length of navigable water open the greater part of the year.

KNOXVILLE AS A CENTER OF TRADE.

KNOXVILLE and Knox county, in which it is, have been generous to railroads; and this policy, steadily but discriminatingly pursued, has

BLEAK HOUSE, THE RESIDENCE OF R. H. ARMSTRONG,
Gen. Longstreet's Headquarters during the Siege of Knoxville, Nov., 1863.

redounded immensely to the city's commercial advancement. It has earned it a name, too, among its somewhat backward sisters of the South, and as well with its forward cousins North, as a city infused with the essence, at least, if not the true inspiration, of progress.

The commerce it has gained by development of the contiguous country has been secured to it largely by these railroad subsidies. Most of the new business of the last few years has been jobbing trade, but manufactures are increasing, and the traffic of the place is notable as much for its diversity, as amount.

The grand total of the commerce of the city is set down by local statisticians at $50,000,000;

nearly a tenth of it manufactures. The characteristic industries of the city are quarrying and shipment of the marbles which abound in exceptional variety in its environs; the coal trade, of which it is a very important center, and lumber and its products, although several of the strictly mercantile lines, like the trade in groceries and dry goods, exceed these in the sum total of business from them derived.

For its marble business the city is most widely known. It is the greatest center of that trade in the land. And although $1,000,000 worth of the dressed and rough product were distributed throughout the forty-three States of the Union from Knoxville last year, the business is yet in its infancy, and it promises by its growth to bring the city additional fame in the years to come.

It is a profitable commerce, also, that accrues to Knoxville from the prevalence of excellent coal in the country round about. Residents of Knoxville are largely interested in these coal fields; and with iron and limestone in juxta-deposition to coal, the time full surely approaches, in the very nature of things, when these resources will be utilized thoroughly, to Knoxville's especial enrichment. The coal trade of the city at present is upwards of $1,250,000 in value a year.

Several large saw and planing mills and factories of fine interior building finish, have

MARKET SQUARE, EAST SIDE.

been established in recent years at Knoxville. With the forests hard by, and the facilities of both river and rail to bring the raw material for it in, this industry, still also in its incipiency, is likewise of great prospective import. It sums up $500,000 or more annually now.

Knoxville's manufacturing status is however only that of a good beginner. A better point for the location of such industries as manufacture of wagons, and small woodenware, could scarcely be conceived. But, on this subject more may be said in its proper place anon. For the production of steel by the new process of the trade, by which the metal is made direct from the iron ores, its position is considered by the experts really superior to that of Birmingham or the other Southern iron centres, by reason of the uncommon abundance and propinquity both, here, of the materials for it. A cheaper freight rate in any direction, because both ways the grade is down, is also in its favor. The city has not yet reached the stage in finance in which these ventures originate; but through its commercial bodies and syndicates, it offers ample encouragement to capital to embark in them and co-operates to the best of its power.

SIGNS OF THE CITY'S PROGRESS.

THE Census Bureau, in its bulletin of city populations recently issued, admits (in a foot note, however, and grudgingly it would seem) that Knoxville in 1890 was a city of 40,000 souls. It had barely 10,000 twelve years ago. At the rate of its growth of late, it has all of 50,000 now. And its stature in commerce is that of a city of very considerably more.

practically a unit. These three municipalities are, Old Knoxville, the largest of the three by far, and North and West Knoxville which, in the march of improvement, have risen alongside. The signs all point to a consolidation of the three very soon. North and West Knoxville have been settled by the overplus from the old town; they are residence districts chiefly, West Knoxville, of the two, most in favor with the people of fashion and wealth. In numbers and area, however, they are nearly on a par; and their joint population is a fifth of that of the old city itself.

It is in this robust fashion that Knoxville

GAY STREET, LOOKING WEST.

Knoxville, the trade center, is a trinity of three cities in one; politically distinct, but

matures. But the upbuilding of suburbs and extension of commerce, are not the sole signs of

POST OFFICE AND GOVERNMENT BUILDING.

this ambitious city's growth. There are tokens of the forces that are bearing the community forward, and as well of fortunes already attained, in the important and expensive buildings and public improvements, that are the corollary of an active real estate market and steadily enhancing property valuations thereby. There are structures in Knoxville of much architectural merit; costly edifices both public and private; types of the builder's art comparable with the best work in the land; such, for instance, as the County Court House, the Post Office, the Girls' High School, the French & Roberts and Harris Blocks, and the mansion of E. C. Camp; this last of native stone, finished in rare woods and marbles, representing an outlay on the part of its owner, a miner of coal and man of affairs, of $125,000, exclusive of its site.

A CENTER ALSO OF INSTITUTIONS.

KNOXVILLE is a seat of institutions, City, County, State and United States, second only in Tennessee, to Nashville, the capital itself. The University of Tennessee occupies an imposing pile grouped upon an elevation in the midst of the town. At "Lyons View," a picturesque bend of the river about five miles out, the State's asylum for the deaf and dumb is maintained. And as the shire town, not merely for Knox county, but for East Tennessee, the government has provided it with a costly marble-fronted Federal building for the accommodation of the resident officials of the Pension, Internal Revenue, and Judiciary departments of State.

Knoxville is in latitude 35.30 N. and longitude 7 W. from Washington, mountain-enclosed, as we have seen, a quarter of a mile, approximately, above sea level. Its climate is exceptionally even, free from extremes of summer heat and winter cold; its hygienic conditions of drainage, water supply, sunlight and all, naturally superior; and when it has completed the work of systematic sewerage which, lately, it has vigorously undertaken, it should be as healthful a place as any in the world. And with its mellow mean of 48 winter and 73 summer, and its charming surroundings of mountain and vale, it is growing in favor as a stop-over station, on the railroad routes from the Northwest region to the Land of Flowers.

SOCIAL CONSIDERATIONS.

KINDLY and warm, likewise, is the social air of Knoxville, as it is manifest in the hospitality extended to the stranger within its gates by the Chilhowie Club, an organization of its merchants, and by the Knoxville Chamber of Commerce and Board of Trade. Here verily is a community tolerant, politically; typical, over all in the South, of the connubiated Blue and Gray. Welcoming the man who brings his wealth of industry, or enterprise, or capital to participate in its privileges and advantages; and tolerant of its negro minority, recognizing it, always, as a hereditament of the soil, to the manor born and raised.

Exampling its manly spirit in its martial brigade of militia, its ball club and boat club, and its half-mile track. Exhibiting its general enlightenment in its schools of every order, its free public library, its patronage of art, science, music, letters, its taste for the wholesome drama. And disclosing its general morals in the spires of its numerous churches, its enforcement of Sunday observance, and its usually orderly demeanor.

In the home of old Parson Brownlow, the field of Fort Saunders and the tomb of Sevier, Knoxville has its heirlooms of a rapidly vanishing past. But of these as family reliques, it makes but a modest boast.

For Knoxville begins an epoch, again, with this, its hundredth year.

And the future is bigger with promise than ever the past has been.

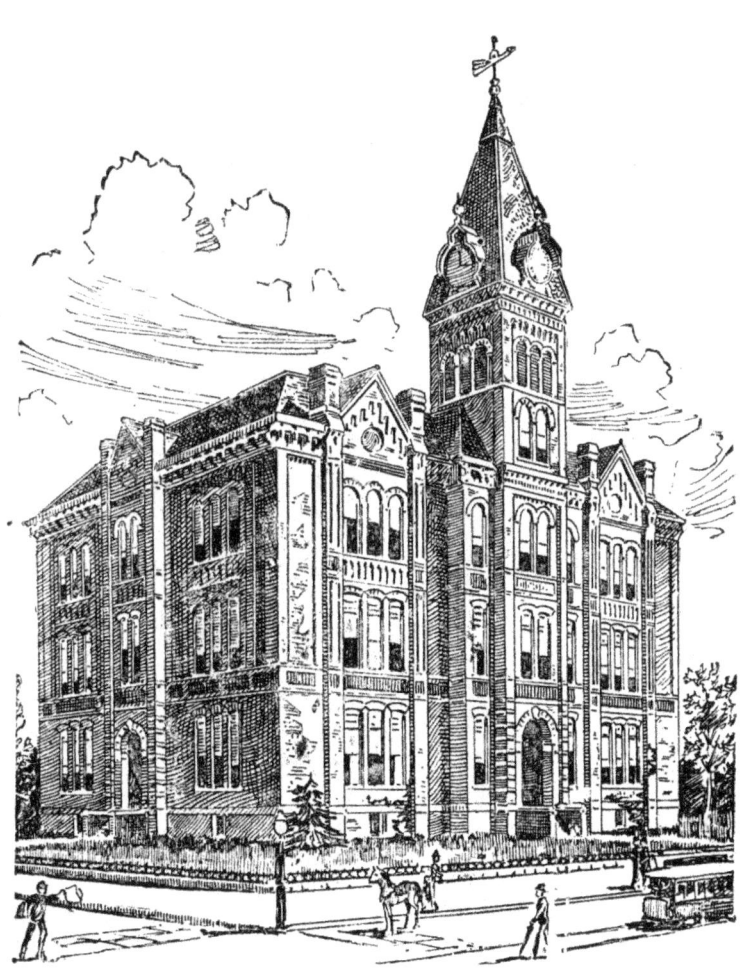

GIRLS' HIGH SCHOOL.

Bauman Bros., Architects.

THREE KNOXVILLES; IN REALITY HOWEVER, BUT ONE.

WE shall consider the three Knoxvilles herein, to the end of our task, as one; for such they are known to the world outside, and such in verity they are. Knoxville is three-fold only, as we have said, in the matter of its government; as a trade center it is single, indivisible, inseparable. North Knoxville and West Knoxville are wings merely of the greater encampment of Old Knoxville, new-made, creations of yesterday, likely to be incorporated in the main body to-morrow, as it were. We shall depart therefore from the rule we have just laid down, only when it is necessary, incidentally, to distinguish one from either or both the rest.

The population of Knoxville proper, by the National Census returns of 1890, was, in exact figures, 22,535, a gain in ten years of 12,842, or 132½ per cent; of North Knoxville, 2,297; of West Knoxville, 2,114; of Knoxville the trade center, embracing all three, 26,946. But there was, even then, by the published admission of the census officials, just outlying this urban trefoil of Tennessee, population sufficient to bring up its total, in round numbers, to 40,000 souls.

At the rate of its growth in the decennium past, by 1900 it should have a population of 93,000; with nothing to offset the relatively greater impetus of an enlarged and steadily enlarging volume and mass, a magnitude beyond, perhaps, even that.

And while Prophecy is not, as you will doubtless say, gentle reader, an exact science, it will do no harm to let this estimate stand. It is only fair to presume, with nothing to stay it, an equal measure of advancement in the next ten years, with that of the ten years past.

MUNICIPAL CHARACTERISTICS.

OLD KNOXVILLE or Knoxville proper, occupies a half nearly of the five square miles of the total area of the three cities. It fronts the river, contains the most valuable property and most substantial betterments, comprehends the business quarter almost in its entirety, and is the scene of pretty much all the traffic, wholesale and retail of Knoxville, the trade center, except some little transacted in and about the factories scattered throughout its widespread suburban skirts. It is, in short, the real market place; the core, the kernel, the hub and the hive, of Knoxville's commerce.

THE MAYOR AND THE COUNCIL.

OLD KNOXVILLE, after the fashion of the larger cities of Tennessee, is governed really by a Board of Public Works. This body is all-powerful in its sphere, the administration of the fire, police, street and all other city departments, excepting that of the schools; limited only in the conduct of the municipal business by the legislative authority of the City Council, a body of ten, one from each of the city's wards. This Board of Public Works appoints the heads of the various departments, though some hold too by favor of the council; but the offices of Mayor, Treasurer, Recorder, etc., are elective. Appropriations from the revenue are the province of the council; the Mayor's functions are supervisory chiefly; he is the guardian and conservator of the popular interests and rights.

M. E. THOMPSON, a real estate agent and large property owner, is the MAYOR OF KNOXVILLE PROPER, elected, after a very close contest with three competitors—two Democrats and a Republican—January 16, 1892, to succeed Peter Kern, wholesale confectioner, whose term had recently expired. Mr. Thompson is a native of the city, who, in the ordinary acceptance of the words, has, truly, been the architect of his own fortune.

He began life as a teamster, and for seven years prior to 1873, followed that occupation. In that year he went into the business of a liveryman, and was successful enough to retire from it at the end of ten years. Since 1883 he has been operating largely in real estate, and his judgment, business tact and faith in the city's future, applied whenever the golden opportunity offered, have secured him an ample share of its enhancing realty.

He owns the Palace Hotel and the Palace Stables, and residence property, and business sites in various parts of the town. He is now planning to build himself an elegant home, becoming the position he holds as chief magistrate of the city. He is a Democrat in politics, but, from his experience and interests, is believed to be a man who will discharge the duties of his office with due consideration for the welfare of all.

The Board of Aldermen elected with him is as follows: Ben. F. Boyd, Matt M. Nelson, R. J. Jarnagin, Jas. P. Kennedy, Albert Payne, S. A. Bailey, John P. Murphy, Geo. W. Callahan, Gregory J. Ash, and Lon C. Mabry, representing, in the order named, the wards of the city from one to ten inclusive. These are men, alive, like the mayor, to the fact that the growth of the city requires a broad, liberal and forward municipal policy, and a progressive administration.

FINANCES OF KNOXVILLE PROPER.

The total assessment for taxes in Knoxville proper in 1891 was $12,567,893, of which $10,451,006 was the assessment laid on the real estate of the citizens. At the rate that was levied, $1.25 on the $100 of valuation, this produced a revenue for the support of the city government of $157,098. License collections amounting to $63,000, poll taxes of $4,326, market rents, back taxes, and other receipts, bring the total ordinary revenue of the city up to the sum of $275,000 a year or thereabouts. This revenue is expended usually upon the different branches of the public service about in proportion as it was last year, i. e.:

Upon streets, new buildings, reconstruction, repairs, and public improvements generally, $61,000; for schools (inclusive of the funds derived from the State), $41,250; for interest and current debts, $37,500; police, $21,000; street lights, $17,000; fire department, $14,500; official salaries, $12,300; public health (sanitary service) and hospital, $8,500; water supplied the city, $6,500, and for miscellaneous purposes the balance. Expenditures for extraordinary purposes, like the new sewer system, are met by an additional levy of taxes, or the issuance of bonds; but by law the tax rate must not be greater than it is at present.

The whole tax rate is: city, $1.25; county and State, $1, total, $2.25.

The total debt of the city is $1,050,300, all of it funded so as to be in gradual process of extinction. Half this sum was recently incurred to provide for special sewer and other improvements, and more than half the remainder of the debt is a guarantee of railroad bonds. As against this debt, the city counts among its assets $375,000 of Knoxville Southern and Knoxville & Ohio railroad stock; $104,000 of school property, and $124,000 of other public buildings, and resources besides, bringing the grand total of its possessions up to $682,880. But a small part of the last issue of Old Knoxville's bonds has yet been expended, but the work for which they were floated has commenced, with the building of a viaduct over the main street of the town, and the planning of a sewer system, forehandedly designed to apply to its sisters and its suburbs, as well as itself; to Knoxville, in short, as a whole. And the credit of the city, in its corporate capacity, is indicated by the fact that these very bonds, with a hundred competitors offering theirs at the very same time in the very same field, were taken in lump, in the city of New York, at par.

PUBLIC HEALTH, FIRE SERVICE, POLICE.

The sanitary concerns of the city are the trust of a Board of Health. That body reports the conditions affecting the public health normally good, and rejoices in a prospective of sewer-improvement calculated to improve them. The city lies, to use the well-worn realty phrase, "high and dry," 900 feet at the least, above the sea, with gradients affording it excellent natural drainage. It is in a region whose climatic features are a mellow weather mean; whose extremes of temperature, and these but rarely reached, are 97 or 98 in summer, and 6 to 12 above in winter; that has an exceptional proportion of clear and pleasant days; and that counts among other attractions —not least from the hygienic standpoint—innumerable mineral springs; a region, indeed, which is a grand health resort itself.

There is house to house inspection by the health department of Knoxville once a year; police inspection daily; quarantine enforced against contagion when necessary; a free city hospital and dispensary, and private institutions of the sort, besides. Robust persons are easily acclimated. The most common complaints of late are those the flesh is heir to everywhere. The death rate, with a population one-fifth colored, is but 15.46 to the thousand; the mortality of the whites but 13.32 per cent.

An ample and wholesome water supply is everywhere a desideratum of importance in respect of the general welfare; quite as important with regard to the public health as it is for fire protection, or as a business facility. The water at Knoxville is furnished mainly by a private enterprise, the KNOXVILLE WATER CO.

That company has a franchise running till 1913. Its works embrace a pumping plant situated on the river bank about a mile east of the center of the city, a reservoir on the highest point within the corporate limits, and 28 miles of distributing mains ramifying those parts of the city known as Knoxville and North Knoxville. Attached to its mains in these two divisions are 189 street hydrants or "plugs" for the fire service.

The pumping works are equipped with two Davidson compound condensing pumping engines, and a battery of four boilers of 60

the living springs of the mountains, in all its original purity, uncontaminated by the waste of any settlement higher up, large or small.

The Knoxville Fire Department is a paid force of 21, including its chief, W. W. DUNN, an experienced man. Its equipment consists of two steamers, one truck, two hose reels and twelve horses, housed in two fire houses. The underwriters of the city, in common with the citizens, who are most interested in it, consider it an efficient corps. It has, naturally enough, some drawbacks, in a city growing faster than its means, a city whose residence quarter is largely of wood, and which lacks also suburban mains; but its salvage of property exceeds by far its cost to the taxpayer. On

"WESTWOOD," KINGSTON PIKE, KNOXVILLE.
Residence of J. E. Lutz, dealer in boots and shoes, hats, etc.

h. p. each, affording a pumping capacity of 3,000,000 gallons a day. The reservoir is 234 feet above low water in the river, and it covers about half an acre. It is partitioned in the middle and has two discharging pipes of 16 and 14 inches diameter, respectively. This reservoir has a storage capacity of 3,200,000 gallons, and this is about the capacity of the works, although the supply can be largely increased if desired. The company is providing a quantity equal to all present demands.

The water of the Tennessee river at Knoxville is exceedingly clear before it is settled even in the reservoir. There are no towns of any size on the stream or its forks above the city, and it reaches Knoxville direct from

property insured for a total of $91,575, in the year ending July 1, '91, the fire loss was but $15,236, and the insurance loss only $6,778. The pressure and volume of water available for fires, according to the chief, is, generally speaking, sufficient; and no circumstances prevail to make the hazard from fire at Knoxville particularly serious.

The Knoxville police (in the old town) number thirty. "Our negro populace is," says the chief, CAPT. J. J. ATKINS, "the most orderly of any in a Southern city." The community as a whole, he affirms also, is remarkably law abiding. Sunday law is enforced at Knoxville; not even barbers are permitted to do business on the Day of Rest. And gambling and social vice are firmly restrained within bounds.

PUBLIC IMPROVEMENTS.

THE City Engineer, a subordinate of the Public Works department, has charge of the

KNOXVILLE SAVINGS BANK.

street, sewer and bridge work of Knoxville proper, and of public improvements of that character. This position is held at present by M. NICHOLSON, a graduate and experienced man. From him the following information was obtained:

The sewer system which has been adopted, and upon which work has lately begun, is the plan of Engineer R. F. Hartford of Chattanooga. It is what is known as a "separate" system, that is, one of underground pipes or conduits, with no provision for storm waters or surface drainage. It is projected to cover all three Knoxvilles, each to construct, however, its part of the whole; and for the better understanding of it, a description of the "lay" of their land, would not, perhaps, be out of place here.

The area of the three cities is 3,236 acres, or 2½ miles square. The river is the southern boundary of Knoxville viewed as a whole, and its frontage thereon is about equal to the length of its sides, North and West Knoxville included. The Hartford scheme covers the entire water shed of two creeks that flow through the triplet city, as far north as 2½ miles from the river.

Within this area of five miles square, there are 125 miles of streets laid out, but not all graded, 100 miles of this in Knoxville proper. Of this total about forty-eight miles length is macadamized, thirty-five of that in Knoxville proper. The natural grades being, for the most part, heavy—varying indeed from two to twenty-one degrees, the natural drainage was, under the circumstances, exceptionally favorable, and sewers could, until lately, be dispensed with; and only a few made by private parties, two miles, perhaps, in all, had in fact, been constructed. The growth of the city, however, began at last to demand them, and in accordance with popular sentiment in the question the authorities of Knoxville proper last year bonded the city for $225,000 for a starter, and upon expert advice have commenced the sewer work.

At the same time bonds were sold for a like amount to provide for bridges and permanent pavement, and this work also is under way. North and West Knoxville are expected to follow suit to the extent of their means very soon.

The expenditure heretofore for street work, new and old, in Knoxville proper, has been at the rate of $35,000 to $40,000 a year; and this sum, drawn from the regular revenues of the city, will still be available. The principal work undertaken besides the sewers, is a viaduct over the railroad tracks at the crossing

M'GHEE PUBLIC LIBRARY BUILDING.

of Gay street—the Broadway of Knoxville—for which purpose $50,000 has been appropriated.

The owners of an addition over the river from the city, are to build a bridge across to

COURT HOUSE OF KNOX COUNTY, KNOXVILLE.
By courtesy of the Stephenson & Getaz Manufacturing Co.,
of Knoxville.

their possessions at an expense of something like $200,000, and another, a railroad bridge, is also projected. Large sums have been spent in the last few years conditioning the suburbs; parks have been made, and places of resort, railroads built, boulevards planted, and very much more is in contemplation; but this is the work of private parties. The city has done nothing yet, or next to nothing to provide its people with relaxing places. Sewers and pavements, fire alarms, water works, a city hall, schools, hospitals—works of necessity must be first provided; parks and statuary, fountains, boulevards, riverside drives, summit perspectives—these will all, presently, doubtless, as Knoxville grows, have a share of attention.

OLD KNOXVILLE'S MINOR SISTERS.

LET us pause now, for a moment, to glance at the two lesser Knoxvilles.

WEST KNOXVILLE embraces all that part of the city lying between Second and Third Creeks north of the Tennessee river, and south of the line of the East Tennessee, Virginia & Georgia Railroad where it traverses the city; an area altogether of 805 acres. It has a complete municipal organization of Mayor, Recorder and Treasurer, Marshal and Boards of Aldermen, Education and Health. It was incorporated in 1888. Its assessed valuations then were $750,000; for '91 they were $1,750,000. Its tax rate is $1.15, of which five per cent goes to its sinking fund to extinguish its debt of $75,000, which was contracted entirely for public improvements. These include two schools, one high school and one for the elementary studies, (not counting a class-room for its youth of color, or the University of Tennessee and University School, a preparatory academy, both which are in this part of the town), streets graded, macadamized, curbed and guttered everywhere, except those recently opened, electric lights, fire hydrants, etc. It has the only strictly public park in the three corporations, the "Circle," which, however, is yet in a state of unadorned nature.

It is the fashionable residence quarter, with all the social advantages that phrase implies. It has, however, a number of the large factories of the city within its confines, too. Its residents are the people of wealth of the city. Its average assessment for each householder is $5,000 as compared with $65 in the country at large. It has but two saloons (and these permitted only under stringent regulations), and no dens of social vice. Its population is largely of native stock.

JOHN W. YOE, a lawyer, is its Mayor. The Aldermen, his cabinet, are of both parties, but they are a unit for West Knoxville.

NORTH KNOXVILLE is a residence quarter chiefly, but it has extensive manufactures along the tracks of the railroads that pass through it. It embraces an area of 575 acres, beginning at the intersection of Crozier and Broad streets, and situate north of the line of the East Tennessee, Virginia & Georgia Railroad.

It was incorporated in February, 1889, so that its public improvements are all the work of scarcely three years. It has eight miles of streets graded, macadamized and curbed, a new water-works, owned by Boston parties, who are required to furnish filtered water, and a pressure ample for its fire service, is lighted by the Knoxville Electric Light Co., has a chemical engine, a steam road-roller, a $20,000 school for its white children, and an arrangement for the tuition of its colored youth with Knoxville proper, and is looking ahead in the matter of its sewerage and making provision for future growth.

Its tax valuations, upon a low basis of assessment, are $1,500,000; its tax rate, $1.05; the odd fraction for its sinking fund, to extinguish its indebtedness of $100,000, which was contracted for the improvements that have been named. It has legislative permission to issue $75,000 of bonds additional to provide for sewers when the system for Knoxville itself is commenced.

North Knoxville has for municipal administration a Mayor (LEWIS A. GRATZ, an attorney of the Deaderick Block, present incumbent), a Recorder and Treasurer, and a Marshal, a Board of Aldermen of six members, and a Board of Education.

Mayor Gratz is a Democrat in politics, but was elected unanimously. He is now serving his second term. He has been Mayor, in fact, since the city of North Knoxville was incorporated. He has been a resident here since '65, and has been practicing his profession continuously and successfully since he came here.

He is largely interested in North Knoxville real estate, and he has, perhaps, the finest residence in it. He strongly favors a consolidation with Knoxville proper, on the ground of mutual interest, and thinks their union a matter merely of time.

STREET LIGHTS, RAPID TRANSIT, RESORTS.

IN addition to a water supply in common, reference to which has already been made, the three Knoxvilles are provided with the facilities of street and household lights, both gas and electric, telephone service, and rapid transit by means of street railroads, (with incidental attractions of terminal resorts), on a scale embracing them all.

THE EAST TENNESSEE TELEPHONE COMPANY, which has its headquarters in Nashville, Tenn., was organized in 1880. It has lines in Chattanooga and Knoxville, Clarksville, Cleveland and Bristol, Tenn., Lexington, Paducah, Bowling Green, Frankfort and Middlesborough, Ky., and it operates chiefly in East Tennessee and Northern Kentucky.

It has at least 1,000 miles of wire and fifty employes. It has 500 subscribers here, and some 2,150 altogether: in Chattanooga, 650; Clarksville, Tenn., 150; Bristol, Tenn., 125; Lexington, Ky., 350; Paducah, Ky., 200; Middlesborough, Ky., 100, and Frankfort, the Kentucky capital, 50 (these in addition to the number at Knoxville), and it maintains a line from here to Maryville, Tenn., a distance of sixteen miles. In the last two years its business has increased fully 300 per cent. It operates on the Bell-American system. O. F. NOEL, of Nashville, is president; S. J. KEITH, of the same city, vice-president; J. W. HUNTER, JR., secretary and treasurer. Mr. Noel is well known here as formerly a banker and wholesale grocer of Nashville. Mr. Keith is president of the Fourth National Bank there. The directors are Messrs. Noel and Keith, James Compton, superintendent of the Western Union Telegraph company's lines for this district, W. O. Vertrees, a Nashville attorney, and Joseph M. Brown, of Washington, D. C.

Its office here is at 81 Vine Street. A. P. HARRISON is its Knoxville manager. He was formerly engaged with the Cumberland Telephone Co., of Nashville.

THE KNOXVILLE GAS LIGHT CO. which has been established thirty-five years, has for its largest customer the city of Knoxville proper, for whom it lights the streets and public build-

INTERIOR OF THE KNOXVILLE CENTRAL STATION, EAST TENNESSEE TELEPHONE COMPANY.

ings under contract. Its charges to private consumers are $1.50 a thousand feet.

THE KNOXVILLE ELECTRIC LIGHT & POWER Co. furnishes the three municipalities which

RESIDENCE OF J. D. COWAN, OF COWAN, M'CLUNG & CO., WHOLESALE DRY GOODS.

make up the trade center Knoxville, with street lamps of the arc pattern, to the number of 151, for which service the company receives $100 per lamp per year. A large number of arcs are furnished also to private parties at $8, $10 and $12 per month, according to the time they are burned. Some 1,200 incandescent lights are also furnished by it to its customers. No motors are sold by it; but it will shortly embark in that branch of the business also.

It has two plants, one on East Cumberland street, in Knoxville proper, and the other in West Knoxville. One of these plants has a capacity of five dynamos of 30-arc lights each, and the other of four dynamos of 50-arc lights each; and its alternating dynamos, three in number, will supply 1,500 incandescent lights or 500 each. Its engines are four in number of 100 h. p. each; its boilers five, of 100 h. p. each.

Its mechanical complement embraces also 30 miles length of wire and the poles constituting its distributing system, which are valued at $25,000. It operates under the Thompson-Houston arc and alternating, and Schuyler arc systems.

This company was organized in 1888, C. H. HUDSON, general manager of the E. T., Va. & Ga. R. R. is its president; J. C. DUNCAN, secretary and manager, W. H. Simmonds, real estate and insurance agent; R. Z. Roberts, manager of the Southern Car Works; J. M. Greer, of J. M. Greer & Co., dealers in agricultural implements; J. C. Luttrell, of S. B. Luttrell & Co., wholesale hardware, and the president, are the directors.

Its office is at 150 Gay street.

THE KNOXVILLE ELECTRIC RAILWAY Co. operates eighteen and a half miles' length of street railway at Knoxville, thirteen miles with electric motor and five and a half with horses. It has an electric power house thoroughly equipped, twelve motor cars and five trailers and three horse cars, has forty horses, and in its service seventy employes, and represents an investment all told of $500,000, which sum is the amount of its capital stock.

It ramifies the principal streets of the city, traverses the fashionable residence districts, passes the hotels, depots and other public buildings, and affords transit to the suburban resorts. It is a system complete in itself, and is operated independently of any other road, in six divisions, four of them electric and the other two horse lines.

These lines are the following: 1. The main or Broad street electric line, two and a half miles long, extending from the Court House of Knox county to and past the Union depot, with its termination two and a half miles out. 2. The Lake Ottosee electric line, from Hardee and Morgan to Ottosee lake and park, elsewhere mentioned in this work, four miles. 3. The Elmwood electric line, from the same starting point as the Lake Ottosee line, but describing a different circuit of about the same length, past Elmwood park, a place for athletics, to Ottosee, four miles. 4. The Morgan street line, electric, from this same Hardee and Morgan street corner out North Fifth and Washington avenues (considered usually the choicest of all the city's residence thoroughfares), three miles. 5. The Asylum street horse line, making a loop from Market Square past the base-ball park and through the suburb of

"Mechanicsville" to the point of beginning, three and a half miles. 6. The Mabry street horse line, extending from the Court House north on Gay, and out through Mabry street to a termination at the Catholic Cemetery and the Fair Grounds of the city.

The building and extension of these various lines, and their conversion from horse to electric roads, has been an effective agency in the development of the city. Property values have been greatly enhanced, especially along the Ottosee line in Northeast Knoxville, by the conveniences they afford. The advancement in some instances has been as much as 500 per cent.

Great enterprise has been exhibited by the management of these lines, and further improvement is promised by it. It is proposed to give the two horse roads an electric equipment at an early day. This management is as follows: W. G. McADOO, JR., a resident of Chattanooga, president; F. K. HUGER, superintendent of the East Tennessee, Virginia & Georgia Railway, vice-president; M. R. McADOO, general manager. The McAdoos are brothers, sons of W. G. McAdoo, long a professor of the State University here, and an old and highly respected citizen. They are young men comparatively (for such an enterprise). Mr. W. G. McAdoo, Jr., is but 28 years old, and his brother, the manager, only 26. Both have, however, already exhibited business abilities of an uncommon order, Mr. W. G. McAdoo, in the practice of his profession, that of the law, at Chattanooga, and his brother, in his calling, that of a civil engineer, and also in the auditor's department of the East Tennessee, Virginia & Georgia Railway. They own, between them, considerable real estate here, and so also does their associate, Major Huger.

THE WEST END STREET RAILROAD Co. operates about 3½ miles of road in two divisions, both extending from State and Clinch streets, in the heart of Knoxville proper, into and through the district known as West Knoxville. This road was built in 1888 with local capital. It is at present a horse road, but it is the intention of its owners to furnish it with mechanical motors of some modern pattern as soon as business shall justify the change, and this improvement is likely to be made ere long.

The main line of this road proceeds to Circle park, a favorite residence precinct, and a branch runs to the old Fort Sanders battle ground. Fare on this line is five cents also. Settlement of the district it traverses has rapidly followed its building, and real estate hereaway has also advanced.

Hitherto, the west end of the city has been wanting most in transit facilities. The building of a bridge over one of the creeks that severs this section from Knoxville proper has, however, made it so very much easier to approach, that this defect is likely to be remedied in a very short time.

THE FOUNTAIN HEAD RAILROAD is a steam line extending from Broad street at Central Market, in the center of Knoxville, to FOUNTAIN CITY, a place of residence and resort, four and a half miles out, north of Knoxville. It covers, therefore, the growing part of the city, and passes through a residence quarter, and by the new railroad shops for the East Tennessee, Virginia & Georgia, which, when in full operation, will employ 1,500 hands.

It cost to build and equip, about $125,000. This investment includes the picnic grounds, hotel, etc., at Fountain City, where the company owns a tract of 612 acres. The equipment consists of three engines, seven passenger cars and four freight cars. The fare is five cents to Arlington and ten cents to Fountain City. The time occupied in transit from the

FOUNTAIN HEAD HOTEL, SUBURBS OF KNOXVILLE.

city to the Fountain City terminus is twenty-five minutes. The road is operated independently of any other here. It is owned by

Messrs. CULLEN & NEWMAN, wholesale crockery dealers of Knoxville (mention of whom is made elsewhere herein), and by Eastern parties, resident, most of them, in New York.

While Knoxville—in lump, of course regarded—as must be confessed, by even its blindest admirers, is sadly deficient in the matter of public parks, the three communities leaven with a pride that must soon provide them. Meanwhile the terminal pleasure resorts maintained by the city railroads, afford a substitute for them.

Chief of these are the pic-nic grounds at Fountain City, just referred to, and the park

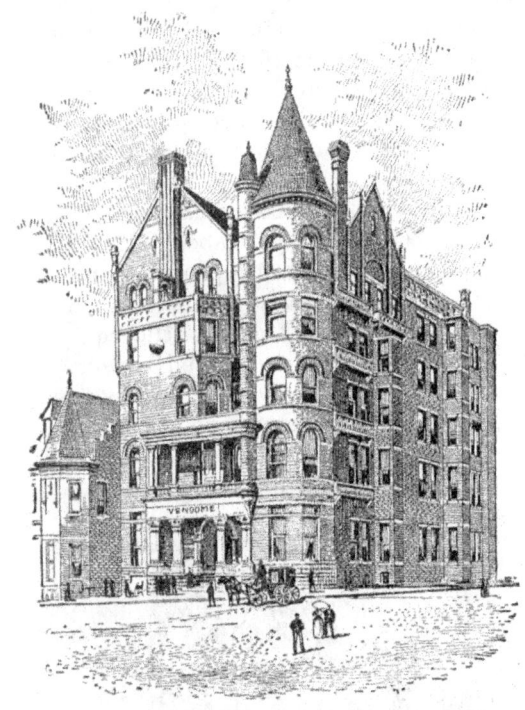

HOTEL VENDOME.

and lake of Ottosee, two and a half miles northeast of city, at the end of the lines of the Knoxville Electric Railway. Ottosee is a picturesque spot of 50 acres, whose natural charms have been heightened by the many improvements made upon it. It is a sanitarium and pleasure ground both; it has mineral springs bubbling from the soil, whose waters are curative of various disorders; and on this account it is frequented pretty much all the year. These waters are highly commended by the medicos of the city, and baths have been provided, to make them available.

The lake Ottosee covers 12 acres. There is a boat house on it with boats for hire. What with shady nooks, and bowers and arbors; and rustic benches and swings and a "zoo" for the children and a pavilion or summer theater for their elders, Ottosee has been made a very pleasaunce for the recreative Knoxvillian, old and young, to relax in.

And for those who love aquatics of a more robustious fashion, the river flows by all Knoxville, affording a clear and unruffled course of as many miles' length as may be desired; for the patrons of the turf there is the track of the Knoxville Driving Park Association, soon to be enlarged from a half to a mile course; and for the curious-minded stranger many more attractions—the old Capitol of Tennessee; the field of Fort Sanders; the Confederate and National God's acres; the homestead of the Brownlows; the Longstreet headquarters; Island Home Farm, a model old manor, and Lyons' View, most charming of seats for a State's institution to shelter its deaf and dumb.

HOTELS OF THE CITY.

To the traveler approaching a strange city for the first time, one subject is usually uppermost—the question of "what hotel?" At Knoxville as everywhere else there is room for choice; but the best are those described as follows. There has been, it is true, some talk of late, of a new and grander project than any of its sheltering folds at present: but not because those it has now are inns of inferior order; simply to enlarge the city's already excellent accommodations for transients. To "boom" it a little, perhaps as well, like the plan to hold an exposition.

But to return to the question under discussion—the Knoxville Hotels—

The HOTEL HATTIE, situated most centrally at Gay and Clinch streets, has lately been enlarged, newly furnished, and provided with the most recent electrical and other appointments. The house is now nearly twice the size it was before these improvements were made. It has elegantly furnished rooms, arranged both single and *en suite*, and accommodations for 250 guests. Attached to it is a first class restaurant, in which meals can be had at all hours, day or night.

The "Hattie" is headquarters for the drummers, whose patronage is usually considered an evidence of a superior table and entertainment generally. It is owned and conducted by JOHN C. FLANDERS, owner besides of considerable valuable farming land adjacent to the city and one of the firm of J. C. Flanders & Son, who are proprietors also of the PALACE HOTEL, described in the paragraphs that follow. Rates at the Hattie are $2, $2.50 and $3 a day.

The PALACE HOTEL, the largest at Knoxville, is situated corner of State and Commerce streets, adjacent to the jobbing center. Street cars, running to all parts of the city and its suburbs, pass close by.

The Palace is a new house comparatively, and has all the modern improvements—sample rooms, elegantly fitted bar, cafe and billiard hall, steam heat, electric lights, elevator, fire escapes, etc. It was built in 1889, by the Mayor of old Knoxville, Mr. Mel. E. Thompson, of the very best materials, and is furnished throughout handsomely and luxuriously. The cut on this page shows its external appearance; but it gives no hint of the comfort and elegance that reign within, the superior service, and excellent *cuisine*; for the Palace is famous for its table with traveling men and tourists who make the town.

Knoxville is fast becoming a half-way and stop-over station for tourists bound either North

PALACE HOTEL.

or South, and is beginning to be, with its equable seasons and many attractions, both a summer and winter resort. For this class of transients,

journeying for pleasure, or pleasure and business combined (for your traveling public is very apt to have both for its bent), for this class,

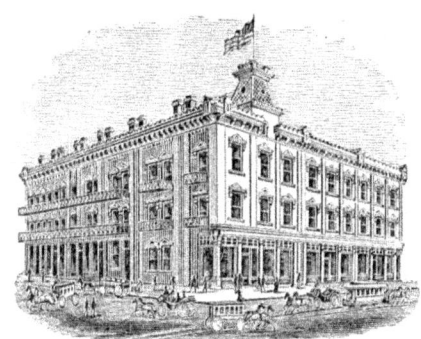

THE HOTEL KNOX.

we repeat, the Palace can be specially commended. It is near the Union depot—only half the distance, indeed, of any other house, and has an experienced and capable management.

It is owned and conducted by JOHN C. FLANDERS & SON, owners also, as we have said, of the Hattie House here. Mr. Flanders, the elder, has lived here for a lifetime, and has been in the hotel business for more than twenty years. He is one of the few hosts who have made hotel keeping a success.

Rates at the Palace are $2 to $3 a day. It has accommodations for about 125 guests.

The HOTEL KNOX, formerly the "New Schubert," a cut of which is on this page, is situated at the corner of Gay and Cumberland streets, the exact business center of the city, and is a house that, in its appointments, service and *cuisine* will compare with any first class hotel in the land. It has 100 sleeping rooms, commodious and well lighted sample rooms, electric lights, bath, bar and billiard rooms, barber shop, transfer and telegraph office, and is the only house here, in fact, with complete advantages of the sort; and a first class restaurant is run in connection with it. It was built in 1875 and was run for a time thereafter by Herman Schubert, from whom it derived its original name, and in 1890 passed into the hands of CHAS. McNABB, for whom it was entirely refitted and refurnished.

Mr. McNabb is a man of experience in the business. He takes considerable pride in sustaining the reputation the house has acquired as the finest here.

The Knox's rates are $2 to $2.50 a day, according to the accommodations furnished.

The LAMAR HOUSE, long the leading and best hotel of the city, has lately been refurnished and refitted at a cost of $5,000. It is an old house, with a reputation like the St. Charles at New Orleans, the Peabody at Memphis, the Maxwell at Nashville, and the Pulaski at Savannah, of an old-fashioned architecture, and at the same time old-fashioned comforts and thorough service.

It has a sodded lawn with a fountain and shrubbery and rustic seats where its guests can enjoy their *otium cum dignitate* after partaking of its excellent fare, and for that and other advantages has the patronage of the commercial men and theatrical people whose wayfaring life and luxurious tastes, posts them on

SECOND BAPTIST CHURCH, WEST KNOXVILLE.

the inns where they can take their ease at a moderate rate for the entertainment.

The Lamar has 200 rooms. Its regular rate to transients is $2. Special rates are made, however, to histrionic and commercial people. It has all the late electrical conveniences; cars from the depot run by it. MRS. LAURA WHITEHEAD & Co., are its proprietors; MR. ARTHUR THOMPSON, manager.

EGAN'S CAFE AND RESTAURANT consists of two parts or departments, a restaurant and lunch counters and a saloon, both first-class of their kind, centrally situated and enjoying the patronage of the best and most substantial people of the town.

They are at 125 Gay street, opposite the Mechanics' Bank, and make a specialty of the best fare and refreshments the market affords.

MR. TOM EGAN, the proprietor of this establishment, has been in the business here for years, and has acquired a fortune by running a place which is first-class in every respect.

EDUCATION AND ÆSTHETICS.

KNOXVILLE—all three of it too, in this particular, be it remembered—is as much the educational center of East Tennessee and adjacent parts (not to speak of its right to literary and artistic distinction, to which it has also claims), as it is their trade, financial and manufacturing nave. It is a community, as a whole considered, liberal in its cultivation of the field, and tree of knowledge—the field in general and the tree in detail—by medium of common and higher schools, training schools for the negro race, academies, colleges of business practice, and of medicine and dentistry, universities, conservatories of music, classes in art, newspapers, public libraries, the drama, legitimate and transitory—all the fruits and flowers, in fact, of this broad field, from the A B C's to the muses and the humanities. And it expends, all told, a very generous share of its income and resources, for the advancement of intelligence among its youth; in this respect and policy aligning itself with the most forward and aspiring communities of the land.

As for public schools, where all may imbibe at a living fountain, rich and poor, high and low alike, the old city supports nine of them, three especially for its youth of color. The six school buildings owned by it are valued at $104,500; one, the girls' high school, cost $40,000, and another, the ninth ward school, $20,000. The attendance at these nine schools, last year, was 3,370, of which number 770 were the children of the blacks.

Sixty-two teachers are employed at an average salary of $550 a year. The sum applied to maintenance of the schools, last year, was $41,500. Under the system in vogue in Tennessee, the school funds are drawn from the State and county levies of taxes. From these sources, $32,350 was received by the school district of Knoxville; and the city added, for its part, nearly $10,000 more.

These public schools of Knoxville are governed by a School Board, and are managed by a

Superintendent who is its executive officer. ALBERT RUTH, a teacher of thirty years' experience, holds that office at present. In the methods employed for discipline and instruc-

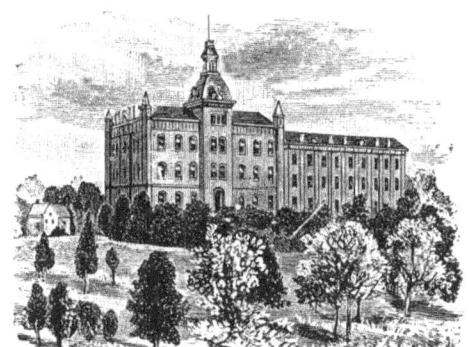

KNOXVILLE COLLEGE (COLORED).

tion, the Knoxville schools differ little from those of other cities. The high school course is so framed as to make it preparatory for college. Instruction is given in all the grades in vocal music. Latin in the high school excepted, no foreign languages are taught. There are no normal, kindergarten, technical or training schools or classes. Parents supply the text books for the children. The system, in short, is that of the common school, pure and simple.

North and West Knoxville, have each a public school, in addition to these, and West Knoxville has a high school besides.

The Parish Schools of the Catholic Church, and others that are under private management, supplement the work of these public schools in the elementary branches. An especially large proportion of the scholastic population of the city is under such private tuition; barely a half the children reported of school age attend the public schools.

Of the higher institutions of learning at Knoxville, the most notable is the old—in an impetuous age like this, the ancient, indeed, and venerable, UNIVERSITY OF TENNESSEE, which was established in 1794 by the General Assembly of "the territory south of the Ohio." It crowns the summit and mounts the slopes of University Hill in West Knoxville, almost within bowshot of historic Fort Sanders, with the twelve buildings that house its various departments, and a campus of 40 acres.

It is an institution fulfilling all the elements of that homely, but apt definition of a university, "a place where anybody may study anything." In its organization the Prussian School System, so well exemplified in this country at Ann Arbor, Mich., has been followed. It fitly rounds out, with its perfected facilities for higher instruction, literary, scientific, agricultural, mechanical, engineering and pedagogic, the scheme of popular education as it is understood in Tennessee.

The latest additions to it are schools of law, medicine and dentistry. There are 275 free scholarships in this institution at the disposal of the members of the State legislature, or established as rewards of merit for contention in the high schools of the State. CHAS. W. DABNEY, LL. D., is its president. It has a numerous, efficient, and as a whole, distinguished faculty.

JUDGE HENRY H. INGERSOLL, a graduate of Yale, and a lawyer of learning and very extensive practice, is at the head of the law department of this university. He is assisted by a corps of ten able lecturers.

The TENNESSEE MEDICAL COLLEGE, situated corner of Cleveland street and Dameron avenue, in North Knoxville, one of the highest points in the city, was founded in 1889. It is, therefore, a comparatively new institution; but it has this advantage in that very fact: It is modern in its methods, appointments, and facilities for mastery of the healing art.

It was established by professional men of lifelong experience, with the assistance of others prominent socially and in a business way. It originated with DR. J. C. CAWOOD, one of the most prominent physicians of the South, who is its dean, and DR. C. E. RISTINE, equally notable, its registrar, and its organization was promoted by the following distinguished Tennesseeans who are its Board of Trustees: Col. A. J. Albers, of Sanford, Chamberlin & Albers, wholesale druggists; J. T. Shields,

TENNESSEE MEDICAL COLLEGE.

president of the City National Bank; C. M. McGhee, railroad magnate and capitalist; Perez Dickinson, of Cowan, McClung & Co.;

Frank Smith, professor of literature in the University of Tennessee; H. M. Aiken, president of the Holston National Bank; Judge J. G. Rose, of Morristown, Tenn.; W. M. Rule, editor of the *Knoxville Journal*; Dr. B. B. Lenoir, Col. E. J. Sanford, wholesale druggist and capitalist; Rev. Dr. J. H. Keith, John H. Inman, of the Richmond Terminal Railroad System; Gen. R. N. Hood, president of the Third National Bank; Hon. Howell E. Jackson, United States Senator from Tennessee, and C. M. McClung, secretary, with the Governor of Tennessee *ex-officio*, a member of the board.

VIEW FROM THE GROUNDS OF THE UNIVERSITY OF TENNESSEE.

Its faculty has for members, the leading lights of the medical and dental professions here, for it is a college of dentistry as well of surgery and medicine. These instructors and the subjects taught by them are as follows:

The Dean, Dr. Cawood, principles and practice of surgery and clinical surgery; Dr. C. M. Drake, descriptive and surgical anatomy, and clinical surgery, and the direction also of the pathological laboratory; Dr. J. W. Hill, orthopœdic, operative and clinical surgery; the registrar, Dr. Ristine, obstetrics and clinical gynæcology; the secretary of the faculty, Dr. R. M. C. Hill, materia medica and general therapeutics, and clinical medicine; Dr. J. M. Masters, opthalmology, laryngology and otology; Dr. Campbell, superintendent of the State Insane Asylum here, mental and nervous diseases; Henry R. Gibson, medical jurisprudence; Dr. W. C. Bailey, theory and practice of medicine and clinical medicine, and also direction of the bacteriological laboratory; Dr. C. M. Wilson, gynæcology and clinical gynæcology; Dr. B. D. Bosworth, physiology and microscopy; Dr. R. N. Kesterson, (dean of the dental faculty) dental surgery and operative dentistry; Dr. J. S. Cottrell, mechanical dentistry and dental metallurgy; and besides these, nine demonstrators—Dr. B. B. Cates, of anatomy and operative surgery; Dr. Thos F. Fitzgerald, of chemistry; Doctors H. M. Lee and C. H. Brooke, assistants for anatomy; Dr. D. H. Williams, of pathology and microscopy; Dr. P. A. Pennington, of operative dentistry; Dr. H. F. Henderson, of mechanical dentistry; Dr. H. S. Keener, of operative dentistry and chief of dental clinics, and Dr. T. B. McBride, of mechanical dentistry.

It has the inestimable advantage of location in the most healthful and pleasant city of its size in the South; but it would be supererogatory here, after what has been already said of Knoxville, to recount the climatic and scenic charms of the place.

Its new College building, that shown in the engraving accompanying this matter was completed in December of 1890. It is a five-story building, constructed of stone and brick, and affords as complete and ample arrangements for didactic, clinical and laboratory teaching as any school in the South. This building contains two large, well ventilated and lighted lecture rooms, furnished with opera chairs; a large and completely equipped chemical laboratory; a microscopical and pathological laboratory, which, in arrangement and equipment, is unsurpassed; a bacteriological laboratory; a large, airy and well-lighted dissecting room; students' library and reception room, together with other provisions for prosecuting practical work in medicine, surgery and dentistry. The museum, which occupies two stories, well filled with models, dry and wet preparations, anatomical and pathological specimens, forms a rich and unique collection, which is utilized in illustrating the lectures upon the different branches. And large acquisitions to the museum have lately been made. A hospital soon to be erected, adjoining the college building, will contain a hundred beds and afford a large field for practical experience in all classes of diseases and injuries, and will require the services of two resident assistants. These

Members of the faculty and hospital staff of the college, are chief and local surgeons of the East Tennessee, Virginia and Georgia Railway System, and are thus enabled to show to the class many interesting cases in railroad surgery.

The UNIVERSITY SCHOOL of Knoxville, is situated at 303 and 305 Highland avenue. It was founded in 1889 by MESSRS LEWIS M. G., BAKER, M. A., and CHARLES M. HIMEL, both from the University of Virginia. They conducted their school during the first session, at 184 W. Main street. At the close of this first session, they bought a lot and erected a building at a cost of $15,000. It is a large brick building of two stories and a basement, and it is furnished with every modern invention for heating and ventilating, and the most recent school apparatus. The accompanying cut shows its external appearance.

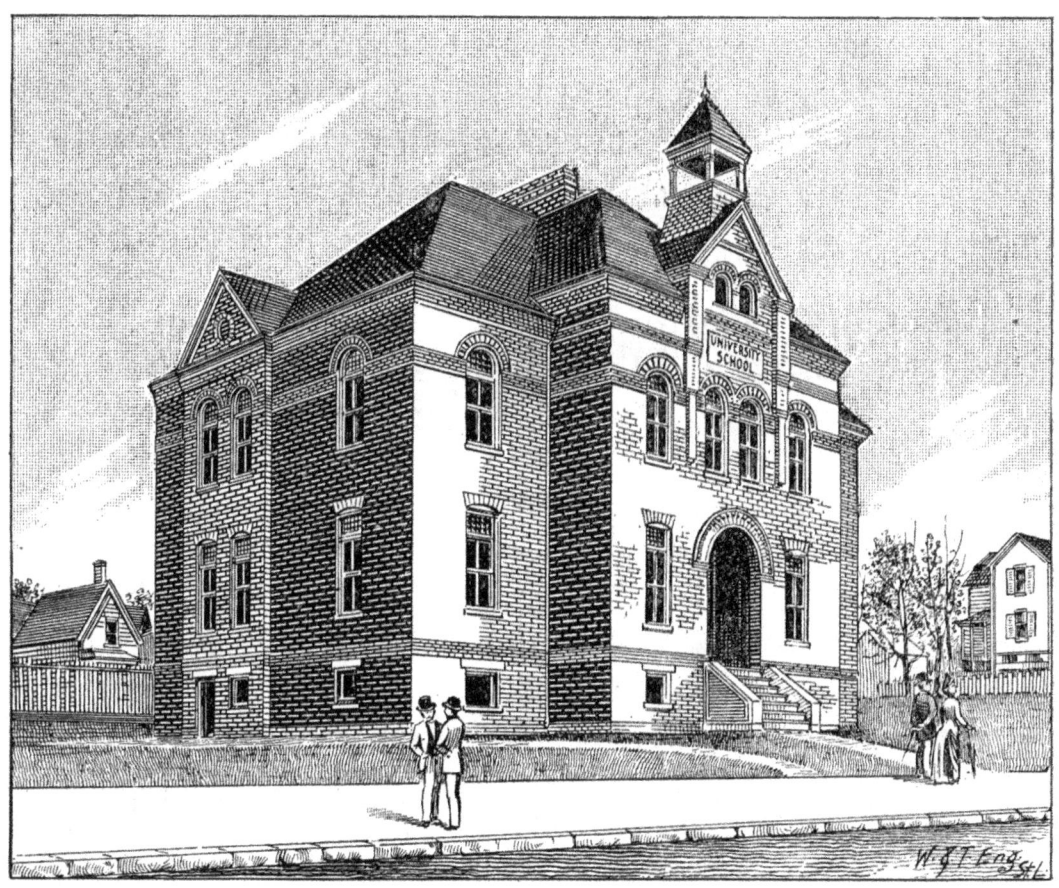

UNIVERSITY SCHOOL OF KNOXVILLE.
Baker & Himel, Principals.

assistants will be chosen from the graduating class at the end of each session. The two standing the best examination will be selected.

This school is situated in the midst of the fashionable residence quarter of the city known as West Knoxville, and it draws its patronage from the best people of the city. It was incorporated in 1891, with Lewis M. G. Baker, Chas. M. Himel, C. S. Newman, J. W. Caldwell and J. L. Thomas, as incorporators. Lewis M. G. Baker was elected president, and Chas. M. Himel, secretary and treasurer.

Besides its regular academic department, this school has a primary department designed for boys from seven to twelve years of age. It has a boarding department also, the number in which, at present, is limited to twelve. The work of the school is to prepare students for the best colleges and universities, and for business life. Messrs. Baker and Himel are assisted by three competent and experienced teachers, and each teacher has special subjects to which he devotes his entire time and attention. The number of pupils is limited, and

Company and the Knoxville Savings and Development Company. The secretary, Mr. R. S. Collins, ranks among the most skillful American penmen, and his equal as such can hardly be found in the entire South. The law department of the college is under the management of Judge A. G. Howe, B. L., a graduate of the law department of the Indiana State University, who is a regular practitioner at the Knoxville bar.

This college occupies the entire third floor of the Public Library building, one of the handsomest structures of the city, and has quarters affording accommodations for about 400 pupils.

The course of study is thorough and practical, as hundreds of young men and women who are occupying responsible places will testify. There were enrolled last year over 300 students

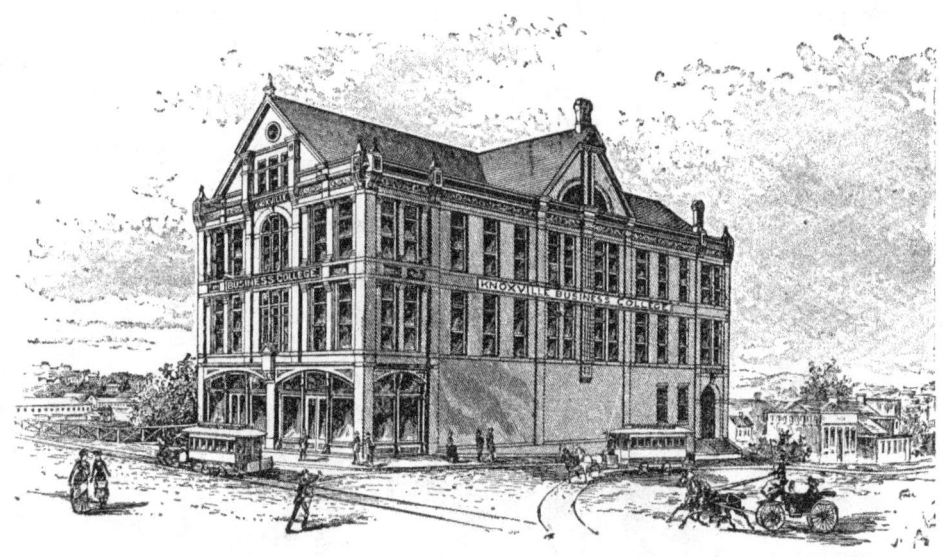

KNOXVILLE BUSINESS COLLEGE.

these are carefully selected. The management is on the "Honor System," by which means principles of honesty and manliness are inculcated, and the boys are made to feel, that unless they are upright and studious, the University School is not the place for them.

The KNOXVILLE BUSINESS COLLEGE is said by those acquainted with its methods and results, to be one of the best commercial schools of the South. Its success is to be credited largely to the fact that the faculty are experienced men in their respective lines of instruction.

The president and proprietor, Mr. J. T. JOHNSON, is a live business man, and, besides ownership of the Knoxville Business College, is a stockholder and director in two corporations of Knoxville—the Southern Accident

from six different States. The college is in continuous session, and students may enter at any time. Information concerning it is supplied upon request for its catalogue, which will be mailed free to any part of the country.

YOUNG'S COLLEGE OF SHORTHAND, of which A. E. BROYLES, agent for the Caligraph typewriter and type-writer supplies, is proprietor, and MISS EMMA SPERRY, instructor, was established in 1884, and it has hundreds of its graduates occupying good mercantile positions hereabouts.

Mr. Broyles is an expert stenographer himself, and Miss Sperry has had five years experience of the business. They give lessons by mail as well as to students who sit under them. This school is in the McCALLUM BLOCK.

There is, at Knoxville, also, an institution, which, in connection with the topics under discussion herein just now, could hardly be passed, without, at least, a reference to it. That institution, the TENNESSEE SCHOOL FOR THE DEAF AND DUMB is situated in a sequestered bend of the river, a few miles out of the city. It was founded in 1845, and has 140 inmates. A new building to accommodate 200 has just been completed. It has grounds of eight acres area; and near it, the colored unfortunates, similarly afflicted, are domiciled. At both, the methods pursued are progressive. Lip reading and speech are taught, and the trades, likewise, in an industrial department.

M'CALLUM BLOCK,
Occupied in part by Young's College of Shorthand.

The SLATER TRAINING SCHOOL of Knoxville, is a normal and industrial institution for colored youth, which is one of the beneficiaries of the "Slater fund," bequeathed in trust to the American Missionary Association of New York, to further the cause of education among the negroes of the South. Hence the name of it. The Slater fund is, however, insufficient to maintain it without other assistance, and it is dependent, largely, upon the bounty of the philanthropic throughout the land. Knoxville is a liberal contributor to it, and it has a small income from nominal fees for tuition. It was founded in 1869 by MISS EMILY AUSTIN, and at present it has a rudimentary purpose only.

UNIVERSITY OF TENNESSEE.

THE PRESS OF KNOXVILLE.

SINCE the *Sentinel* suspended a few months since, Knoxville has but two dailies, the *Tribune* and the *Journal*. The Knoxville TRIBUNE is successor to the *Herald*, which itself was successor to the *Register*, established in 1813, and the first paper that was published in the State. The *Tribune* is owned by a stock company of which J. H. MORRISON is general manager. It is an eight-page six-column paper, of 4,200 circulation daily, and it issues a weekly for its farming patrons, which has a subscription list of 10,000. In politics it is Democratic.

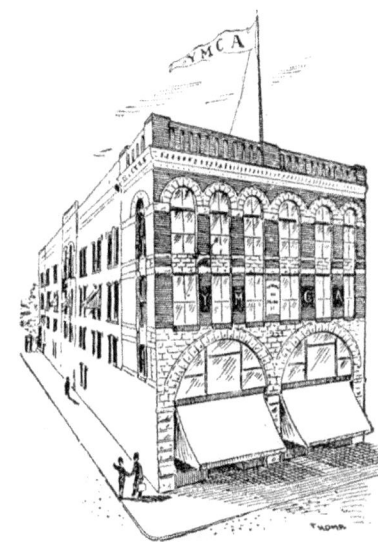

Y. M. C. A. OR BORCHES BUILDING.

The *Daily Journal* is descendant in the second generation from *Brownlow's Whig*, which was established in 1839. Its editor and manager, WM. RULE, has been connected with it since '59. It is an eight-page, six-column paper, with about 3,000 daily circulation, independent, influential and enterprising. It represents an investment of about $40,000, and is solidly established.

LETTERS, ART, SONG AND DRAMA.

THE LAWSON MCGHEE Library Building and the collection of 8,000 volumes of standard literature it contains, was the gift to Knoxville of the public-spirited citizen whose name it fitly bears. It is the free and school library of the city. The university has also an extensive library of standard works.

Knoxville as yet makes no contention with Boston as regards its culture; but it has its share, nevertheless, of cultivated people, and it has produced, in its day, some little original literary work; under which head we may cite, Dr. Ramsay's "Annals of Tennessee," and Dr. Hume's "Loyal Mountaineers," not to mention old Brownlow's biography of Clay, and other works of the kind, all which have proceeded "lang syne" from the Knoxville job press. And long ere a Craddock had woven in fiction the spell of these Smoky mountains yonder, others, ruder in fancy, perhaps, than she, but still betimes, had blazed the way, as pioneers, in that very same realm of romance.

Little could reasonably be expected of Knoxville yet in the matter of art; it has, nevertheless, a school, if nothing more, for instruction in drawing, painting and modeling, the master of which has studied abroad. In music, however, proficiency in which is a commoner accomplishment, it cuts a braver, and, size and situation considered, a somewhat noteworthy figure. It has an unusually large number of ambitious, musical-minded amateurs; it supports liberally, concert, opera and oratorio; and music, vocal and instrumental, is, very generally, a pastime of its homes.

The only theater at Knoxville is "STAUB'S." It is one of a number in Tennessee, controlled en circuit, by a single management. It is an old house but a large one; sufficient, perhaps, for the place and the times.

From books and music and the play and all that, it is an easy transition to the clubs, and organizations, and social life generally of the people of Knoxville. The most notable of the clubs of the city is the CHILHOWIE, to which most of the more prosperous business and professional men belong. The CHAMBER OF COMMERCE is strictly a commercial body, devoted to the advancement of the city's business interests. It busies itself with projects for new hotels, expositions, factories and that sort of thing; it has, at least, advertised the city extensively, and has done some effective work in heralding the attractions of the town.

The martial spirit characteristic of the Southern youth has exemplification at Knoxville in several military companies of numerous membership. The city supports a ball club, and a boat club, recently organized, the CHEROKEE. For the rest it has lodges of pretty much all the fraternal orders, churches of every denomination, mission homes, and other organizations, formed and maintained, mostly under the auspices of the churches, for charity's sweet sake.

In its social phases, Knoxville is, in a word, characteristically many-sided, city like, metropolitan.

SCENE ON THE TENNESSEE RIVER.

REAL ESTATE AND BETTERMENTS.

THAT very conspicuous feature of the progress made by Knoxville in the expansive period of the last few years, to which we have heretofore alluded, namely, the activity prevailing in real estate, and in building, and other improvements of a permanent character, is a condition of things worthy more, indeed, than mere remark. Here, then, before we turn our attention to aspects strictly commercial, let it be considered.

To begin with, let it be understood that there has been no "boom" at Knoxville, in the sense of that term out West. The enhancement of real estate values has been tremendous, in some instances, 500 per cent within five years; but in this there is nothing abnormal. The city grows and waxes great, by virtue of growing surroundings. There has been of late, to be sure, a season of dulness; this, however, is but natural; no market is always lively; and prices hold up well, if business is slow, because the promise and prospects of Knoxville justify them.

The record of transfers of realty at Knoxville, for '91, was not, at the time this compilation was made, accessible to us; the status of Knoxville, among the capitals of American commerce, great and small, is, apparently, a matter of indifference to the official recorder of deeds. We are able, however, to say that the real estate business of the city has been very large, both in number of transactions and values. It amounts, all told, to a total of several millions. And it supports something like fifty or sixty regular dealers in property and lands, the most prominent of whom are mentioned hereinafter.

PROSPEROUS CONDITIONS.

The substantial Knoxville real estate firms of STEELE & MCMILLAN and FRENCH & ROBERTS are authority for the statements made hereinafter—that is to say, the facts are theirs, drawn out by interview; the grouping of them, and the conclusions therefrom, are, however, our own.

Suburban development, and building improvement everywhere, are the distinguishing phases of late, of the Knoxville real estate market. Here, for example, are the names of the concerns engaged in the work of upbuilding and extending the outer precincts of the city, and the titles they give their projects. The KNOXVILLE REAL ESTATE EXCHANGE, which has laid out "Ukala Park," or Longstreet's Heights, and is building an overhead cable railway to it of ingenious and novel construction; the CHEROKEE LAND CO., which proposes to bridge the river, and to found, really, another city across it, with co-operative laundry, restaurant and other such institutions; the MIDDLEBROOK PARK ASSOCIATION, whose property is about four miles out; the FOUNTAIN CITY CO., already mentioned (page 21); the Lake Ottosee, or KNOXVILLE LAKE PARK SPRINGS CO.; the BROAD STREET LAND CO., which is exploiting the "Arlington" addition, on the line of the Fountain Head Railway; the LONSDALE LAND CO., operating in the suburbs to the northwest; the ROSEDALE LAND AND IMPROVEMENT CO., whose tract is northwest of the city, near the railroad shops; the EDGEWOOD LAND CO., which has two tracts in market, one of them, "Edgewood," north of the city; the RIVERSIDE IMPROVEMENT CO., and the CIRCLE PARK LAND CO, of West Knoxville, and the WEST END LAND CO, of North Knoxville; the KNOXVILLE DEVELOPMENT CO., which has no particular addition; and, besides these, the NORTH KNOXVILLE LOT AND BUILDING ASSOCIATION, and eight or ten other Building and Loan Associations, local or national, or both in scope. And, as a center of trade and population, as well as of real estate projects, Knoxville is also headquarters for the land department of the East Tennessee, Virginia & Georgia road, the Lenoir City Co., original owners of the town site of the flourishing city of Lenoir, and the Knoxville Industrial Investment Co., an auxiliary of the Chamber of Commerce, which is intended to further the establishment of manufacturing and other industrial enterprises by bonuses of land, subscriptions to stock, and like assistance.

ARCHITECTURAL IMPROVEMENTS.

AND as for the building improvements, indicative of an uncommon degree of advancement, the following, of late and therefore modern construction will serve. The marble Federal

Courts and Postal Building, which cost $500,000; the Court House of Knox county, $125,000; the woolen mills, $75,000, without their equipment of machinery; McTeers, Payne, Hood & Co.'s seven-story wholesale house, $60,000; the Commerce Building, $60,000; the Harris Building, $60,000; St. John's Episcopal church, $55,000; the Girls' High School, $40,000; the Vendome Hotel, French & Roberts' Block, and Deaderick Block, office buildings, $30,000 each, and a dozen others as costly, devoted to office business or purposes of trade.

Besides these buildings, residences like the following: E. C. Camp's palatial mansion, the cost of which has been $125,000; the Ross Flats, old and new altogether, $40,000; S. B. Luttrell's house, $30,000; at least fifteen that will average $20,000—in this class Col. Swepson's, W. C. Fulcher's, J. D. Cowan's, Major Huger's, W. W. Woodruff's, Sam McKinney's, C. J. and C. M. McClung's, the Sanfords', father and son, W. B. Lockett's, A. J. Alber's, Jos. M. McTeer's, C. M. McGhee's and Perez Dickinson's; the Vandeventer residence, $18,000; and more than 100 homes erected in North and West Knoxville in the past three years that cost from $8,000 to $15,000 each. A list which is Knoxville's manifest, at once, of its prosperity and its rise.

ENHANCED VALUES AND PRICES.

The work of sewer and street improvement, which has been entered upon in Old Knoxville, and the character of the street railroad facilities of the city, are subjects already given attention in our general description of the city, pages 17, 18 and 19.

The general advancement in the price of Knoxville real estate, which is the measure of enhanced values, has been all the way from 40 to 500 per cent in the last five or six years. A general average for the whole would be something between 50 and 100 per cent. The greatest advancement has naturally been in the suburbs, in which parts, it is a rule of the real estate men, property usually quadruples in value, if it doubles itself inside.

Knoxville property is, however, compared with the prices prevailing in other cities of its size and rank, still very low. It is the lowest of any Southern city; cheaper at all events, relatively, than in Chattanooga, Nashville or Birmingham.

The principal thoroughfare of the city is Gay street. It is a street of both wholesale and retail business. None of its wholesale property is in market, but it is valued at $500 to $750 a foot front, without improvements. Ground in the wholesale district, a block off this street, has been sold for $600 a foot. Retail sites on Gay street are held at $1,000 to $1,500; near Market Square, such ground can be bought at $125 to $150 a foot; the best property of this sort is reasonably worth $300 to $1,000.

Inside residence property on fashionable streets, is worth $20 to $150 a foot; residence property further out $8, and $10 to $30; in the outskirts, suitable for the homes of working people, at from $2.50 to $10.

Manufacturing sites are available well down town at from $10 to $30 a foot; in the suburbs, two or three miles out, at $50 to $150 an acre. Some sites for this purpose can be had for the asking.

RENTS AND OTHER CONSIDERATIONS.

The income that can be derived from property here justifies these prices. For example: The Deaderick Block cost $30,000; its rentals aggregate $7,500 a year; it returns twenty per cent net; the McCallum Block earns about the same; the Borches Block cost $30,000; it earns $4,000, or thirteen per cent, and the Minnis Block about that too. These are office buildings, and the growth of the place makes their accommodations largely in demand.

Rentals are usually a fair gauge of property values. At Knoxville it is true, owing to the very growth of the place, they are somewhat high, but there are compensating circumstances to tenants in the flourishing state of affairs that makes them so. Long leases are not the fashion here. A building or warehouse suitable for ordinary jobbing or manufacturing purposes, brings from $1,800 to $2,000 a year. Rents for first class retail locations are about the same figure. Offices fetch from $10 to $25; a four-roomed house $10 to $20; one of five or six rooms, $16 to $30; one of eight, perhaps $40.

The expense to build here is ten to twenty per cent less, on an average, than in other places, by reason of the plentiful supply of building materials and labor available. Taxes are lower than in most cities; indeed, the moderate Knoxville scale of assessment considered, they are the lowest, perhaps, in the land.

The ruling rate of interest for real estate loans is eight per cent, and a half, generally, of the value of the property can be obtained upon mortgage security.

There are seven or eight building and loan associations established, and in prosperous condition; and these stand ready to assist the thrifty man to secure a home.

THE SUBJECT IN GENERAL.

THERE are few cases to be met with of troublesome titles; most trace back to the original grants of the North Carolina Colony, which Tennessee, to begin with, was.

Water is supplied at the rate of about $8 per annum for an ordinary family; some householders rely entirely on cisterns, which cost from $10 to $25. Gas is $1.50 a thousand, 10 off for cash.

The city grows rather evenly at all points away from the river. The business quarter is spreading chiefly east and west from Gay street, and the East Tennessee, Virginia & Georgia track, where it terminates in the city. The residence district moves steadily northward and westward; West Knoxville is the favorite district of the well-to-do.

The real estate business has been somewhat slow of late, owing to the general dulness prevailing throughout the southern section of country. It is beginning, however, to show some signs of revival. The improvement projects mentioned at the beginning of this subject matter, however, are all meeting with success, and money is still coming in from outside sources for investment. The owners of large properties, like E. C. Camp, S. B. Luttrell, Perez Dickinson, the Knoxville Real Estate Company, and the Cherokee, Lonsdale and Edgewood Land Companies, are inclined to be liberal and enterprising and public-spirited in their methods of trade.

COUNTRY LANDS.

THE advantages of Knoxville for business, and its attractions for residence, are set forth in detail in the various chapters of this work, and need not be especially emphasized here. It is sufficient to remark upon that subject that as the knowledge of its salubrity, its rich surroundings, and its progressiveness spreads abroad, it challenges attention as a city with no uncertain future.

One word more is perhaps necessary in this connection. Most of the local dealers in real estate "handle," as the phrase is, country, as well as city lands, and some, in fact, make a specialty of the trade in farming, mineral and timber properties in East Tennessee and Kentucky, and adjacent North Carolina. This is a mountainous region; but it has a very fair proportion of rich agricultural and pastoral domain. The valley lands contiguous to Knoxville are, some of them, of unsurpassed fertility. Wheat, corn, oats, barley and truck flourish on these lands. They can hardly be excelled for strawberries and melons. Such lands can be obtained in quantity to suit, from an acre up, at from $25 to $50 an acre with improvements, $10 to $40, without.

The following sketches give an account of some of the leading dealers in Knoxville real estate, and Tennessee lands.

LEADING DEALERS IN REAL ESTATE.

COLE & PRATT, dealers in real estate, at 336 Broad street, handle their own property chiefly. They have considerable of it—fine residence and business property both; also suburban acreage, the latter on Sixth avenue and along the line of the Fountain Head dummy line of railway.

Mr. Cole has been a resident here about four years, and all the while has been interested in realty. Mr. Pratt has had his home here two years. He is one of the directors of the National Manufacturing Co., described on another page of this work.

E. H. SCHARRINGHAUS, real estate agent, of 246 and 248 Gay street, has been established in this line here about two years. He makes a specialty of trade in city and suburban property.

He has some very desirable suburban tracts, that have been subdivided into lots 50 x 150 feet, and wide avenues, which tracts offer the investor excellent bargains, and give home-seekers the desired opportunity of buying plots at reasonable prices, on easy terms. He also has choice business property and manufacturing sites, and gives special attention to the renting of houses.

He is secretary of two associations, viz.: The HOME BUILDING & LOAN ASSOCIATION and the NORTH KNOXVILLE LOT & BUILDING ASSOCIATION. He was instrumental in the organization of both these associations, and their entire success is owing, in a great measure, to his ability and energy.

He is a native of Covington, Ky., and came to this city from Cincinnati, Ohio, where he was also formerly actively engaged in the real estate and insurance business, and in building and loan concerns.

The HOME BUILDING & LOAN ASSOCIATION was organized in this city in 1890, and has, upon its stock book, many of the best and representative citizens of the city. Mr. W. H. SIMMONDS is its president; W. W. LEE, vice-president; E. H. SCHARRINGHAUS, secretary, and the CENTRAL SAVINGS BANK, treasurer.

The estimate of time necessary for this stock to mature is seven years. Its loans are confined to Knoxville and its suburbs, but membership is open to all.

Though but so recently organized, the Home has gained such headway that the people here look upon it with confidence and speak of it in terms of commendation.

It has many advantageous features over other associations, chief of which is its liberal withdrawal clause. All profits are pro-rated semi-annually among the stockholders, according to their investment, which dividends are credited in the pass books, so at any time the cash surrender value of stock can be readily seen by shareholders.

At withdrawal all dues are returned, and the entire dividend paid as well. These dividends have heretofore amounted to 19 per cent per annum.

The conditions are equalized by the plan of this association, for investments, with cash surrender value at any time, give a poor man, who is unable to carry stock to maturity, as much benefit in proportion as his more fortunate brother.

The NORTH KNOXVILLE LOT & BUILDING ASSOCIATION, of 246 Gay street, was organized in 1890 by parties resident here, in company with others not resident, for the purpose of purchasing an available suburban tract, subdividing it and selling it on the instalment plan to home builders. It procured itself a charter and has since been successfully engaged in the business. The largest stockholder in it is Mr. O. J. CARPENTER of Covington, Ky.; the next largest, W. H. SIMMONDS, insurance and real estate agent of this city, and the third largest, E. H. SCHARRINGHAUS, real estate agent here and secretary also of the Home Building & Loan Association. Mr. Simmonds is president of the company and Mr. Scharringhaus, secretary and general manager. The latter is from Cincinnati, where he was actively engaged in the insurance and real estate business. He has been prominent in these lines also since he came here two years ago.

This company began operations by the purchase of a tract divisible into 190 lots. This tract is in North Knoxville about a mile and a half from the heart of the city proper. Two-thirds of it has been disposed of already upon the very liberal terms (to buyers) of $2 a week or $8 a month. Numerous residences have been built upon it and a number more are to go up in the spring. No lots have or will be sold to colored people, and an effort has been made to attract the best sort of settlers only.

About fifty lots still remain to be sold on the same terms as the others. These lots are 50 x 150 feet and front on streets sixty feet wide. They have, in accordance with the custom prevailing here, a ten-foot alley in the rear. Water is available and street cars will reach the tract at an early day. The car line is now within eight squares of this land.

These lots afford an excellent medium for those who desire to save rent charges. As an investment they will pay largely. The company has been so successful in disposing of them that it will shortly subdivide similarly, for sale, another tract like this.

The HOMESTEAD INVESTMENT Co., of Knoxville, which has offices at 117 Prince street, opposite the Federal Building, is a building, loan and savings association, organized and conducted upon the methods that prevail with such associations generally in this country.

It has certain safeguards, however, with respect to its management, which are not so commonly characteristic of these fiduciary concerns. It is required by statute, to deposit $25,000 in securities, as a pledge for its outside loans business, and is subject to regular examinations by State officials.

Its officers are bonded, the secretary for $5,000, and the treasurer for $10,000. The securities given it for loans are deposited with three solid banks of Knoxville, and there remain until regularly redeemed, and are therefore not like those exacted by private money lenders, specially to be negotiated and sold.

Leading citizens of Knoxville are its directors: F. C. Beaman, Homer Gilman, W. S. Cagle, J. F. J. Lewis, T. C. Holloway, J. E. Dosser, S. P. Fowler, and C. B. Jennings. MR. BEAMAN is its president, MR. GILMAN first, and MR. CAGLE second vice-president; MR. LEWIS, secretary and general manager; MR. HOLLOWAY, treasurer; MR. FOWLER, of counsel, and MR. JENNINGS director of agencies for it.

The COVENANT BUILDING & LOAN ASSOCIATION, of Knoxville, has been remarkably successful. Its plan of operation differs little from

OFFICES OF THE COVENANT BUILDING AND LOAN ASSOCIATION.

those of other building associations; its advantage lies in the character of its management.

Its president is W. P. WASHBURN, of Washburn & Temple, leading attorneys, not of Knoxville alone, but of East Tennessee. Mr. Washburn has shown his capacity for affairs by the fortune he has accumulated, not entirely in his profession, but from business ventures and investments here. The vice-president is Mr. W. E. GIBBINS, the managing member of the partnership of W. W. Woodruff & Co., perhaps the largest wholesale hardware firm south of the Ohio river. The treasurer, ALEX. ALLISON, a druggist, is a man of high standing and business ability. The secretary, W. M. ASHMORE, is a book-keeper and accountant of many years' experience, and, as the author of one or more books of forms that are used by several other associations, is recognized as one of the ablest and most expert persons here as regards building and loan matters. W. BORIGHT, attorney, and manager of the loan department, is a man of extensive acquaintance with business matters generally, has had many years experience in the loan business, and is an expert in making abstracts and examining titles. M. V. HAMMACK, superintendent of agencies, has had varied and successful participation in agency business, thoroughly understands building and loan matters in all their details, and displays great judgment and discrimination in selecting agents. S. BURGER, of V. Burger & Son, wholesale dealers in produce, is one of the directors and a member of the executive committee. He is a very careful, conservative business man, who has built up a business house of long standing, and who has the confidence of the business community of all this section of country.

The Covenant was organized in '89. It has a Tennessee charter, authorizing it to issue stock to the extent of $25,000,000, and has been required, under the stringent laws of the State respecting building and loan associations, to deposit a $50,000 guarantee bond with the State Treasurer. It has been doing business now for two years, and its reports show an average profit of 24 per cent.

Its stock is held at $100 per share, payable in instalments of sixty cents per month, earnings to apply on payments. Paid up stock is sold at $50 per share, cash down, and on this class of stock 6 per cent per annum is earned, payable semi-annually; and, in addition, the

THE ROSS FLATS. R. Z. GILL, ARCHITECT.

holder receives $100 for each share at maturity. The Covenant has sold, to date (January 1, '91), of this class of stock, $161,000. It has made loans to this same date, aggregating about $200,000, and all on improved property.

Under its charter it has the privilege of doing an inter-state business, and, accordingly, has established 150 agencies in twelve different States, between Pennsylvania and the Gulf. Each branch manages its own affairs, under the general supervision of the home office, excepting in the matter of loans, which are all examined into by the manager of the loan department at headquarters.

The average proportion of valuations loaned last year was 39 per cent, which is a very safe procedure, and no loans have or will be made on unimproved property, except for the purpose of improving.

ness, and we can safely predict for it as prosperous and remunerative business in the future. The building it occupies is on the principal business street of the city. An engraving of it accompanies this matter.

The SOUTHERN BUILDING & LOAN ASSOCIATION of Knoxville, enjoys distinction among the organizations of its class, as one of the most notably successful in the land. It was organized in 1889, just three years ago; and yet it has already issued shares of its stock to the aggregate value of $10,000,000, and the subscriptions therefor range from 3,000 to 5,000 shares of $100, par value, a month; that is to say, $30,000 to $50,000 of new business every 30 days.

OFFICE OF THE SOUTHERN BUILDING AND LOAN ASSOCIATION OF KNOXVILLE.

The Covenant, in the beginning of its business, occupied rooms in the Deaderick building, and only employed four office men. Since it has moved into quarters at 115 Gay street (the old People's Bank property), its business has so rapidly increased that it has been compelled to add to the working force four additional helpers. In the new quarters it is fitted up very nicely, and has the use of a fire-proof vault in which all valuable papers and books belonging to the association are kept.

The books show that it has sold, since commencing business, about $3,500,000 in instalment stock. Considering the opposition that it has to fight against, this is an excellent busi-

Its assets are $2,000,000, nearly every dollar of them secured by first mortgage liens; its net surplus is $300,000 and its cash income $75,000. Its management, indeed, has been so careful and satisfactory to all concerned, that less than twenty-five per cent of its stock has lapsed or withdrawn; which is very much less than the usual proportion.

Its annual profit has been, thus far, about twenty-four per cent, and this has been obtained by economical and prudent conduct of its business, and by having no idle funds.

The Southern is an organization of National scope. It does business in sixteen States of the South, Southeast, Southwest and Northwest, through its Eastern department at Baltimore, Maryland, and its Western at Austin, Texas, its HOME OFFICE 138 PRINCE STREET, KNOXVILLE, and its local boards, 400 in number, which are stationed wherever there are a sufficient number of members to justify it. Its plan of operations, in other respects, differs little from those of other institutions of the sort. Its special characteristic is the responsibility and business character of its management.

S. B. LUTTRELL, its president, is of S. B. Luttrell & Co., a leading jobbing hardware house of Knoxville, and is president also of the Mechanics' National Bank of the city. CHARLES DAWES, vice-president, is cashier for Cowan, McClung & Co., the leading dry goods house of this part of the South. W. H. COLLETT, secretary, has disbursed and received millions of pension money in his capacity as a government official without a discrepancy. He has been used to handling finances. M. L. Ross, the treasurer, is of M. L. Ross & Co., wholesale grocers here, and is president of the Knoxville Chamber of Commerce.

S. M. JOHNSON, general manager, has had a vast and varied experience of building and loan concerns. It is to his efficient direction of the affairs of the association that its remarkable prosperity is largely due. J. P. HEAP, a prominent attorney, has charge of the company's loans business.

The directors are the above named gentlemen and GEO. W. ALBERS, wholesale druggist, and B. A. JENKINS, capitalist and president of the Tennessee Coal Mining Co.

Tennessee has stringent laws regulating associations of this character, and one of the State officials is charged with the duty of inspecting them regularly. The Southern, of course, is subject, like all the rest, to this examination.

To provide suitable accommodations for its fast-increasing business, this association will erect an office building for itself during the present year.

The ROSEDALE LAND AND IMPROVEMENT CO., which has its offices at 56 Union street, was organized in 1890 for the development of suburban Knoxville, by the purchase of large tracts and their subdivision for sale as building lots. In pursuance of this purpose a tract of 100 acres situated only about a mile and a half from the Post Office, northwest of the city proper, and near the new shops of the East Tennessee, Virginia & Georgia Railroad, was acquired by the company; and subdivision was made of it into lots, 50 by 150, fronting upon 80-foot streets, and with a good wide alley in the rear.

This property is eligibly situated. It is high and sightly; is higher, in fact, than any residence property in old Knoxville. Considerable of it has been disposed of already to home builders; the improvements that have been made have enhanced the valuations of the lots generally throughout the tract, and as they proceed must advance prices still more. No conditions whatever have been made by the sellers as to the character or value of these improvements, but they are, for the most part, substantial and attractive structures.

Naturally, with so large a tract, the company still has many lots on hand. The price to buyers now is $250 to $300 a lot, according to situation.

The company has $65,000 capital stock. The principals in it are substantial men, who, during many years residence here, have shown themselves entirely responsible and trustworthy. The president, MR. E. J. DAVIS, is president and general manager also of the East Tennessee Coal Co. and of the Jellico Coal Mining Co. He has lived here some twenty-one years and has been identified with such enterprises pretty much all that time. He is, in fact, one of the solid men of the city. He has been an alderman, and his residence on Oak street is a very fine mansion, indeed.

The secretary, MR. B. A. JENKINS, is also largely engaged in coal mining. He is president of the Tennessee Coal Mining Co., and a director of the East Tennessee Coal Co. He is also interested in the Co-Operative Town Co. of Elizabethton, Tenn., and in other such projects.

J. M. MEEK, capitalist and dealer in realty, of 43 Deaderick Block, is a lawyer by profession, but is not actively engaged in practice. He has devoted the last eight years of his life to the more congenial pursuit of a trader in real estate. He is a wealthy man, and is the owner of considerable property here himself. The Meek Block, the largest building of the city, is his.

He makes a specialty of the sale of country lands, which he has listed with him in very great variety, and of loans on mortgage security.

Mr. Meek has been prominent here in business and public affairs for years. He was one of the convention that reorganized the State for its readmission into the Union, in 1865. He was commissioned Attorney General for the Second Judicial district of Tennessee, by President Johnson, in 1866, and again, in 1883, U. S. District Attorney, for the district of East Tennessee, by President Arthur. He has been a member of the Legislature of Tennessee, also, and has held other preferments indicative of his abilities and popularity hereabouts.

JOE M. WILSON & Co., 65 West Clinch street, opposite the Post Office (Joe M. Wilson, the "Co." of the firm name being nominal, merely), are also, leading real estate agents, of Knoxville.

SIMMONDS & HENDERSON, over the State National Bank, are leading real estate agents of Knoxville. They do not do a commission business, but handle their own property, of which both own considerable.

They are largely interested in developmental projects here, the WEST END LAND Co., and the RIVERSIDE IMPROVEMENT Co., for instance. These enterprises are described on other pages of this work. Mr. Simmonds is president of the Riverside Co.

They handle suburban lands, largely, and also mineral and timber lands, and they have business property suitable for both manufacturing sites and stores, on hand and for sale.

Personal mention is made of other affairs of these gentlemen, in the sketches herein, of the projects they are promoting.

H. B. WETZELL & Co., dealers in timber and mineral lands, at 44 Deaderick building, have been established in that line here about four years. They have done a very considerable business since then, and have been entrusted with numerous commissions, both to buy and sell.

In 1888 they bought, for the Unaka Lumber Co., of this city, a tract of land in Unicoi county, Tenn., covered with white pine, poplar, cherry, ash and walnut, to the extent of 150,000,000 feet of standing timber. This is one of the most valuable bodies of such timber in the South, and the sale of it is an illustration of the sort of business this firm does.

They have sold timber lands of this character (in North Carolina, mostly) for as low as $2 an acre, and they have listed with them now such bargains as the following: 15,000 acres of coal lands in the Jellico coal region of Tennessee, on the Knoxville & Ohio Railway, valued at $400,000; 10,000 acres of poplar lands in Swayne county, N. C., valued at $40,000; 450 acres of placer gold claim in Jackson county, N. C., from which one man can pan out from $2 to $6 a day; 120 acres of gold-bearing quartz lands in Macon county, N. C., which will average $23 production to the ton mined.

They have mineral and timber lands in the two Virginias, Kentucky, Tennessee, and the Carolinas listed with them. They were in business in the timber and mineral districts of the Northwest before they came here, and are experts in that line.

They came here from Grand Rapids, Mich. MR. WETZELL was in the lumber business there, and his partner, MR. G. A. RUMSEY, was president of the Rumsey Lumber Co., of Big Rapids, Mich.

W. C. CROZER, civil and mining engineer of 36 and 37 Deaderick Building, has been engaged for more than thirty years in the practice of his profession in the States of Kentucky, West Virginia, Virginia, Tennessee, the Carolinas, Georgia and Alabama, and has acquired, by service in the location and construction of railways and turnpike roads, the survey and improvement of rivers and other waterways, the examination and reporting upon mineral and timber lands and titles, etc., an extensive and intimate acquaintance with the people, resources, transportation facilities and necessities of those States.

He began his engineering career before the war in the construction of turnpikes in Kentucky. During the war he was detailed as resident engineer of the United States Military Railroad from Nicholasville, Ky., to Knoxville. He has been division engineer of the Cumberland & Ohio, Cincinnati Southern, and Kentucky Central railroads; resident and division engineer of the Kentucky & Tennessee Railroad, principal assistant engineer of the Nashville & Charleston, and the Tennessee & Coosa Railroads; chief engineer of the Poplar Mountain Railway of Kentucky, and of the Nashville & Charleston road. He has also been assistant engineer under Major King and Col. Barlow in the government's improvement of the Cumberland and other Southern rivers.

He refers inquirers as to his experience and ability to ex-Comptroller of the National treasury, Durham, now a resident of Danville, Ky.; to ex-Gov. McCrary, of Kentucky, now Congressman from that State; to Col. Barlow and Major King, U. S. A., just referred to; Col. G. B. Nicholson, chief engineer of the Cincinnati Southern Railway; John R. Proctor, director of the Kentucky Geological Survey, and Gen. R. N. Hood, president of the Third National Bank of Knoxville, and also of the Knoxville & Augusta Railway.

Mr. Crozer will make topographical and plain surveys of town and city sites, will examine and report upon railway, mine and timber properties, will survey for and construct railways, water works, sewerage systems, and furnish plans and specifications for the same; or will act as agent for parties buying or selling or engaging in such projects; and having unbounded faith in the resources of this part of the country will take an interest in such properties in payment for his services.

He has complete maps, reports, etc., of the principal enterprises hereabouts, of the sort referred to, and will furnish information concerning them with pleasure.

CHARLES WARING, Surveyor and Engineer, of 58½ West Clinch street, has been following that line about thirty years, and has been in it here for twenty-one years. The work he has done here stamps him a competent man for surveying farms, city and suburban lots, railroad work, water and sewer systems, etc. He has, in fact, been remarkably successful, and he is the most prominent man in his line here.

RESIDENCE OF MRS. D. J. EGGLESTON.
Geo. F. Barber & Co., Architects.

He makes a specialty of the business of examining titles, and furnishing abstracts. Having given that business his attention for over twenty years, he has accumulated appointments for it valued at over $50,000, and is now in the possession of the most complete set extant of record books, maps, charts, etc., relating to property hereabouts.

LAWYERS OF KNOXVILLE.

THIS real estate business of the city, and the law business centralized here by reason of the fact that Knoxville is the seat of Federal as well as State courts and institutions, attracts to it a very great deal of legal "talent." Among the successful practitioners at the bar here, the following are perhaps the most distinguished:

INGERSOLL & PEYTON, constitute a law partnership of exceptional ability.

Judge Henry H. Ingersoll, of this partnership, was born in Oberlin, Ohio. He graduated in both the literary and law departments of Yale College; was admitted to the bar in 1865 and moved to Greenville, Tenn., where he practiced law for ten years before coming to Knoxville. He began practice of the law just after he was twenty-one years of age, and he has devoted his entire life to his profession.

In 1879 he was appointed a member of the Court of Arbitration, and occupied that position on the Supreme Bench of the State of Tennessee for two years. Many of his opinions have been reported, and are considered the very highest authority upon the subjects involved. In 1889 he was elected Grand Master Mason for the State of Tennessee, and served in that position with honor to himself and to every member of the order in the State. He is a Knight Templar of high degree, and is held in much esteem by the members of that body. He has always been actively identified with the educational interests of the city in which he lives, and has never failed to extend a helping hand to those wishing to prepare themselves for usefulness in life.

Mr. Masterson Peyton of this firm, is a native of Stanford, Ky. He graduated from the Kentucky University, at Lexington, Ky., and the law school in Louisville, Ky., and was admitted to the bar in 1880. While on a visit to Knoxville, in 1887, he formed a partnership with Judge Ingersoll, and since that time they have practiced together. Mr. Peyton has been prominently connected with many of the business enterprises of the city. He was the organizer of the Central Savings Bank, and of a number of other institutions here.

The practice of the firm of Ingersoll & Peyton, is chiefly in the Chancery Court of Knox county, Tenn., and in the Supreme Court of the State, in the United States Circuit Court and the United States Supreme Court. They give special attention to Supreme Court practice for other lawyers who live in East Tennessee, so far away that they do not care to come and try their cases in this Court; and they represent a number of corporations of Knoxville and elsewhere, and have a very large corporation practice. Among the Knoxville corporations represented by this firm, are the Central Savings Bank, and the Louisville & Nashville Railway Company; among others, the Boston Safe Deposit & Trust Company of Boston, the Norfolk & Western Railway Company, and the Finance Investments Companies of Philadelphia.

The office of this firm is over the East Tennessee National Bank, corner of Gay and Union streets.

WASHBURN, TEMPLETON, PICKLE & TURNER, 36, 37 and 38 Deaderick Building, is a law firm, established Jan. 22 last, by the consolidation of two others, both of which ranked in point of patronage and ability at the head of the local bar. These two were the firms of Washburn & Templeton, and Pickle & Turner.

The members of the new firm are all well known throughout this part of the country.

Mr. W. P. Washburn is a native of Massachusetts, but a resident here for 36 years. He has been practicing law since 1857. He is president of the Covenant Building & Loan Association, (elsewhere referred to in this work) and vice-president of the Knoxville Gas Light Co., and has interests in several other local business concerns.

Jerome Templeton is a native of Tennessee, admitted to the bar in 1874. He is a director of the State National Bank of Knoxville, and he also has interests in other Knoxville enterprises.

Geo. W. Pickle is a native of Knox county. He read law with Dan Voorhees of Indiana, and was admitted to the bar of Tennessee in 1870. He is Attorney General and Reporter for the State of Tennessee.

Wilbur R. Turner is a Georgian by birth, and a lawyer of fifteen years steady practice in Tennessee.

This firm is general counsel for the Knoxville, Cumberland Gap & Louisville Railroad,

KNOXVILLE IN GALA ATTIRE.

Reunion of the Blue and Gray, October 7th, 1889.

the Mechanics' National Bank, the State National Bank, the Knoxville Fire Insurance Co., and for other important corporations and individuals here.

LUCKY & SANFORD, attorneys, of 123 and 125 Prince street, are largely engaged in corporation practice—sometimes for and sometimes against these embodied creations of the law. They are general counsel for the East Tennessee National Bank, the Knoxville Southern Railroad, and the Coal Creek Mining and Manufacturing Company (which, with 50,000 acres of coal lands, is one of the great corporations of the State), and for other such concerns besides.

But they have also distinguished themselves as opponents of corporations at the bar. They have won, but lately, a celebrated case of this character, that of McDonald, Shea & Co., *et al*, railroad contractors, against the Chicago, Cincinnati & Charleston Railway; a case involving $581,528, the full amount of which they recovered for their clients. Able counsel were opposed to them, and powerful interests antagonistic; but they succeeded nevertheless.

Mr. C. E. Lucky, of this firm, is a native of Washington county, Tenn. He is a graduate of Hamilton College, New York. He read law under the late Supreme Justice Nelson, and was admitted to practice here in 1871. He has pursued the vocation he adopted then, steadily since.

His associate, Mr. Edward T. Sanford, is a younger man, but he has demonstrated abilities for his profession of a high order. He is a son of Col. E. J. Sanford, president of the Knoxville & Ohio Railroad. He is a graduate of both the literary and law departments of Harvard, and was admitted to the bar here in 1888. He and Mr. Lucky have been in partnership since 1890.

WELCKER & GAUT, attorneys, of 24 and 25 Deaderick Building, have been in partnership only since May, 1891, but both had been practicing long anterior to that date. Mr. Welcker is a Tennesseean by birth, and a resident here for four years past. He was admitted to the bar July, 1871, and was district attorney of the Third Judicial Circuit of the State from '72 to '78. He is a director of the Fountain Head Suburban Railway, of Knoxville, of the Farmers' and Traders' Bank, and South Knoxville Street Railway Company.

Mr. Gaut is also a native of the State. He was formerly engaged in the practice of his profession at Cleveland, Tenn., and has been following it here for about two years. Welcker & Gaut are attorneys for the Fountain Head and South Knoxville Railways, and for other local corporations. Their specialty is corporation, land and commercial law practice.

HENRY H. TAYLOR, attorney of 33 Deaderick Building, was born and raised in Carter county, Tennessee. He read law for some time prior to his admission and received his license in Virginia in 1867.

In 1870 he came to Knoxville and soon established himself in a lucrative practice. For the last twenty years here, his ability as a chancery lawyer has received a full measure of recognition. He takes no criminal cases; but he has much business of a civil character in the Supreme Court of the State. He has never sought office; has applied himself strictly to his practice and has accumulated considerable property hereabouts by means of it.

COMFORT & SPILMAN, attorneys of 16 and 17 McCallum Building, hold, with an extensive general practice, and a high degree of success in their profession, a position of rank among the lawyers of the city. Mr. Comfort is a Virginian by birth, but has been a resident of Knoxville for twenty-six years. He is a graduate of Princeton, N. J., and was admitted to practice at the bar of Tennessee in 1868. He is treasurer and one of the regents of the State University here, and is one of the most experienced and thoroughly informed of the Knoxville attorneys.

Mr. Spilman is a younger man but has also exhibited, since he settled here, the right kind of qualities for general practice. He was admitted to the bar in 1888 at Springfield, Ill., and shortly thereafter came to Knoxville. He organized the Wholesale Grocers' Association of Knoxville and was, until recently, its general counsel and manager. He has other business interests besides.

D. R. NELSON, attorney, of the Deaderick Building, is one of the local counsel of the East Tennessee, Virginia & Georgia Railroad, and is attorney for other corporations here. He makes a specialty of land and corporation business. He is a native of the State, and has had lengthy experience of his profession.

He has been remarkably successful in securing judgments of court favorable to his patrons; especially so in behalf of his clients, the railroads.

Mr. Nelson was admitted in Loudon county in 1872. He has represented the district embracing Loudon, Blount and Monroe counties (the Sixth Senatorial District of Tennessee) in the State Legislature.

G. S. W. McCAMPBELL, attorney-at-law, of Gay and Clinch streets, is a native of Knox county, and a college graduate, with the B. A. degree. He has been a teacher in the free schools of the State and also in college.

He graduated from the law department of the University of Tennessee here, and read law with Judge George Andrews, ex-Supreme Justice of Tennessee; and he has been regularly engaged in practice for the last eight years; for three years of that time here.

He has made a specialty of commercial law and collections; he has, in all probability, the largest collection business of any lawyer here; and he has a good chancery practice also.

He represents, as counsel, such corporations as the McCormick Harvesting Machine Company, the Walter A. Wood Reaping and Mowing Machine Company, the Geiser Manufacturing Company, and the Greer Machinery Company.

C. R. McILWAINE, attorney, of the Deaderick Building, is a Virginian by birth, and a graduate of the law department of the University of Maryland. He has been a resident of Knoxville about six years, and has been practicing his profession here for four.

His practice is general, except that he takes no criminal cases. His specialty is the law of real estate titles and conveyancing. He is, in fact, the leading abstract and title lawyer of the city. He gives considerable attention, also, to collections.

W. H. SHAVER, attorney, of 58½ West Clinch street, has been established at Knoxville now going on three years. He practices in all the courts, State and Federal, and makes a specialty of real estate titles, conveyancing and land business generally, collections and commercial practice. He is considered a very efficient counselor, and is increasing his patronage every day.

FOWLER & FOWLER, attorneys, of 117 Prince street, maintain two offices, the one here, and another at Clinton, Anderson county, Tenn., a place about twenty miles from Knoxville, which is a center of the law business of the coal regions. Mr. S. P. Fowler is the resident partner; J. A. attends to affairs at Clinton.

They have been established here since 1886, and have acquired, during the five years since, an extensive practice, chiefly in land and chancery suits. They are attorneys for business houses, and for several corporations of this part of the State, and one or other of them is a director in the same; among others, the Knoxville Trunk Company and the Homestead Investment Company.

ALFRED G. HOWE, attorney and solicitor in chancery, of 121½ Prince street, began practice at Knoxville in 1885, and in his specialty, land business, has acquired a very great reputation. He does not confine himself solely to that branch of the business, however. He has a general practice, largely commercial, and he pays considerable attention to collections.

He is a native of Indiana, and was admitted to the bar there in 1870. He had five years' experience there before he came here.

SAYLOR & MOORE, of 119½ Prince street, are a prominent law firm of Knoxville—the most prominent, in fact, of the younger generation of lawyers here. Mr. Saylor was admitted in 1889 at Knoxville, and Mr. Moore in 1887 in Jefferson county. They have been established in partnership here now about three years. Their specialty is commercial practice.

OSBORNE & MILLER, lawyers of 121 Prince street, have been established in partnership here about four years. Mr. Osborne, however, had been engaged in the pursuit of the law for some time before they began together. Mr. Miller was practicing in another part of the State also, before that.

They have built up a profitable patronage for themselves, both as civil and criminal lawyers, and are ranked among the most successful of the younger practitioners of the city.

THE BUILDERS' TRADE.

THE building permits issued during 1891 for Old Knoxville, numbered 324, involving values aggregating $377,017. For 1890 they were about the same. For the city, as a whole, they have been something like $800,000 to $1,000,000 a year during this time. It is estimated, by competent authority, that at least $2,000,000 has been expended for new residences in the last three years to house the incoming population. Considerably more than that has been laid out for business structures, factories, etc.

In the betterments thus raised, a tendency is clearly exhibited toward a finer and more substantial architecture than was characteristic of the city before. This tendency is apparent in the examples of superior edifices given in the pages preceding (31 and 32), relating to real estate and the improvements thereto.

The material chiefly used for business superstructures, is brick and stone; for residences, wood, in this case, because it is cheaper, and for the climate, serviceable. The city is favorably situated with respect to the supply of these materials. Lumber comes to it from Georgia, near by; brick, clay and stone abound in its vicinity.

FIRST BAPTIST CHURCH, KNOXVILLE.
Bauman Bros., Architects.

Building work is unquestionably cheaper here than in most cities, partly for that reason, and also because of the abundant labor supply attracted by the growth of the place. Lumber costs from $6 per thousand, for common, to $18 for framing; brick laid in the wall, $8.50 to $20, according to its character. The very finest of interior finish and planing mill work is done right in the city.

There are six or eight architects, and perhaps twenty regular builders engaged in the trade at Knoxville.

ARCHITECTS AND BUILDERS.

BAUMAN BROS., architects, of 122½ Gay street, plan and execute work every year that will aggregate $500,000 in value, a total indicating their rank in the profession. They stand, indeed, at the head of it here, both with respect to quality and quantity.

The following, among other important architectural performances, are credited to them: The First Baptist Church on Gay street, a Gothic type which cost $30,000; the Broad street M. E. Church, also of the Gothic order, $35,000; the Third and Fourth Presbyterian Churches, which cost—the former, $25,000, and the latter, $6,000; the Deaderick office building, a structure on which $30,000 was expended; the Harris & Caswell Building, $60,000; the Court House of Knox county, the construction of which they supervised, $100,000, and besides these, the Commerce Block, McTeer's, Payne, Hood & Co.'s, and many more of the most impressive buildings of the business quarter of the city.

Of the costlier residences here, the following are their work: Col. Swepson's, at Fort Sanders, which cost $15,000; Mrs. Margaret Hays', in the West End of the city, $9,000; J. C. Woodward's, in the same district, (said to be the handsomest in Knox county) $20,000; and others besides. Most of the school houses here were built by them, for example, the Girls' High School; and an addition to the Deaf and Dumb Asylum is also theirs.

At present, they are supervising construction of the new St. John's Episcopal Church, the plans for which were furnished by J. W. Yost, of Columbus, Ohio. It is of Georgia marble, will cost $50,000, and will doubtless be the handsomest structure of the early English Gothic order here.

They are native here, established since 1872, and enjoy a large measure of professional reputation everywhere the influence of Knoxville as a commercial capital prevails.

JAMES R. TORRANCE, architect, of the Sedgwick building, corner of Union and Prince streets, came to Knoxville from St. Paul, Minn., in the spring of 1891.

Mr. Torrance is a native of Scotland, and received his professional training in that country. He has filled important positions in various parts of the Union, and, in order to improve himself as far as possible in his profession, has traveled extensively in Europe for that special purpose.

Among other buildings here completed under his direction may be mentioned the "Odd Fellows' building," Mabry street; the residence of E. D. Davis, at Lake Ottosee, and that of Geo. A. Gammon, in North Knoxville.

He is also a modeler in clay, and has executed some important commissions in that line, too.

Mr. Barber has had some fifteen years' experience in the profession in this and other States, and has been located here for three years.

Publication of the book was begun about two years ago, and, as a work filled with new and practical ideas on building, together with a

RESIDENCE OF F. E. McARTHUR, OF THE McARTHUR MUSIC HOUSE.
Geo. F. Barber & Co., Architects.

GEO. F. BARBER & CO., architects, designers and publishers of the "*Cottage Souvenir No. 2,*" a book of architectural designs, which has been circulated already extensively, both in this country and abroad, have offices at Knoxville in the building 126½ Gay street.

great variety of beautiful designs and plans for those contemplating building to select from, it has proven a great success. It is a volume of about 200 pages containing over 200 designs, plans and drawings of artistic dwellings that would cost from $500 to $10,000 to build, with estimate of expense for each. The styles of architecture in the book are new, and are very attractive. It will be mailed to any part of

C. C. SULLINS' FLATS.
R. Z. Gill, Architect.

the United States or Canada upon receipt of its price, $2 a copy.

Other designs will also be furnished by the firm, and any commission entrusted them will receive prompt attention.

R. Z. GILL, architect, of 71 West Clinch street, has been established at Knoxville now going on three years, during which period he has executed work that stamps him a man of superior abilities in his profession, and as one of originality and experience also. He has planned and superintended construction among others, of the following fine buildings of Knoxville and its vicinity: S. B. Luttrell's Queen Anne residence, on the banks of the Tennessee river, in South Knoxville, which cost $15,000 to build; the Ross block of flats on Church and Walnut streets, a $20,000 job; W. H. Pace's residence, Raleigh, N. C., an $8,000 job, and the Cumberland Hotel, at Harriman, Tenn., a $55,000 job.

He will estimate upon and undertake work of any character and for any part of the South. He does not find it necessary to compete eagerly for commissions, however, because his services are always in demand. Here, where he is so well known, his work is appreciated.

He was the first to introduce here the style of building known as flats; these, and hotels and public buildings are his specialty.

Mr. Gill is a native of Urbana, Ill. He graduated in architecture from the University of that State, after instruction under Prof. N. C. Ricker, and, after graduation, was with Holabird & Roach and F. S. Allen, architects of considerable note and business. He is a member of the Chamber of Commerce, and is the owner of considerable real estate, and he lives in a handsome residence in the western part of the city.

The GALYON & SELDEN Co. is a recent incorporation which is successor to the firm of Galyon & Selden, and which, like that firm, is engaged as a contractor, builder and lumber dealer, and manufacturer of building material, at the intersection of Park street and the East Tennessee, Virginia & Georgia tracks. Its principals are L. A. Galyon and A. K. Selden. It has works there that cover three acres, including its yards, and over 300 feet of side track, and it is the employer of about sixty hands steadily. Its mills are thoroughly equipped; it has a dry kiln of original pattern, of 8,000 feet capacity, and a dry house of 10,000 feet storage capacity, which facilities enable it to fill orders promptly. It is a shipper of lumber and finishing material to all parts of the State, and as a con-

RESIDENCE OF MRS. LOU. M. ROGERS.
R. Z. Gill, Architect.

tracting company, gets its share of the local work in the building line. Galyon & Selden were successors to L. A. Galyon, senior member of the firm and senior principal in the company, who has been in the building trade here for eight or ten years. Before he and

GALYON & SELDEN CO.'S MILL AND LUMBER YARDS.

Mr. Selden went into partnership in this business in August, 1890, the latter was of Caldwell & Selden, grocers of Knoxville. Mr. Galyon assumes general management of all the outside business of the company, and Mr. Selden is its office and financial man.

HARVEY ABRAMS, contractor and builder, of Broad and High streets, had a lengthy experience of that business in New York and other places, before he settled here. He was at first engaged here at a large salary to supervise the business of the Stephenson & Getaz Company, and he resigned that to go into business on his own account.

While with the Stephenson & Getaz Company he supervised construction of the East Tennessee Medical College, the Luttrell Street Methodist Church, West Knoxville University and other important jobs.

Since he began for himself he has executed contracts for several fine residences here, and he is now engaged on the St. John's Episcopal Church, a $60,000 job.

Repair and reconstruction of brick work are specialties with him, also the raising and moving of brick buildings. His energy and enterprise have attracted attention here, and he is fast taking the lead in his line.

COOLEY BROS., contractors and builders, and manufacturers of and dealers in sash, doors, blinds, mouldings, brackets, lumber, lath, pine shingles, flooring, and other building materials, have a factory at No. 1 Chamberlain street, which, with its accessories of yards, side tracks, and other parts of their works, covers six acres of ground. It is equipped throughout with all the latest improved expediting and labor-saving devices, and is as complete in that particular as any establishment of the sort in the State.

In it they employ usually thirty hands, and in work of all kinds, outside and in it, 100 hands. They have side tracks accommodating eight or ten cars at a time, and they are in receipt of about ten or fifteen car loads a month, of pine direct from Georgia mills, and of poplar, walnut, and cherry woods from other parts besides.

As building contractors this firm does, perhaps, the largest business in that line here. During the last eight or ten years, since they began in the trade, they have executed such contracts as the following: The Ross flats, which number five tenements, and cost $20,000; the residence of M. O. French, an $8,000 job,

RESIDENCE OF HARVEY ABRAMS, BUILDING CONTRACTOR.

and of C. M. McClung, the same, and that of W. C. Fulcher, a $7,000 job; and of business blocks they have constructed several. They have, among other contracts in course of execution, a very fine residence for R. R. Swepson, to cost $18,000, and one for Mrs. Margaret Hayes to cost $10,000, and the Y. M. C. A. building, and Science Hall of the University of Tennessee.

Their extensive business operations have made them well known hereabouts. They are natives of the State, resident in Knoxville for twenty years, and are stockholders in the banking and other solid concerns of the city that are described herein.

SCENERY, EAST TENNESSEE, VIRGINIA & GEORGIA RAILWAY.

KNOXVILLE THE TRADE CENTER.

ITS RAILROAD, BANKING, DISTINCTIVE AND JOBBING BUSINESS AND MANUFACTURES.

WE come now, after the preliminaries of general description, to a survey of Knoxville in its business aspects; to Knoxville, the center of railroads, the banking center, the jobbing center, the center of certain characteristic industries, the center of manufactures. And first as to its railroads.

Knoxville may be likened, in the matter of its railroad communications, to a gigantic squid; with a kindlier tentacle extended to what lies within its reach, be it said, however, than this denizen of the depths which in form it resembles; embracing firmly, to be sure, the commerce of its field, but to conserve, rather than destroy; and clinching, at their extremities, the arms of other great octopuses like itself—the trunk lines of the land.

Its railroads, in this similitude, are the limbs of the creature, which is Knoxville; in number, five, one major, because a system in itself, and four short and minor ones. The greater arm—the system, is the East Tennessee, Virginia & Georgia; the others are the Knoxville & Ohio, the Knoxville, Southern and Marietta & North Georgia consolidated, the Knoxville, Cumberland Gap & Louisville, and the Knoxville & Augusta.

Only four of these arms have, however, so to speak, independent life and volition, and one of the four, the Knoxville & Augusta, sixteen miles long, is local only and insignificant. The Knoxville & Ohio is attached to the East Tennessee, Virginia & Georgia system, and it works in conjunction with it; and is, in fact, in the matter of management, an integral part of that great Southern transportation line.

THE FAVOR SHOWN TO RAILROADS.

How much of life blood our squid has supplied these limbs as they budded from it (to continue the use of the figure), in the shape of financial wherewith, of subsidies and rights of way and stock subscriptions, is apparent in the following-named contributions:

To the Knoxville Southern, $275,000, paid for stock in the venture; to the Knoxville, Cumberland Gap & Louisville, $225,000 subscribed, but as yet unpaid, for good and sufficient reasons; to the Knoxville & Ohio, $100,000, the joint contribution of Knoxville and Knox county; and to the Western North Carolina, which is still under way, $100,000, likewise by the county, the bulk of whose people, it should be remembered, live really in the city. A total of $700,000, not to speak of other valuable gifts and concessions, depot and spur sites. After which fashion Knoxville, the trade center, demonstrates its innate desire for progress.

And this is, in part, the material return the roads have made for these favors: The Knoxville & Augusta's bridge, spanning the river; the shops of the East Tennessee, Virginia & Georgia, employing, when running, full 1,500 hands, in addition to those of its traffic departments; the central depot of the same road, and its official headquarters.

Since we have already explained and endeavored to illustrate, at the very outset of our story of Knoxville (in the initial chapter, in fact, of this work), its position of advantage with respect to the rest of the world, by means of its railroads, we need not repeat the statement then made of its railroad ramifications. One of its roads, however, as a main stay of the city's commerce, deserves especial attention, the East Tennessee, Virginia & Georgia.

A veritable Briareus itself, this East Tennessee, Virginia & Georgia; hundred-handed, clasping for Knoxville, as its beneficiary, four whole States and parts of others; bound to the city by the ligatures of reciprocal interest. A Briareus, too, growing every day; likely, it is said, to wed very soon another cyclopean system. And this is its description:

THE EAST TENNESSEE, VIRGINIA & GEORGIA.

THE EAST TENNESSEE, VIRGINIA & GEORGIA RAILWAY SYSTEM embraces five roads, having a total mileage of 1,800. These five roads are the East Tennessee, Virginia & Georgia main line, traversing East Tennessee, Alabama and Georgia, 1,192 miles long, upon which main line Knoxville is situated; the Memphis & Charleston Railroad in its entirety, 330 miles long; the Mobile & Birmingham, 163 miles long; the Knoxville & Ohio, beginning at Knoxville and proceeding to Coal Creek and Jellico, Tenn., great Southern coal centers, a road 66 miles long; the Waldens Ridge Railroad, 52 miles long, from Knoxville to Harriman's Junction. Besides these there are two other short connecting links of the system, aggregating 60 miles length.

Bristol, Tenn., seated upon the line dividing that State from Virginia, is the most northerly terminal of the line; Memphis, on the Mississippi, the most westerly; the port of Brunswick, on the coast of Georgia, the most southeasterly; Mobile, on the Gulf Coast of Alabama, the most southerly.

The East Tennessee division of this system runs from Chattanooga through Knoxville to Bristol; the Georgia division, from Chattanooga to Brunswick; the Alabama division, from Rome, Ga., to Meridian, Miss. (including various branches reaching Birmingham, Bessemer and Akron); the Birmingham & Mobile Railway, from Selma, Ala., to Mobile, and the Memphis & Charleston Railroad, from Chattanooga to Memphis.

Thus it will be seen, that this system has terminals at Memphis, the largest interior cotton center of the country, and connections there with all the Southwestern systems of railroad, and with lines to St. Louis and Kansas City; that it has three great Southern iron centers also, for division termini, viz.: Bristol, Chattanooga and Birmingham, and besides that, two seaports, Brunswick and Mobile.

At these points it makes connection with all its sister systems of the Southeast, and through them also with lines to Northern cities. Its fast freight line, the PAINT ROCK, transports a large share of the traffic from Eastern cities South-bound, and *vice versa* that of Southern trade centers.

Connections are made with lines to Eastern and foreign ports at West Point, and Norfolk, Va., by means of the Richmond & Danville Road to the former, and the Norfolk & Western to the latter. From these two Virginia ports there are steamship lines to New York, Boston, Providence, Baltimore, Philadelphia and Europe. New York freights, by this water route, usually go by the Old Dominion Steamship Company; Philadelphia freights, by the Clyde Line, and Baltimore freights, by the York River Line.

This system traverses the greatest coal fields of the South, the prodigiously rich and productive iron district of East Tennessee and Alabama, the cotton fields of Georgia, Alabama, Mississippi and Tennessee, and the long leaf pineries of Georgia and Mississippi. It has, therefore, a very profitable coal, iron, cotton and lumber traffic; but it has, likewise, a vast miscellaneous traffic of commodities exchanged between the East and South, and between the Southeast and the West and Northwest.

The principal freight traffic over its East Tennessee division, upon which, as we have seen, Bristol, Knoxville and Chattanooga are the leading cities, is in coal, grain, marble, live stock, lumber, ores, zinc, spelter, and of manufactured products, car wheels, light T rails, railroad fastenings, bar iron, finished handles, dressed marble, flour (from the three mills of Knoxville largely), cotton and woolen goods also of Knoxville manufacture, saddlery, brick, sewer pipe, and drain tile, and jobbing commodities. This classification would apply also to the Georgia division, with the addition of yellow pine, phosphate rock, naval stores, cotton, and the special manufactured products of the country traversed by the division; and as well to the Alabama division, over which pig iron and iron ore, and the production of numerous cotton mills on the line, is also transported.

The time made from Knoxville by freight, over this road, to Louisville, is 26 hours; to Cincinnati, 36; to Memphis, 42; to Baltimore, 80; to Philadelphia, 90; to New York, 96; to Mobile, 60, and to New Orleans, 72 hours.

The number of freight trains run from Knoxville over the line, is 30 to 50 daily; of passenger trains 17 each way; the number of passenger trains run on the system, 51 each way

STATION AND GENERAL OFFICES OF THE EAST TENNESSEE, VIRGINIA & GEORGIA RAILROAD, KNOXVILLE.

daily. Passenger time over the lines of this system, from Knoxville to Chattanooga, is three hours and a half; to Bristol, four hours;

C. H. HUDSON is its general manager; EDWIN FITZGERALD, traffic manager; T. S. DAVANT, general freight agent; B. W. WRENN, general passenger and ticket agent, and C. A. BENSCOTER, assistant general passenger and ticket agent.

A MOUNTAIN GRADE.
On the Line of the East Tennessee, Virginia & Georgia Railway.

Its general offices and headquarters are at Knoxville, and it has established there also shops employing 450 hands, which number will be increased to 1,000 or more when the new shops, now under construction, are completed. It was the first road to enter the city, and it is the most important of the roads affording it communication with the great world outside.

The natural wealth of the country tributary to this road, particularly in those parts adjacent to Knoxville, and especially in marble, iron, coal and timber, may fairly be characterized as stupendous. It would be difficult, however, within the brief compass of a sketch like this, to set forth these resources properly. But the road has not been behindhand in presenting its advantages, by means of printers' ink; valuable pamphlets, descriptive of East Tennessee, and other sections ramified by it, have been prepared for general circulation by its traffic management.

to Atlanta, eight hours; to Nashville, ten; to Cincinnati and Louisville, the same, eleven hours; to Memphis, fifteen; to Washington, D. C., twenty-two, and to New York, twenty-six. The trains of the line are rapidly being vestibuled, and a through vestibuled train has lately been put on between Cincinnati and St. Augustine, Fla., passing through Chattanooga, Tenn., and Rome, Atlanta and Macon, Ga., to make the trip in thirty hours.

The East Tennessee, Virginia & Georgia is operated independently of any other system. It cost as a whole, $96,000,000, and its operating expenses are about $6,000,000 a year. It has 5,000 employes. Improvement is continuously being made in its road-bed, rolling stock, terminal facilities and appointments generally. Its management can truly be said to be in competent hands.

The other two principal lines of Knoxville are the following:

THE MARIETTA & NORTH GEORGIA RAILWAY.

THIS line, now consolidated with the Knoxville Southern Railroad, is 204 miles long. It is operated independently of any other line, but has close traffic relations (through the Knoxville Belt Railroad) with the Knoxville, Cumberland Gap & Louisville Railroad, and connection here also with the East Tennessee, Virginia & Georgia Railroad, the Western & Atlantic Railroad at MARIETTA, GA., and the Knoxville & Augusta Railroad, *en route*, and by its Murphy Branch with the Western North Carolina of the Richmond & Danville Railroad System at Murphy, N. C.

This road, as a narrow gauge, started nearly fifteen years ago from MARIETTA, GA., to run north and northeast into the mineral region of Northeastern Georgia and Western North Carolina. In 1887 the construction of the KNOXVILLE SOUTHERN, beginning here, was taken up under the same management, and on completion of that line to a junction at Blue Ridge station with the extension of the Marietta & North Georgia Railroad, the entire line, from Knoxville to Marietta, was made standard gauge, and is now the main line of the consolidated project. The division of the Old Marietta & North Georgia Railroad still, however, uses narrow gauge track from BLUE RIDGE STATION on the main line for 25 miles to MURPHY, N. C., and connects there, as we have said, with the Western North Carolina, an "R. & D." road.

Connection is made at MARIETTA under traffic arrangements with the Western & Atlantic Railroad, and solid trains from Knoxville run through the 18 miles from that terminus to Atlanta.

Proceeding from Knoxville, this road runs through an agricultural country, past several unimportant stations after leaving the suburbs of the city, until it reaches LOUISVILLE, 14 miles from Knoxville, on the southern bank of the Tennessee river; and six miles further, after traversing a region where the marble quarries furnish occupation to the residents, and freight to the railroad, the old Quaker Settlement of FRIENDSVILLE is reached.

This town was founded fifty years ago by the disciples of old Wm. Penn, and many notable people have lived here. W. E. Forster (one of the leaders in the English House of Commons) had friends and relatives here, and has paid several visits to the place.

It is in the midst of a very rich agricultural country, and to say that it is an orderly, thriving, prosperous and happy community, with such a people, is, perhaps, to make rather a supererogatory remark.

ALLEGHANY is the station where the passengers for the summer resort of Alleghany Springs disembark; McGHEE STATION is at the crossing of the Little Tennessee river, just below the mouth of the Tellico river, and 32 miles from Knoxville. It is the head of steamboat navigation on the Little Tennessee river, and the outlet for the Tellico river valley, and is likely to become an important point.

Next, 44 miles from Knoxville, is MADISONVILLE, the county seat of Monroe county, an old village, doubled already in population since the construction of the railroad, and of increasing business importance.

TELLICO JUNCTION, 56 miles from Knoxville, is at the crossing of the Athens & Tellico Railroad, a line 20 miles long, extending from Athens to the iron ore beds, where the Tellico river debouches out of the Chilhowie mountain range.

At 61 miles from Knoxville is the new town of GRADY, named for him, who was in his day, the apostle of the New South; and at 67 miles, WETMORE station is reached. This and the siding, called by the old name of the place, "Savannah Farms," are in the plain at the foot of the mountain where the Hiawassee river breaks through an Alpine gorge and flows to the southwest to join the Tennessee river, and Wetmore is at the head of navigation on the Hiawassee river, with weekly steamboat connection for

TENNESSEE SCENERY.
On the Line of the East Tennessee, Virginia & Georgia Railway.

Knoxville and Chattanooga. There are large deposits of iron ore in this vicinity, saw mills, stone quarries, beautiful scenery and mineral springs. Hiawassee Gap affords, by report of the United States engineers, the best opportunity for railroads from the Northwest to reach the Southeast, and several lines are, in fact, projected to reach this point.

The scenery from McGhee to Wetmore is fine. The Blue Ridge mountains are in sight on the southeast of the road all the way; but at Wetmore the road plunges into the heart of the mountains through the gorge of the Hiawassee, continues along the stream until, at CRESCENT station, 73 miles from Knoxville, it crosses to the south bank, which it follows nearly to the North Carolina State Line, where, by some bold engineering, it leaves the river valley and runs through the mountains to DUCKTOWN.

At one place (beyond Wetmore), the cliffs abut the river so that the train actually skirts them on a shelf cut out of solid rock. Here the passenger may look down and see below the Hiawassee river so pent in that it literally "runs on edge." No one knows the depth at this place; the width of the river between the banks is only nineteen feet, while the usual breadth is from 200 to 300 yards.

Copper mines were opened, in 1853, at Ducktown, and worked to some small extent by miners; and later, to a much larger extent by speculators, for several years. From 1867 to 1875 the mines and furnaces here were in full blast, under the able management of Julius E. Raht. Over 1,000 men were then employed. Mr. Raht's death, and the decline in price of copper, put an end to work there until the completion of this railroad, and now mining is reviving again in this field; operations are conducted by an English company, which, it is expected, will work on a larger scale than ever before, in the production of sulphuric acid, for use with the phosphates of South Carolina, Georgia and Florida, as well as of copper and iron ore.

Beyond Ducktown again, the road descends into the Ocoee valley, crosses into Georgia and ascends Ocoee river to BLUE RIDGE, where the Murphy branch begins; passes southward through Ellijay, Jasper and Tate, where there are extensive quarries of marble of various colors, Canton and Woodstock, until, finally, 204 miles from Knoxville, the pretty and brisk town of MARIETTA, the end of the line, is reached.

Difficulties attending the consolidation of the two roads—financial troubles chiefly—have forced this line into the hands of a receiver, and it is now operated by James B. Glover, who holds that position, and whose offices are at Marietta.

THE KNOXVILLE, CUMBERLAND GAP AND LOUISVILLE RAILROAD.

A NEW line extends from Knoxville, over a course a little east of north and seventy-two miles long, to MIDDLESBOROUGH, KENTUCKY, the scene of wonderful recent improvement through manufacturing and developmental projects. Here connection is made by it with direct trains to Louisville and Cincinnati, and points on the Chesapeake and Ohio Railroad, via the "L. & N." system, and via Norton, Virginia, over the Norfolk & Western and R. & D. systems for all Eastern cities. This is the "K., C. G. & L." road, whose initials are explained in the sub-head above.

Middlesborough is too well known to require minute description. The Watts' Steel and Iron syndicate's furnace and steel plant there, is considered the finest in the United States; that and the South Boston Iron Works, which contracts for the manufacture of ordnance for the government, and has here a factory for electric machinery, large wood-working factories, a brewery, etc., make this—though the city is not yet three years old—a very important manufacturing center already.

The station at Middlesborough is three miles from the great tunnel at Cumberland Gap, which was built by this road, and which is also used by the Louisville & Nashville, and Great Southern Railroad for its Clinch river and Virginia extension, and will probably be used by other railroads now projected. Leaving Middlesborough, over that precocious city's Belt Railroad, with its twenty-six miles of coal, ore and spur tracks for the development of its industries and those of the region around it, the passenger on the "K., C. G. & L." stops for a moment at the northern entrance of the tunnel, and then after three-fifths of a mile under Cumberland mountain, reaches CUMBERLAND GAP, an important station, center of the traffic of the great Powell's valley from Lee county, Va., south. At this point the Louisville & Nashville Railroad (Virginia extension) diverges to go on one mile to HARROGATE, and turning sharply to the east, pursues its way up the valley of the Powell's river to Big Stone Gap and there connects with the Norfolk and Western Railroad to Norfolk, on the coast of Virginia. Continuing southerly towards Knoxville, over the "K., C. G. & L., HAMILTON SPRINGS, a mile from Cumberland Gap, is reached, and three miles further on, the town of ARTHUR.

HARROGATE station is the site of the stupendous "FOUR SEASONS" HOTEL, unequalled in the South except by the Florida palaces of entertainment. The laying off here of miles of beautiful drives, the many beautiful villas and chalets that are now being constructed, and along with these a Sanatorium and Casino, show carefully considered plans for making this one of the great pleasure and health resorts of the United States. Harrogate is reached from the main line of the "K., C. G. & L." Railroad through a spur track from ARTHUR, or by the short drive over the ridge from Hamilton Springs; or by the suburban trains constantly running on the Louisville & Nashville Railroad, between Middlesborough and it.

Two miles more towards Knoxville is a branch seven miles long to the southwest, constructed down Powell's valley to reach the iron fields which furnish the principal supply of ores for the Middlesborough furnaces. This line may be extended down the valley very easily towards Careyville. Eight miles further, the road following down the valley of Gap Creek, crosses Powell's river, and at POWELL'S RIVER STATION there are saw mills supplied with timber, both by rafts down the river and from the surrounding country.

After a gradual ascent of the huge ridge which lies between Powell's and Clinch river, near the divide of the waters of the two streams, comes TAZEWELL STATION, four miles from TAZEWELL Court House, county seat of Claiborne county, Tenn.; six miles further LONE MOUNTAIN STATION, where the road makes a bend to avoid the foot hills of Lone Mountain, which stands out against the horizon on the southwest of the road. Six miles further still, along a line following Sycamore Creek, Clinch river is reached, and at CLINCH RIVER STATION, lumbering and other enterprises are rapidly developing, and zinc ore is brought in for shipment.

Two miles further on, at OAKMAN STATION, are extensive limestone quarries, and at POWDER SPRINGS, quarries of marble. The road then runs through a delightful country until LUTTRELL, thirty miles from Knoxville, is reached. This is the shipping point for a considerable scope of country; quite a town has sprung up here, and several small factories.

At CORRYTON, twenty miles from Knoxville, is the junction point with the MORRISTOWN & CUMBERLAND GAP RAILROAD, constructed largely by the same parties in interest as those who built the one which is the subject of this sketch. The Morristown & Cumberland Gap forms a branch line forty miles long, connecting CORRYTON with MORRISTOWN, and passing on its way through the heart of Richland valley, Grainger county, LEA SPRINGS, RUTLEDGE, the county town, and "BEAN STATION," (which was a settlement and bore the name when the word "station" meant the place where stages changed horses,) and the well known watering place, TATE SPRINGS. Continuing thence towards Knoxville, the next station is MALONEYVILLE. This is established on the large farm bought by Knox county many years ago for its poor house, and other charitable, penal and reformatory institutions; but the construction of the railroad has made the land valuable, so that a part has been laid off for a village, and enterprises, like quarrying, brick making, etc., established.

The road then bears southwest through an agricultural country, with stations for the convenience of local traffic, until it reaches the beautiful suburb of Knoxville, called BEVERLY. The population is principally on the side of the Black Oak Ridge, north of the station, and from one-fourth of a mile to a mile distant. From this point the road is practically in the suburbs of Knoxville; using the Belt line or Dummy line, it encircles the city, and, running along the river bank with spur tracks to the steamboat landings, comes into Knoxville proper, at the intersection of Main and Cumberland streets.

The length of the Knoxville, Cumberland Gap & Louisville main line is seventy-three miles, but its connections with the Knoxville Belt Railroad and Middlesborough Belt Railroad, and its spur tracks to ore banks, add largely to the mileage operated by it.

This road has been of very great service already to Knoxville. It makes a modern highway of steel of the old trail at Cumberland Gap, which has been used for a century as a wagon road—the same that was famous during the war as one kept open, at an enormous cost to the Government, as the only practicable means of reaching the Tennessee valley.

The officers of the K., C. G. & L. are: Clarence Cary, of New York, president; H. T. Pollock, of London, England, vice-president; L. F. Winne, Knoxville, superintendent; M.

R. Gay, Knoxville, treasurer; W. A. Bly, Knoxville, assistant general freight and passenger agent. Its principal offices are at 218 Main street, Knoxville.

Incidental transportation facilities are the following:

The KNOXVILLE BELT RAILROAD, a corporation of $200,000 capital, was organized by parties interested in transportation and development projects at Knoxville, in 1886, owns the terminal grounds, city tracks, etc., used by the Knoxville Southern, the Marietta & North Georgia Railroad, and the Knoxville, Cumberland Gap & Louisville Railroad, lines already described herein, and furnishes connections, for these roads, with the East Tennessee, Virginia & Georgia Railroad system, with the steamboat landings and manufacturing quarters of the city, and controls, practically, the railroad portals of Knoxville. It is the owner, also, of valuable river landing properties here.

As its name implies, it is projected to encircle the city, but is now only partly completed. Extension of it is under consideration, and track-laying, it is expected, will be resumed in 1892. W. R. TUTTLE, also president of the Brookside Cotton Mills, is its president; CHARLES SEYMOUR, secretary and counsel; M. R. GAY, treasurer.

The KANSAS CITY, FORT SCOTT & MEMPHIS, and MEMPHIS & BIRMINGHAM lines, which enjoy nine-tenths of the passenger business between this part of the country and the Trans-Mississippi region, maintain a passenger agency at Knoxville for that city and its tributary country, and are represented here by MR. C. M. BAKER. He has been their agent here ever since these lines were completed to a union at Memphis, some five years ago.

This company's joint business from here is done over the East Tennessee, Virginia & Georgia line, by which passengers are carried to Memphis for it. Thence it transports them through Arkansas, Southwest Missouri, Indian Territory and Kansas, to its western terminal at Kansas City, or affords them connection with all the Southwestern and Northwestern lines en route. It is the most direct line from here to the Central West or the Rocky mountain country. It runs through Pullman and chair cars, and is a first-class road in every respect.

This company's ticket office is located at 75 West Depot street, only a short distance from the Union Depot.

RAILROADS PROPOSED.

OF railroads in prospect for Knoxville the most important projects, and the ones most likely of realization, are the Tennessee Midland, a line from Memphis through Nashville to Knoxville, a hundred miles of which have been built from Memphis westward, and the air line from Knoxville to sea at Port Royal, S. C., part of which also is constructed.

There are other enterprises in process of development also, of this same sort, one in particular of a Northwest and Southeast line, with Knoxville as one of its principal stations, and another in the opposite direction, from Bristol to Memphis, via Knoxville and Nashville. From its very position, and the rank it has reached, Knoxville is bound to be one destination, at least, for all the roads traversing the great valley over which it is regnant, or penetrating the mountains of mineral at its back. As the nearest large city to the few available routes from Chicago and the Central West, to the South Atlantic seaboard, it is one of the points that, perforce, must be taken into serious account, by any such projects.

THE TENNESSEE RIVER.

AND then the river, in which Knoxville has a facility for transportation, by no means to be despised. The Tennessee river is now navigable over the whole of its course. The French Broad and the Holston, its head waters, are navigable also above the city of Knoxville, the former for 100 and the latter for 40 miles. Two packet lines ply on the stream, one above and the other above and below the city both. These are the FRENCH BROAD TRANSPORTATION Co., which has two boats running to Dandridge, on the French Broad river, and the other, the FARMERS' AND MERCHANTS' TRANSPORTATION Co., running to Dandridge, and also to Kingston, 85 miles down stream from Knoxville. Both are backed by Knoxville money.

MISCELLANEOUS CONCERNS.

CLOSELY related to the transportation concerns of the city are the following:

HARRILL'S TRANSFER, formerly known as the Knoxville Transfer Co., is the leading concern of the kind in the city. It has the patronage of most of the merchants, for whom it does hauling to and from the railroad depots, steamboats, etc.; it has the best facilities for moving household goods and furniture, and, in its specialty, the hauling of heavy weights, like safes, marble, machinery, monuments, etc., has practically no rival here.

Mr. G. W. Harrill, its proprietor, began in the business here twenty-five years ago, with a single team, and with six bags of coffee for his first load. Now he runs twenty teams, large and small, and employs as many hands. His equipment embraces twenty wagons and trucks and forty horses. His stables, situated on Fifth avenue, corner of Lamar street, are 50x200 feet. His headquarters are at the stables and at the East Tennessee, Virginia & Georgia freight depot.

Mr. Harrill has acquired valuable resources during his twenty-five years' business here, and has other interests besides this transfer. He is president of the company operating the Crystal Ice Works here, which have a capacity of 65,000 pounds daily. These works are described on another page of this book.

The Merchants' Transfer Co., of 218 Gay street, is operated by Mr. E. S. McClung, a prominent merchant of the commission line here. He is engaged at the same place in the grain, hay and produce business.

This transfer business was established by him about nine years ago. He runs eight teams, and does the heavy hauling for about twenty-five of the leading jobbers and business men of the city. His specialty is the hauling of railroad freights and the moving of furniture. He has an order office at the railroad depot here.

KNOXVILLE AS A FINANCIAL CENTER.

COMMERCE with seven States in whole or in part, naturally makes Knoxville an important financial center. No less than eleven banks thrive by supplying the sinews of trade for this commerce. Six of these banks are organized under the National banking laws, and five with State charters; two are savings banks and one is a banking and trust company.

The six National banks are the East Tennessee, the Third National, City National, State National, Mechanics' National, and the Holston National. The five State banks are the Merchants', the Farmers' & Traders', the Knox County Bank & Trust Co., the Knoxville Savings, and the Central Savings Bank.

The combined capital and surplus of these eleven banks is, according to late reports made by them, $1,666,700, and of this aggregate, $1,250,000 is cash capital. The deposits, all told, in the eleven, amount to something like $2,500,000, a figure lower than usual; and the loans and discounts approximate that sum. Their total resources are in the neighborhood of $4,500,000.

The bulk of the business is naturally done by the six National banks, which have two-thirds of the capital embarked in banking at the city, and a like proportion of the total resources. The two savings banks are both in prosperous condition; their growth and success is an indication of a thrifty and industrious working population. Knoxville as yet has no clearing house, and no account is available of the clearings and exchanges of the banks, even for so much as comparison. The banks do about all the banking and broking business of the town, but, by a great deal, not all its financial business.

Fully $100,000 of capital is employed by private parties doing a money lending and note-shaving business. Then there is also a vast financial total of pension disbursements internal revenue collections, postal and other government transactions, city and county funds officially handled, insurance and general collections business done. The sum total of all these transactions is upwards of $1,500,000 a year; between that and $2,000,000, which is the practical benefit Knoxville derives from its governmental institutions.

Thus, for instance, the lump sum of the business of the money order department of the Post Office at Knoxville last year was $583,293, a total equal to the business of a pretty good bank. The total revenue collections last year, in the district of thirty-six counties of East Tennessee, headquarters for which has been fixed at Knoxville, was $161,049; the city is a center of pension disbursements also for a large district; its own municipal affairs involve $250,000 to $300,000 a year; the county of Knox has transactions approximating this sum, and the insurance premiums collected by the local agencies alone, were upwards of $100,000.

The banks here confine themselves, (State as well as National) to commercial loans only. The mortgage loans business is entirely in the hands of individuals and loans corporations. The usual rate of interest is the same as the ruling rate of commercial discount, gilt edged, viz.: Eight per cent. Exchange varies with the season. Loans on mortgage are made, generally, at a half of valuations.

NOTES ON THE KNOXVILLE BANKS.

THE EAST TENNESSEE NATIONAL was established in 1872, and is the oldest bank in the city. It has $175,000 capital, and the largest surplus of any bank here, viz.: $246,204.

The MECHANICS' NATIONAL BANK of Knoxville was organized in 1882, and is the second oldest banking institution of the city. It has a paid up capital of $100,000, and a surplus of the same amount, and at the time of its statement of December 2d, 1891, had $23,500 of undivided profits besides. Its total resources at that time were $705,760, of which $558,000 were loans and discounts. The deposits with it then, aggregated $445,500.

Since its organization, it has paid $105,000 in dividends. These figures show how successfully it has been managed.

Its officers are representative business men of the city. S. B. LUTTRELL, its president, is of S. B. Luttrell & Co., wholesale hardware, and is president also of the Knoxville Real Estate Co,; M. L. ROSS, vice-president, is of

M. L. Ross & Co., wholesale grocers, and is president also of the Chamber of Commerce of the city. E. G. OATES, cashier, and W. B. SULLINS, assistant cashier, are both experienced banking men.

The directors are W. P. Washburn, of Washburn & Templeton, attorneys; J. W. Borches, grocer; J. T. McTeer, of the wholesale clothing house of McTeers, Payne, Hood & Co.; W. L. Russell, of the Jones Brick Co.; S. P. Evans, of the Coal Creek Coal Co.; J. C. Luttrell, of S. B. Luttrell & Co., and Messrs. S. B. Luttrell, M. L. Ross, and Cashier Oates.

The principal correspondents of the Mechanics', are the National Park Bank of New York, and the Merchants' National of Louisville.

The Mechanics' is at 122 Gay street.

The THIRD NATIONAL has $300,000 capital, and $50,000 surplus and undivided profits. R. N. Hood is its president. It was organized in 1887.

The CITY NATIONAL has $100,000 capital, and $64,000 surplus. It was organized in 1888.

The STATE NATIONAL BANK, of Commerce and Gay streets, occupies handsome quarters there, the appointments for which, a combination of oak and cut glass, were made in Louisville. It was organized in 1890, and has $100,000 capital paid in. An entire change in its management was effected in '91.

In September last, when a statement was made by it in accordance with law, it had a surplus and undivided profits of $3,500, loans and discounts of $171,455, deposits amounting to $88,152, and total resources of $247,665.

This bank, considering the time it has been doing business, has been one of the most successful of Knoxville's financial institutions, especially so since January 1, 1891. Since then its business has more than doubled. This success is due largely to the character of its management, the *personnel* of which is a guarantee here, where they are known, of sound business methods.

Its officers are: JAMES C. WOODWARD, a Virginian by birth, but a resident and business man here for several years, president; WM. H. SIMMONDS, also an old resident and business man of the city, vice-president; JOHN L. BOYD, an experienced man, cashier, and HAL. S. HARRIS, assistant cashier.

The directors are: Messrs. Woodward, Simmonds, Boyd and Harris; W. H. Dawn, contractor and builder; S. T. Harris, capitalist; Wm. M. Baxter, solicitor for the East Tennessee, Virginia & Georgia Railroad; Jerome Templeton, of Washburn & Templeton, attorneys; F. C. Bearden, of Bearden & Ferguson, contractors; Walter Woodward, president of the Citizens' Building and Loan Association, and one of the wealthiest men of the city; H. B. Lindsay, attorney-general of the State, and J. C. J. Williams, attorney.

The State National has facilities for a general banking business equal to those of any bank here. Interest is paid by it on time deposits and exchange is drawn by it on the principal cities of this country, Mexico and Europe. Its reserve agents are the National Park Bank, of New York, and the Second National, of Louisville, Ky., besides twenty other regular correspondents.

The HOLSTON NATIONAL is successor since October last, to the Holston Banking & Trust Co., established in 1890. It has $100,000 capital, and $5,000 surplus.

The MERCHANTS' BANK was organized in 1881. It has $100,000 capital, and $7,000 surplus.

The FARMERS' & TRADERS', organized last year, has $100,000 capital.

The KNOX COUNTY BANK & TRUST Co. began business in 1890. It has $100,000 capital, of which $60,000 is paid up.

The KNOXVILLE SAVINGS BANK was organized in 1888. It has $50,000 capital, $15,000 surplus, and $140,000 deposits; the CENTRAL SAVINGS has $25,000 capital, $2,500 surplus, and 450 depositors. It has been established about two years.

UNDERWRITING BUSINESS OF KNOXVILLE.

KNOXVILLE has one local fire insurance company, the Knoxville Fire, one local life company, the Central Guarantee, and one accident company, the Southern Accident. It had another fire company, but that lately has gone out of business and turned its risks over to an underwriting firm.

These local corporations are mentioned in the notes to this chapter.

The fire agents of the city are organized as a Board of Underwriters. No account of the life business done in the city is available; but it can be said that it is large. All the big life companies have representatives working in Knoxville and its field.

The fire insurance business of Knoxville is estimated at $100,000 in aggregate of premiums a year, not counting the country business of the general agencies, which is probably that much more. There are sixteen regular agencies in the city, the most notable of which are those described in the following paragraphs.

The city's paid fire department is, as we have said, considered by the underwriters a very good one. The water supply is also believed to be fairly sufficient. The fire losses of the year preceding July, 1891, were but $15,250, and the insurance loss, $6,775 only, on property jeopardized which was valued at $91,575.

INSURANCE AND KINDRED BUSINESS MEN.

MCMULLEN & VANDEVENTER are insurance agents, doing also a real estate and loans business, at 11 Asylum street. As insurance agents, they represent the following solid companies: Imperial, of London; Northern, also of that city; Queen, of America; Scottish Union and National, of Edinburgh; Germania and Underwriters' Agency, of New York; American, of Philadelphia; Connecticut, of Hartford; Michigan Fire and Marine, of Detroit; Fireman's Fund Co., of San Francisco, and the Southern and Home, both of New Orleans, La.

They are also agents for the Northwestern Mutual Life Insurance Co., of Milwaukee, and the Southern Accident Co., of Knoxville.

They carry extensive lines of business insurance here, and do considerable also in the country.

As real estate agents, they handle suburban Knoxville property, and mineral and timber tracts chiefly. And as loan agents, they are investing considerable outside capital in local mortgage securities.

Mr. McMullen, of this firm, is a native of Alabama, but has been a resident of this city for the last twenty years. He has been in the insurance business here pretty much all that time. He is a director of the Southern Accident Insurance Co., of this city, and owns property also. Mr. VanDeventer is a native of Iowa. He came to Knoxville four years ago. He has been in loans, real estate and insurance pretty much all his life, and for three years here. He is a real estate owner, bank director and capitalist. He manages the loan and real estate business of the firm, and Mr. McMullen their insurance concerns.

W. H. SIMMONDS & Co., general insurance agents, of the Branner Building, 246½ Gay street, are the representatives of ten companies, in this city, among them fire, lightning, tornado, contribution, employer's liability, boiler explosion and general accident insurance. They are local agents for some of these, and State agents for others, with sub-agents in various cities and towns in this part of the country.

These ten companies are the following: The Liverpool & London & Globe, of London, whose stock is held at a higher premium than any insurance company in the world; the North British and Mercantile of London, also an extraordinarily staunch English company; the London & Lancashire, of Liverpool, Eng., scarcely less notable for its strength than those just mentioned; the German-American, of New York; Springfield Fire & Marine, of Springfield, Mass.; the Merchants', of Newark, N. J.; Georgia Home, of Columbus, Ga.; Equitable Fire, of Nashville, and the local company, the KNOXVILLE; also the American Casualty Insurance & Security Co., of Baltimore, Md.

This agency was established in 1889. The partners in it are W. H. SIMMONDS, his son, R. H. SIMMONDS, and H. D. HALL. Mr. W. H. Simmonds has been in the insurance business here for the last twenty years. He is vice-president of the State National Bank of Knoxville, and president of the West Side Land & Improvement Co., the Riverside Land Co., and the Home Building & Loan Association. Mr. R. H. Simmonds has been an underwriter for five years, and Mr. Hall for two. The latter is well known throughout all this part of the State as formerly a traveling man for Nashville houses.

E. P. KING, the well-known insurance man of 59 West Clinch street, who conducts, probably, the oldest agency doing strictly a fire insurance business in the city, is a native of East Tennessee. He came to Knoxville some years ago, and soon afterwards purchased a half interest in the agency in which he is principal now. It was then conducted by Brooks & Goodall. Since that time he has given his entire attention to it, and has purchased the remaining half interest.

The companies represented by him are well known throughout the country. While liberal in spirit, they abide by the board rules and comply with all laws affecting insurance. His list comprises the Western Assurance, and British America, of Toronto, Canada; the Westchester, of New York; Syndicate of Minneapolis; "Hamburg Bremen," of Hamburg; Home of Tennessee; Virginia Fire and Marine, Richmond; German, of Freeport; Fidelity and Casualty, of New York; Employers' Liability Assurance Co., and Hartford Steam Boiler Insurance Co.

In connection with his insurance business Mr. King also represents some institutions engaged in loaning money on improved city real estate. The steady and continuous growth of the city makes it one of the most desirable cities of the country in which to place money for investment; and this branch of his business is generally brisk.

The KNOXVILLE FIRE INSURANCE CO., of 148 Gay street, was organized in 1879. It has $100,000 cash capital, and received, in 1891, through its numerous agencies, established throughout the South and West, something like $250,000 in premiums. It has paid in losses since it began business, over $500,000, and it now has $10,000,000 of insurance in force. Its surplus to policy holders, at the time a statement was rendered by it on January 1st last, was over $210,000.

Its officers are leading business men of the city. MAJOR D. A. CARPENTER, its president, is president also of the Knoxville Brick Co., and secretary of the Knoxville Car Wheel Co. He has been mayor of the city, and is a representative business man. W. W. WOODRUFF, the vice-president, is of W. W. Woodruff & Co., wholesale hardware, and is also a man of many and diverse interests. Secretary L. C. FLETCHER, has been connected with the company since January 1, 1891. He is a gentleman of ripe experience as an underwriter.

The directors are: Messrs. Carpenter and Woodruff; C. M. McGhee, capitalist; R. C. Jackson, first president of the East Tennessee National Bank, and a capitalist also; W. P. Washburn, of Washburn & Templeton, attorneys; James M. Meek, real estate agent and capitalist; Jos. T. McTeer, of McTeers, Payne, Hood & Co., wholesale clothing; S. B. Luttrell, of S. B. Luttrell & Co., wholesale hardware; John E. Chapman, of Chapman, White, Lyons & Co., wholesale drugs; C. M. McClung, of C. M. McClung & Co., wholesale hardware, and M. L. Ross, wholesale grocer and president of the Knoxville Chamber of Commerce.

The company owns the building it occupies, situated at 148 Gay street. This building is shown in an illustration herewith.

DAWES BROS., of 23 Deaderick Block, are leading underwriters of the city, representing as general agents the following staunch fire, life and accident companies:

The Orient Fire of Hartford, Connecticut; the Farragut Fire of New York; the United States Fire, of the same city; the Delaware Fire, of Philadelphia, Pa; the Norwich Union, Guardian Assurance, Phœnix Assurance, and Manchester, English companies, and, incidentally, the Knoxville companies. They are special agents also for Knoxville and East Tennessee of the United States Mutual Life Insurance Co. of New York.

They have been established about five years here, and have built up a handsome business. They make a specialty of the insurance of city property, and important lines on business property are entrusted them also by owners here.

OFFICES OF THE KNOXVILLE FIRE INSURANCE COMPANY.

MR. SAM DAWES, of this partnership, manages the business. His brother and partner, CHAS. DAWES, is cashier for a leading wholesale dry goods house here, that of Cowan, McClung & Co., and is vice-president also of the Southern Building & Loan Association.

This firm also does a general real estate and loans business. As loans agents, they have at command large amounts of capital which they loan at current rates, on terms to suit the applicant, and in amounts from $500 to $50,000.

STEELE & MCMILLAN, real estate and fire insurance agents, of 57 Clinch street, have been established in that line here for about

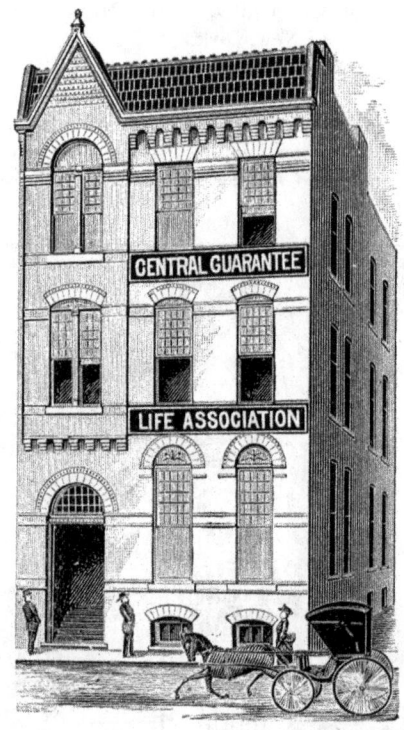

OFFICES OF THE CENTRAL GUARANTEE LIFE ASSOCIATION, KNOXVILLE.

three years; both had however, been in other lines of trade here before that, which gave them opportunity to acquaint themselves with the property and property owners hereabouts. Both have been resident here for very many years.

As real estate agents, they handle both city and country properties, and make a specialty of Knoxville suburban realty, now considerably in demand, and of mineral and timber tracts in this and the adjacent States. They also do a large mortgage loans business.

As insurance agents, they are the representatives of some twenty fire companies, embraced among that number the most substantial doing business in the land.

HICKMAN & MCSPADDEN, general insurance agents, of 144 Gay street, represent here the following well known Fire, Tornado, and Plate Glass Companies:

The Hartford, of Conn.; the Fire Insurance Co., of Philadelphia, Pa.; the Caledonian, of Scotland; the Niagara, of New York; American, of New York; Providence-Washington, of Rhode Island; Granite State, of New Hampshire, and Sun Mutual, of New Orleans, La.; some of which are fire companies exclusively, and some also tornado.

They also represent the New York Plate Glass Insurance Co., of New York.

The members of this firm were formerly principals in the East Tennessee Fire Insurance Co. of this city, now out of business. They occupy the offices formerly in use by that company. Mr. Hickman was its secretary, and Mr. McSpadden was with it in a managing capacity. They both have other interests here, and are men of solid resources. Mr. Hickman is a director of the Savings Building & Loan Association of this city, and a director, also, of the Knoxville Savings & Development Co.

THE CENTRAL GUARANTEE LIFE ASSOCIATION is one of the institutions of the city of which its citizens are justly proud. It was organized in 1887, and occupies, as a home office, the building at 117 Prince street, which is shown in the accompanying engraving. It has members throughout the South and is rapidly gaining in popular patronage and favor.

It has recently been placed under the management of NEWCOMB F. THOMPSON, who has formulated and copyrighted new plans of insurance that promise to place the association in the front rank of life companies. Mr. Thompson is president also of the association. He is an insurance manager of many years experience. He was Southern manager of the Commercial Alliance Life Insurance Company of New York, from the time that company was organized.

The present plans of the Central Guarantee are original with Mr. Thompson, and leading experts and actuaries have pronounced them the most attractive of any now before the public. The same payments made to this association that are made to the old regular companies, assure from two to five times greater advantages to the insured than these companies promise, for the Central Guarantee plans release the usual reserve accumulation on insurance policies, and treats it as surplus, invested on the building and loan plan, and thus secures the highest earning power of its funds, with the advantage that these funds are left at the point where collected, instead of being sent elsewhere and invested at an unprofitable rate of interest. The system is one of constantly increasing insurance, as against a constantly diminishing one under the old plans. It appears to be a perfect solution of the life insurance problem, as the plans cover under one simple policy contract, the entire field of life insurance.

The association has among its directors the leading business men of Knoxville. Ex-Mayor Kern is treasurer and one of its directors; E. J. Sanford, president of the Knoxville & Ohio Railroad and vice-president of the East Tennessee National Bank, is another; A. J. Albers, wholesale druggist; R. N. Hood, president of the Third National Bank; D. A. Carpenter, president of the Knoxville Fire Insurance Co., and N. Cuquel, merchant tailor and an old citizen, are the other members of the directory.

The association, in short, appears to have a very bright future before it.

The SUN LIFE INSURANCE COMPANY OF AMERICA, is a Kentucky company, organized in Louisville, with its principal offices in that city. It began business in August, 1890, and established an office here early in 1891. Its representative in Knoxville, is L. P. KNOKE, of 23 and 24 Minnis Building, 19 Asylum street. The territory allotted him embraces Knoxville and its environment in Tennessee and Kentucky. He has been an insurance agent for many years. He was formerly with the Western & Southern Life Insurance Co., of Cincinnati, Ohio. He has met with considerable success.

The Sun has $150,000 capital, and has $100,000 deposited with the State Treasurer of Kentucky. During its first four months' existence, nearly $2,500,000 business was done by it. Its officers are leading men of Louisville, and its stockholders, seventy-one in number, are representatives of the property, commercial and financial interests of that city.

Albert S. Willis, ex-congressman, and a leading lawyer of that city, is its president; M. W. Adams, insurance agent, vice-president, and George H. Lake, secretary. In its Board of Directors are such men as Jno. B. McFerran, Thos H. Sherley, Harry Weissinger, Jno. A. Lyons, Dr. H. W. Graham, Chas. D. Pearce, H. H. Littell, A. G. Mumm, Chas. Gheens, H. V. Sander, and W. H. Thomas.

Its plan is what is known as the Industrial. Its policies are issued upon weekly payments of from five cents to $1.90 per week, according to the ability of applicants to pay. Industrial Insurance has been in vogue now for forty-two years. Its benefits have been thoroughly demonstrated.

The UNITED ORDER OF THE GOLDEN CROSS, a fraternal order of over 18,000 members, with commanderies or lodges in every State of the Union, and in all the large cities, was incorporated on July 4th, 1876, and has the office of its Supreme Keeper of Records, or Grand Secretary, in Knoxville, at 57 West Clinch street. W. R. COOPER holds that office and resides here.

This order has, therefore, been established fifteen years. During that time it has paid in death benefits over $2,000,000. These death benefits are in sums of $500, $1,000 and $2,000, according to the amount of insurance taken. The insurance feature, indeed, of this order's plan has been a pronounced success.

The expense of joining it is only $3.50 for initiation, fees, etc. Ladies are admitted. A fundamental principle of the order is that members must be strictly temperate and moral. Assessments for death benefits are graded as to age. The *Golden Cross*, a journal published by the order, explains its features more in detail.

L. W. SCHUERMANN, pension claim agent, of 12 Sedgwick Building, has been established here in that line for two or three years. He has built up in that time quite a patronage—

KNOXVILLE OFFICES OF THE SUN LIFE INSURANCE COMPANY OF LOUISVILLE.
L. P. Knoke, Agent.

not here merely, but throughout Western North and South Carolina and Eastern Kentucky and Tennessee. He will prosecute good quartermasters' and other claims, as well as those of soldiers and sailors, and their widows.

He is also an insurance agent, and as such, the representative of the CENTRAL GUARANTEE LIFE, of this city, and the SOUTHERN ACCIDENT INSURANCE CO., of Knoxville also.

Mr. Schuermann has been a resident here since 1863. He was in the Federal army as a lieutenant of artillery, and is, therefore, an old soldier himself.

R. G. DUN & Co's Mercantile Agency, has one of its numerous district or sub-agencies established at Knoxville, with Mr. HENRY FENTON in charge. The office has been located here about eight years, and he has had charge of it for four. He has been with the company in other places also, and has acquired the necessary experience and tact to serve the company's patrons promptly and efficiently.

His district embraces a territory of fifty-two counties, comprising portions of East Tennessee, Western North Carolina, Southwestern Virginia, and Northern Georgia.

Merchants generally, know the purpose and utility of this agency, and many of those in this district have availed themselves of its advantages, both as subscribers to its reference books, and as patrons of its collection department. The latter is, certainly, of all the collecting agencies of the land, the best equipped. It has its own attorneys, and the most thorough system yet devised for liquidating mercantile claims.

The office of R. G. Dun & Co. here, is at 253 Gay street, where may be found an efficient staff under Mr. Fenton's management, and a well equipped office with fire-proof vaults, in which the records for the district are deposited every night; and all possible efforts are put forth there to the end that the patrons of the agency may receive prompt and conscientious service.

CHARACTERISTIC TRADE.

MARBLE, coal and lumber, are characteristic lines of trade at Knoxville, although not the largest items of its business, either singly or collectively. They have an especial importance, however, as the basis, all three, of manufactures, and by reason, also, of the promise they hold out of increase, that makes them worthy particular mention.

Marbles, of the finest quality and most infinite variegation, abound in Knoxville's tributaries; building and monumental marbles, chiefly, such as are favored for fine interior finish. So plentiful and so superior are they, indeed, that it is as much a phase of eminence to say "Tennessee marbles" as "California gold" or "Colorado silver," or, for a closer parallel, "Mexican onyx" or the "granites of Vermont."

While East Tennessee is the principal seat of this industry, Hawkins and Knox counties especially, it exists also in vast deposits in other parts of the city's trade territory, in adjacent parts of North Carolina, for instance, and quarries are worked in those parts also. But the business the city participates in mostly, and from which it derives its fame as a center of the trade, is that which accrues to it from quarries at its doors; by distribution of the rough product throughout the land, and of the finished product prepared in works established here, that are the largest in the world.

The marble quarrying business of Tennessee began in Hawkins county, one of the northern tier of counties on the eastern side, along the Virginia line. It extended from there into Blount and other counties of the valley, and finally had its rise in Knox county, just outside Knoxville, which is now the greatest field for it in this country.

In Hawkins county, which is Knoxville's trade territory by virtue of railroad advantages, there were, in 1890, six large quarries of this rare material; at the same time there were in Knox, twenty-two quarries, producing some sixty tons a day, and besides these, three large mills sawing and polishing the stone in the city itself. The annual trade of the city now, in this commodity, is estimated, by one in the trade, to be $1,000,000 a year. There are fifteen dealers in and manufacturers of it doing business at Knoxville, as the center of the industry; they employ 1,000 hands, and pay in wages $375,000 a year.

The quantity in the ledges round about here seems to be unlimited; beds of marble extend along the East Tennessee, Virginia & Georgia road, where it approaches the city for 100 miles; nearly on the line of the other roads centering here also, and along the river besides. It is so general a constituent of the crust of the earth hereabouts, indeed, that the only question concerning it is, where it can be best and cheapest worked.

This Tennessee marble is remarkable for its extraordinary diversity of veining and tints. In the æsthetic classifications of the trade, it is gray, pink, "peach-bloom," "maiden's blush," etc.; it mantles with other delicate complexions that a belle might envy, as its charms are disclosed by the dressing and polishing processes of the mills; and it discloses, in its final and perfected stage, shades the most exquisitely blended, colors and ground work harmoniously combined, and is comparable at times with nothing short of onyx or agate, or gems themselves.

Sketches and illustrations disclosing the *modus operandi* of the business, the methods employed by the quarrymen, millmen and dealers generally in the business, follow. Representatives of each and every branch of it, have mention in these sketches; and a perusal of them will afford a fair idea of the trade without further dissertation. We may premise, however, with this remark: Regular auction sales, of the rough product, are now held at Knoxville by leading dealers in this incomparable building finish, and monumental material; train loads of it are frequently made up for shipment to the larger distributing centers; and contracts are entered into by those in the business here, to furnish it for important structures anywhere in the United States.

THE MARBLE MEN OF KNOXVILLE.

THE TENNESSEE PRODUCERS' MARBLE CO., of 31 and 32 Deaderick Building, is an organization of the leading quarrymen and manufacturers of Tennessee marble products, entered into for mutual protection and to correct certain evils of the trade (but not for purposes of monopoly) in March, '89. Seven-tenths of the operated quarries in lower East Tennessee are in this combination, and every variety of Tennessee marble yet discovered can be furnished in unlimited quantity by it.

Something like $300,000 of capital stock is represented by this organization. Its managing officers are: W. H. EVANS, of Baltimore, president; JOHN J. CRAIG, one of the oldest residents and best known men of this city, vice-president; and JOHN J. CRAIG, Jr., his son, secretary and treasurer.

The directors are these officers and Wm. Pickel, of the Pickel Stone Co., St. Louis, the largest dealers in marble in the West; D. J. Bailie, one of the largest wholesale marble dealers of New York City; James McDonough, of the Great Western Marble Works of Cincinnati; C. R. Evans, marble dealer of Baltimore, and W. B. McMullen, president of the Southern Monument Company, of this city.

The quarries controlled by this company are on the line of the East Tennessee, Virginia & Georgia road in Knox, Blount and Loudon counties, Tennessee. Their aggregate production is, approximately, 100,000 cubic feet per annum. Every variety and color, as we have said, yet found in the State, is produced in one or the other of them: dark pink, gray and variegations of these, of every sort.

J. ED. ROSS, dealer in block marble, of 55 Union street, operates the "Old Knoxville quarry," as it is called, situated at the forks of the Tennessee and French Broad rivers, about four miles from the city. This is the quarry that furnished the marble used in construction of the Post Office and Government Building here; all that was used in the building of the New York State Capitol at Albany, and pretty much all that was used in the building of the costly and imposing Commerce Building at San Francisco, Cal.

AUCTION SALE OF MARBLE BY T. S. GODFREY.

Marbles from this quarry are very beautiful, and at the same time exceedingly durable. The quarry affords dark and light pink, "peach blow," "maiden's blush," and the gray varieties, and Mr. Ross makes a specialty of the trade in the "maiden's blush," which is largely in demand for inside decorative work, like counters, wainscoting, etc., and for monumental work also.

Mr. Ross does a car-lot business solely. He is a shipper via the Knoxville, Cumberland Gap & Louisville road, (and thence over its connections,) and by boat also, to all the large centers of trade. He has a big business with New York City, and with the larger centers of the West. The quarry produces about 1,500 cubic feet a month, or ten car-loads.

Mr. Ross is a native of this part of the country. He has been in the marble business for twelve years. He is a brother of J. M. Ross, also a large marble man here.

T. S. GODFREY, of Room 51, Lamar House, is proprietor of two notable quarries of this vicinity, the famous "Gray Knox" situated five miles from the city, on the Tennessee river, at the mouth of the French Broad, and the "Stinette," eight miles out on the East Tennessee, Virginia & Georgia road, the latter a quarry yielding an extraordinary variety of beautifully variegated marbles.

This quarry has an output of 5,000 cubic feet a month. It is practically inexhaustible. It supplies Eastern and other markets with a vast amount of furniture marble and marbles used for interior decoration, which are preferable to any imported, because they are impervious to stain of any sort.

The "Gray Knox" quarries have an output as large as the other, and the two make Mr. Godfrey, probably, the largest producer of block marble in the land. The "Gray Knox" affords a material unsurpassed for building purposes; it is both beautiful and durable. The marble used in construction of the new Post Office at Chattanooga was supplied by it, and that building is said to be the finest public structure in the South.

Mr. Godfrey has been operating these two quarries about five years. He employs 175 hands, and has the amplest transportation facilities by means of the East Tennessee road's ramifications and connections, and the Knoxville, Cumberland Gap & Louisville roads juncture with the "L. & N."

The first large auction sale of block marble ever made in this country was recently held here, under Mr. Godfrey's direction. It was attended by purchasers from New York, Philadelphia, Boston, Chicago, Cincinnati, and

FIRST TRAIN LOAD OF MARBLE SHIPPED FROM KNOXVILLE.
John M. Ross, Shipper.

Montreal, Canada, and was an entire success. It marked an era in the trade, indeed, and it is Mr. Godfrey's intention to hold such sales hereafter semi-annually.

An illustration showing this sale is on the opposite page.

JOHN M. ROSS, dealer in rough Tennessee marbles, at 55 Union street, owns and operates five quarries, all within five miles of this city, and employs in them 60 hands. These quarries produce dark and light pink, "peach blow," "maiden's blush," and gray marbles, to the extent, all told, of perhaps 50,000 cubic feet a year. He is a shipper of these to all parts of the country, but chiefly to Tennessee, Pennsylvania, Ohio, Missouri, Illinois, Maryland, Massachusetts and New York points; to the larger cities of the country in fact, in which they are utilized for building and other manufacturing purposes.

This city is his headquarters, and his shipments are made chiefly from here. He receives the output of the quarries by rail, river and wagon, and also ships direct from them, and it is said that he does more business than any other single concern in the trade here.

He is a native of the city, and has been engaged in this business since 1878. He is president and treasurer of the Knoxville

Marble Co., which is capitalized for $250,000, and is mentioned elsewhere in this work; and he is largely interested in other financial and industrial concerns here.

He is a principal also in Ross, Burges & Ross, quarrymen and dealers in rough dark Tennessee marble, at Warham, Tenn., and he has recently purchased the business of the Hercules Marble Co., including their quarry and mill of six gangs, located at the junction of the Holston and French Broad rivers, above the city. This mill cost $10,000, and has been known as a leading mill of the country. The stone for the Chattanooga Custom House was sawed by it. Mr. Ross will run it exclusively upon monumental and building stone.

W. H. EVANS & SON, of Baltimore, Md., and Knoxville, are producers of Tennessee marble from quarries they own here, and manufacturers also on the Knoxville & Ohio Railway, near the National Cemetery, just outside the city, of marble products and particularly of tiling and wainscoting, mantels, pedestals, vases and turned work of every description, interior work, counters and furniture marble.

They make a specialty of artistic interior work, and furnish estimates therefor or execute contracts in any part of the country. Baltimore is their headquarters, and their principal works are there, and they do a vast

They employ in their mills and quarries in Tennessee, 460 hands, and use ten different varieties of marble, taken from as many different quarries. These varieties are chiefly, Hawkins County marble, Bond and Cedar pink, Gray Knox, Great Bend and Cliff variegated, Cedar Bluff variegated, Caswell dark, and Caswell variegated. They saw from thirty to forty cars of raw material a month, and finish about 1,800 superficial feet a day. These are facts that substantiate the general impression, that this is the largest concern of the kind in the world.

The following, among other important jobs of interior marble work furnished by this firm, merit mention: The Ames and the Exchange buildings at Boston, Mass.; the Masonic Temple, Rand & NcNally building and Grand Central Station, Chicago; the German Savings and Loan Society's building, San Francisco; the Washington Loan & Trust building, Washington, D. C., and the County Court House at Dallas, Texas.

J. E. WILLARD is superintendent for this firm here. His principals are interested also in the Tennessee Producers' Marble Co., of this city, also described herein.

GEO. W. CALLAHAN & BROS., 6 East Depot street, are general marble and stone contractors and builders, dealing in marble monuments

MARBLE WORKS OF W. H. EVANS & SON.

amount of work in that city and its vicinity. They have trade, however, extending well over the United States and Canada, and they maintain mills and yards in Chicago.

and building stone, and contracting for the erection of work of that character. Some of the finest jobs in Tennessee marble done here were executed by them.

They have skilled workmen employed to do fine lettering and carving, and they handle hearths, mantels, founts, tiling and flagging. They will estimate on material to be furnished or work to be done in Virginia, North Carolina, Georgia, Kentucky, Tennessee or Alabama.

This firm is successor to Fenton & Callahan, established in 1885. Mr. Geo. W. Callahan, senior member of the firm at present, was a member of that firm formerly. His brothers, S. P. and J. K., are now associated with him. They bought out the Fenton interest in 1890. Mr. Geo. W. Callahan is a director of the Knoxville Bank & Trust Co.

The PHŒNIX MARBLE CO. has large works situated on the Knoxville & Ohio Railroad at Jacksboro street, and occupying lots of 124 feet by 300 area, with a railroad frontage and street at their back. These works consist of a building containing six gangs for sawing marble, and another building, the machinery of which is run by a separate engine, and is used for rubbing, boring, polishing and fitting the sawed marble from the other department. The supply of block marble for these works is procured from quarries owned by the company, situated about two miles from the city, on the line of the East Tennessee, Virginia & Georgia Railroad; also from quarries on the line of the Marietta & North Georgia Railroad, covering over two hundred acres of land and affording gray, true pink, light and dark pink marble, and besides several varieties of variegated marble showing very beautiful colors and formations. These mills and quarries employ between fifty and sixty hands.

During the last year the company has built over a mile of railroad to these quarries, thus, connecting them with the main line where it passes by, thereby enabling it to move marble more economically and at all seasons of the year. It has always done a large furniture marble business; also in slab marble shipped direct from the saws to finishers in all parts of the country. It has of late been turning its attention to the furnishing of polished marble for the interior of residences, public buildings, banks, etc.

The business of the company was founded twelve years ago, by John P. Beach. The mill built by him was the first finishing mill in Tennessee, for at that time the marble business was in its veriest infancy hereabouts. The Phœnix is a stock company: R. R. SWEPSON, president; JOHN P. BEACH, secretary and treasurer; Directors, T. H. Heald, F. L. Fisher, William Caswell, R. R. Swepson, and John P. Beach.

The long and ripe experience of its officers, derived by the early establishment of the

CONFEDERATE MONUMENT, KNOXVILLE.
Made by Geo. W. Callahan & Bros.

business, together with its superior facilities for producing block marble, enables the company to give many advantages to its customers, and so insures it a large and valuable trade.

The EAST TENNESSEE STONE & MARBLE CO., contractors for building stone and fine interior marble work, at the intersection of the East Tennessee, Virginia & Georgia, and the Knoxville, Cumberland Gap & Louisville Railroads, about one and a half miles from the depot of the former road here, have mills there employing fifty hands. These works cover three acres of a ten acre tract owned by the company, and are equipped throughout in first-class style for the sawing and dressing of building stone, and the making of fine interior marble finish, which is the company's specialty. They do work of this character for all parts of the country, more especially the Northwest, and are shippers of it from the Atlantic to the Pacific, and from the lakes to the gulf. They have superior

THE CITY OF KNOXVILLE.

WORKS OF THE EAST TENNESSEE STONE AND MARBLE COMPANY.

shipping facilities in their location on two tracks here, and they run their mills day and night the year round to keep pace with all demands.

J. E. HART, president of this company, has been in trade pursuits pretty much all his life. He came here from Jacksonville, Fla., where he was formerly in the wheat and grain, milling and elevator business. He is secretary and treasurer also of the Cumberland Coal Mining Co. of this city, and is a man of solid resources. C. M. FUNCK, secretary of the company, was formerly with the Baltimore marble firm of W. H. Evans & Son. The other principals in the company are DAVID GETAZ of the Southern Car Works, and the Stephenson-Getaz Manufacturing Co., C. T. STEPHENSON and R. Z. ROBERTS of the last named establishment also, and JAMES WRIGHT, the pioneer marble man of East Tennessee.

The company was established in 1889. It has $100,000 capital stock.

The SOUTHERN MONUMENT CO., of 113 and 115 Prince street, is a wholesale and retail dealer in foreign and Tennessee marbles, granites and onyx, and in finished work like statuary, mantels, hearths, wainscoting, headstones and tiling. As its name indicates, its specialty is cemetery work, for which it has comprehensive and superior facilities. It is a shipper of both finished and unfinished work of this character, not merely to all parts of Knoxville's trade territory, but to Eastern centers, and as far away also as Texas and Arkansas.

Estimates are furnished by it on application.

It has $50,000 capital, and the following officers: W. B. MCMULLEN, who has been in the marble business here since 1860, president; H. M. AIKEN, president of the Holston Bank and Trust Co., vice-president; CHARLES PITMAN, also prominent here from his identification with the Phœnix and Great Southern marble companies, secretary and treasurer.

Mr. McMullen is a director of both the Great Southern Marble Co. and Tennessee Producers' Marble Co., the latter an organization of many of the leading quarrymen of East Tennessee.

KNOXVILLE'S COAL TRADE.

KNOXVILLE is an important center of the coal trade of "the valley," which traffic is destined, with the supply at hand, to be of enormous proportions. It is a center of this trade, as we have hinted, as much because the mines of the valley are largely owned by its capitalists as because of its superior distributing and transportation facilities.

The Cumberland mountains, the western rim of the valley, are one vast mass of this mineral fuel, whose contents are enough to supply the Southern States for a thousand years. This coal, too, is of excellent quality; the Jellico, for instance, esteemed throughout the South, which comes from a district within the compass of Knoxville's commercial influence; a district owned largely by Knoxville parties, sixty-five miles from the city, in Campbell county, Tenn., on the East Tennessee, Virginia & Georgia road, at the Kentucky State line. It yields a bituminous and good house and steam coal both.

Knoxville, too, largely controls, in the commercial sense, the Coal Creek district, thirty miles distant, and is headquarters for mines in Anderson, Claiborne, Campbell, Scott, and other counties adjacent. The Briceville mines, which have lately attracted attention by events transpiring about them—events culminating in the forcible manumission of the convicts working in them—are but thirty miles from Knoxville.

These are all highly productive mines. They make coal exceedingly cheap for manufacturing purposes at Knoxville; and they furnish a market for the Knoxville merchant. There are coking coals, too, in the valley of good quality; but so far, these have not been utilized very much.

Coal at Knoxville is worth about $1.25 a ton, delivered. A million tons of it were handled by the nine corporations and larger shippers of the city last year, or $1,250,000 worth. The principal dealers are those mentioned in the following paragraphs:

LEADING COAL CONCERNS.

THE EAST TENNESSEE COAL CO., which has offices here at 56 Union street, was organized and began business as a miner and shipper of coal in 1876. It has rich coal lands yielding a high grade of product at Jellico, sixty-five miles from here on the Knoxville & Ohio road in Campbell county, Tennessee, and Whitley county, Ky., on the State line, and with 250 hands at work therein is producing about thirty carloads a day. It has a vein of this fine Jellico coal, averaging forty-two inches, the quality of which is so widely known as to need no further description.

It is a shipper of this coal to all parts of Virginia, Tennessee, Kentucky, the Carolinas, Georgia, Florida and Alabama, and it supplies railroads and other big consumers largely with it; and all these customers pronounce its product the best steam coal in the market. It is sold, however, also largely for house coal; is conceded, in fact, fully as good, for domestic use, as the best Pennsylvania bituminous coal.

This company has $150,000 capital. Its officers are: E. J. DAVIS, president and general manager; F. C. RICHMOND, secretary and treasurer. Mr. Davis has other important interests here also. He is president of the Rosedale Land & Improvement Company of this city, and of the Jellico Coal Mining Co. He has been a resident of this part of the State for twenty years, and has been engaged in the coal business for fifteen years of that time.

Secretary Richmond was also in the coal business here before he embarked in mining enterprises. He has lived here for twenty years, and is known, outside his connection with this company, as secretary of the Jellico Coal Mining Co. and a director of the Savings Building & Loan Association of this city.

The directors of the company, besides Messrs. Davis and Richmond, are: S. B. Luttrell, of S. B. Luttrell & Co., wholesale hardware men on Gay street; B. A. Jenkins, president of the Tennessee Coal Mining Co.; D. C. Richards, of the Enterprise Machine Works of this city; D. D. Nichols, superintendent of the Columbia Marble Co. of Knoxville, and Philip Francis, superintendent at the mines.

THE MINGO MOUNTAIN COAL AND COKE CO. which has yards here at the corner of Munson and Wray streets, and on Churchwell street, near the K., C. G. & L. R. R., has its mines in Claiborne county, Tenn. There it employs about 200 hands, and its daily output is about 1,000 tons a day, of coal, and 200 of coke, of the sort known to the trade as Mingo mountain coal and coke. Something like 20,000 tons of this product are sent here for sale, by its agent, W. M. CAPLES. The greater part of this stock is sold as grate coal, but some of it also is con-

ENTRANCE TO THE MINES OF THE EAST TENNESSEE COAL COMPANY, NEAR JELLICO, TENN.

COAL CHUTE OF THE COAL CREEK COAL COMPANY, AT COAL CREEK, ANDERSON COUNTY, TENN.

sumed by the manufacturers here as steam coal, and the Knoxville Gas Company uses 8,000 tons of it alone. It is of superior quality for both uses.

Mr. Caples came here from Baltimore, Md., and has been established here since March, 1891. The company has been operating, however, some two years. It has $150,000 capital, and the following officers: JOHN RALSTON, of Middlesborough, Ky., president; O. W. DAVIS, JR., of the same city, vice-president and secretary; C. M. WOODBURY, of the Standard Handle Factory, of this city, treasurer; ROBERT L. RALSTON, of Middlesborough, Ky., superintendent.

The COAL CREEK COAL Co. of 61 West Clinch street, was organized here in 1867, and was incorporated in 1888 by the parties interested at present. It has the largest paid in capital stock of any industrial corporation of the city. Its mines are at Coal Creek, Anderson county, about 31 miles from here, on the Knoxville & Ohio Railroad, and it has 350 men employed there. Its output of 900 tons a day, is probably shipped over a greater number of the States than any other Tennessee coal company has business in. It supplies many large manufacturing concerns here and in other parts of the South, and furnishes both the Richmond & Danville and East Tennessee, Virginia & Georgia railroads with very much of what they use. Its coal is considered excellent for both domestic and steam purposes.

E. C. CAMP, a resident of this city since 1865, notable formerly as a lawyer and U. S. District Attorney here under Grant's Administration, and now, by his extensive investments, is president of this company, and its principal stockholder. He is a director of the Third National Bank here, and of other local concerns. Since April, 1889, when he assumed management of this company, it has never failed to declare its regular dividend, and the employes have never waited a day for their money.

H. N. CAMP, secretary, treasurer and general manager, was formerly a hardware dealer in Illinois, but has been resident for nine years here. He is a brother of the president. These officers, with S. P. Evans, capitalist of this city, E. M. Camp, a resident of Knoxville also, and Chas. McKarsie, formerly superintendent of the mines, but now a resident of Scotland, are the parties interested in the company.

J. P. CARPENTER'S COAL AND BRICK YARDS, KNOXVILLE.

J. P. CARPENTER, dealer in coal and agent for the KNOXVILLE BRICK CO. (noticed elsewhere herein), is one of the largest coal dealers here, and probably handles more brick than any other concern here. He has large yards at 63 Jacksboro street, which are also on the track of the East Tennessee, Virginia & Georgia road, so that his shipping and receiving facilities both, are first class.

He handles, probably, 500 carloads a year of coal, chiefly the Pioneer coal from the mines at Pioneer, Campbell county, Tenn., considered the finest coking coals in the market, and also excellent steam and domestic coal, quite equal, in every respect, to the famous Jellico

The TENNESSEE COAL MINING CO., which has its main office at 58 Union street, Knoxville, Tenn., and two mines located at Briceville, Tenn., was organized in 1889 to mine and ship coal. It has $65,000 capital, and is the owner of valuable coal lands at Briceville, thirty miles from Knoxville. About two hundred hands are employed in its mines, and about 500 tons of coal shipped per day.

This coal is not excelled in quality south of the Ohio river. As a gas, smithing, steam, or domestic coal it has no superior. This company's product is shipped to all parts of Georgia, Alabama, the Carolinas, Virginia, Kentucky and Tennessee.

TIPPLE HOUSE AT THE MINES OF THE TENNESSEE COAL MINING COMPANY, BRICEVILLE, TENN.

coal. He supplies about 500 families here, and numerous factories besides.

As exclusive agent for the Knoxville Brick Co. (which has a productive capacity of 200,000 brick a day, of ornamental and plain pressed brick), he supplies largely the building trade of the city and its vicinity.

Mr. Carpenter is a native of the city, and lived here until 1881. He then went to Texas, and remained away about ten years, engaged, for the most part, in his vocation, that of a railroad engineer. He set himself up in his present line January 1, 1891, and he has every reason to be gratified with the result of his first year's business lately concluded.

B. A. JENKINS is president, CHAS. H. COWAN, of Cowan, McClung & Co., is vice-president; JOE J. REED, secretary and treasurer, and THOS. J. DAVIS, formerly superintendent of one of the largest coal companies in Pennsylvania is general superintendent of this company's mines.

Theo. F. Burgdorff of the U. S. Navy, and Dr. W. T. Williams and R. W. Montelius of Mt. Carmel, Pa., constitute, in connection with the officers named, the directory of the company.

This company supplies large contracts on short notice, and promptness in shipments and liberal dealing with all its patrons is guaranteed.

The EAST TENNESSEE IRON AND COAL CO., of 122½ Gay street, is, in all probability, the largest owner of coal and other mineral lands in the eastern part of this State. It was organized in 1858, and has been accumulating such properties ever since. Its lands lie chiefly along the Knoxville & Ohio Railway, in Campbell, and Scott counties, Tennessee. It has 50,000 acres, rich in both iron and coal, in these two counties alone.

It is a lessor company only. The PIONEER COAL AND COKE CO., of Pioneer, Campbell county, Tenn., leases from it and has erected a $100,000 plant at Pioneer to utilize the very fine coking coals there, and has several ovens in full blast. Other lessees are now preparing to erect plants on the company's lands, which will be in operation during the current year.

The authorized capital of the East Tennessee Iron and Coal Company is $1,200,000. When fully developed its possessions must be of extraordinary value. Its president and treasurer is A. L. MAXWELL, with whom, and eleven others, it originated; its secretary, C. M. McCLUNG, of C. M. McClung & Co., leading hardware merchants and capitalists here.

Mr. Maxwell is a New Yorker by birth, but he has been resident and engaged in enterprises in the South for forty years. He had an iron works here before the war, which was the largest between Richmond and New Orleans. It was destroyed during the siege of the city. He was a railroad contractor and bridge builder before the war, and many bridges are still standing, North and South, which were put up by him. He has of late, however, practically retired from all business except that of this company, of which he is the head.

The STANDARD COAL & COKE CO., of 56 Clinch street, Knoxville, has its mines at Newcomb, Tenn., on the Knoxville & Ohio Railway, about sixty-three miles from here. It owns there a tract of 6,000 acres of the most valuable coal lands in the State. The product of these mines is a bituminous coal and a gas cannel known as "Standard Jellico," and the output from them will average 1,000 tons of cannel, 10,000 tons bituminous a month. This output is shipped from the mines directly to the points at which it is consumed, which points are situated in all parts of the Middle South. It is handled here in Knoxville by the QUEEN CITY COAL CO., which has yards on Asylum street, convenient to the roads that center here.

This coal is exceptionally popular wherever it has been introduced for both steam and domestic purposes. The demand for it is extensive and grows all the time.

E. E. McCROSKEY and W. W. WOODRUFF, respectively president and vice-president of the company, are residents of this city. RUSSELL A. CLAPP, the secretary, treasurer and general manager; J. C. BROOKS, superintendent of the mine, and R. M. SLEMONS, purchasing agent, reside at Newcomb.

The QUEEN CITY COAL CO., which has offices at 69 West Clinch street, maintains yards here to dispose of its stock in trade, at the crossing of Asylum street and the East Tennessee, Virginia & Georgia Railway. This product is sold in part for domestic use and also largely for steam producing; and many of the foundries and mills here, the rock quarries and rock crushers hereabouts, are supplied with it from this distributing depot. It is a bituminous coal of very fine quality from the Jellico mines.

The company was organized January 1, 1890, and has $10,000 capital paid in. E. E. McCROSKEY, president of the Standard Coal & Coke Co., of Newcomb, Tenn., president also of the Knoxville City Board of Education, and formerly an alderman of the city, is its president; D. B. BEAN, for many years in the coal trade here, treasurer and general manager.

The JELLICO COAL MINING CO., of 56 Union street, was organized here about three years ago for the purpose of developing coal lands lying some six miles north of Jellico, Tenn., on which lands a coal had been discovered quite equal to the far-famed Jellico variety, considered the best all round steam and domestic coal of these parts.

The property acquired by this company lies on the line of the Louisville & Nashville Railroad. Operations have not yet been commenced, but soon will be. It is proposed by those interested, in fact, to begin development of this property this spring. Machinery will be supplied equal to the production of 600 tons daily, and 200 hands will be employed. The mining will be done by means of a horizontal or "entry" shaft.

The parties interested in this venture are solid men. They have subscribed $100,000 for it. E. J. DAVIS, president of the company, is also president of the East Tennessee Coal Co., of this city, and of the Rosedale Land Co. He is a wealthy and prominent man. F. C. RICH-

MOND, secretary, is secretary and treasurer also of the East Tennessee Coal Co., and a director in building and loan and other institutions here; and CHAS. DUCLOUX, treasurer, is assistant secretary and auditor of the Knoxville & Ohio Railroad Co., and is connected with the Knoxville Brick Co., and other local concerns.

C. C. SULLINS & Co., wholesale and retail dealers in coal and coke, have an office at 59 Clinch street, and yards with track connections on East Depot street, of 3,000 tons storage capacity that are usually stocked to the extent of 2,000 tons at least, and that do a business of about ten car loads a day. They are the largest retail dealers here, in both bituminous and anthracite coals, especially the latter sort, and are shippers, besides, to all points in Knoxville's trade territory within a radius of 400 miles. They have fifteen employes and run several teams in Knoxville for delivery purposes, and number among their customers here many of the mills and factories of the place.

Mr. Sullins (the "Co." is nominal merely) has been in this line about three years. He was formerly a general merchandiser here, and is one of the best known business men of Knoxville. He was also formerly an active member of J. Allen Smith & Co., millers of this city, and is still associated with that corporation as a stockholder. He is also a real estate owner here, and has just recently constructed several city houses or flats for rental purposes, a cut of which is on another page of this book.

E. GRAINGER, dealer in coal and coke at 53 to 65 Hardee street, corner of Morgan, does an extraordinarily large retail business. He runs about a dozen teams, and besides several of the factories here, supplies about 500 families with coal. He sells about three carloads of it a day, chiefly Jellico, the best domestic coal sold here, but he also handles the anthracite coal. He receives his coal direct from the mines and has a side track into his yard.

Mr. Grainger is successor to Cruze Bros. His place of business is that formerly occupied by the Black Diamond Coal Co. He is well known as formerly with Knaffl & Locke, wholesale grocers here. He has been a resident and business man here since 1872.

LUMBER AND BUILDING MATERIAL.

THERE are fifteen firms and companies dealing in lumber and the building material made from it, at Knoxville. Several of these concerns operate planing mills; and four run saw mills, cutting the logs as they are received by rail and river from the adjacent forests of the valley and mountains.

These dealers handle about 15,000,000 feet of lumber cut in other parts a year, and the local saw mills cut as much more; so that the total of the trade annually, is 30,000,000 feet, which, at $15 a thousand average is $450,000. In its entirety, the trade represents perhaps, a business of $500,000 a year.

There are two very large saw and planing mills at Knoxville, and five of less importance; two establishments turning out fine hardwood interior finish, and office fixtures as a specialty; two furniture factories, one of them employing a hundred hands; a spoke and handle factory, also employing one hundred persons; and among the dealers are two exporters of lumber and timber, for the most part hardwoods. These do a business of $500,000 more.

East Tennessee has a timbered area, it is estimated of 1,400 square miles. It has 600,000 acres of poplar, wild cherry, red birch or mountain mahogany, chestnut oak, hickory, white ash, basswood, beech, white pine and sugar maple. Yellow poplar is most abundant of these trees, and this region is one of the few remaining notable sources of its supply. The walnut of this section has pretty much all been cut; white pine is rather more abundant than most believe. Poplar, however, chestnut oak, which supplies the finest of tan bark, and the furniture and carriage making woods, are most plentiful; and this country affords a remarkable advantage for lumbering in its numerous mountain streams.

For all this timber there are but two furniture factories at Knoxville; there might be twenty; there are only two carriage shops of any note, and there might be twenty, also, of these. These two carriage works are run on orders and jobbing entirely. The wagons used throughout the valley and mountains, are shipped in from other parts. It is much the same with furniture. In these two lines, with all this timber in the background of Knoxville, are opportunities for manufacture, certain to be grasped ere long.

REPRESENTATIVE CONCERNS.

THE STEPHENSON–GETAZ MANUFACTURING CO., engaged in manufacture of hardwood mantels and all kinds of interior finish, chiefly, however, of native hardwoods, has works covering four acres of ground on the East Tennessee, Virginia & Georgia Railway, one mile west from the depot of that road here. It has $100,000 capital stock, 100 hands employed, and consumes, in the various processes of manufacture, 1,000,000 feet of lumber a year. In respect of its facilities, output and resources, it is the largest concern of the kind, not in Knoxville alone, but in this part of the land.

Its works are as complete in their appointments and equipment as any in the Union, and it can turn out as fine work, promptly and cheaply, as any factory in the country. Its business was established in 1880 by C. F. STEPHENSON and DAVID GETAZ, and from these founders it derives its name. The stock company was incorporated in 1888. Prominent business men of the city are interested, financially in it.

R. Z. ROBERTS, vice-president of the Southern Car Works, and a large real estate owner here, one of the most prominent of Knoxville's business men, in fact, is its president; S. W. GRAVES, furniture dealer here, is vice-president; DAVID GETAZ, one of the founders of the business, general manager, and HENRY ROBERTSON, secretary and treasurer. These officers and J. B. FISCHER, cashier of the East Tennessee National Bank of this city, and a man of numerous other local interests besides, are the directors.

SAXTON & Co., wholesale dealers in and exporters of lumber, of 60 Commerce street, are, in all probability, the largest dealers here in their line. They handle, annually, about 6,000,000 feet of yellow poplar, the product of the mountains of Kentucky and Tennessee, besides other hard woods, and several million feet of poplar, walnut and oak logs. They export to England, France and Germany, the greater part of this, through the seaports of Norfolk, Baltimore and New York. They have also a large New York and New England trade.

They are largely interested also in several of the saw and planing mills of this vicinity.

There are three members of this firm, MR. H. N. SAXTON, JR., a Londoner by birth; F. W. BARTH, JR., son of a leading importer of lumber at Bremen, Germany, with whom the firm has close business relations, and C. G. SCHRADER, a native of Bremen.

KNOXVILLE'S JOBBING TRADE.

TRADE busies the Knoxville of to-day most; this is its principal aim and purpose. The greatest gain to it from that marvelous development of the New South which has been so long in everyone's mouth, is in the way of jobbing. In this respect it begins to rival the most stalwart of its Southern competitors. It is expanding in girth and growing in weight and influence as a wholesale market daily.

Within its own provinces of trade, Southwest Virginia, Southeast Kentucky, East Tennessee, Western North Carolina, North Georgia and North Alabama, not a single adversary of superior magnitude rises to confront it. One solitary competitor only, Chattanooga, the nearest trade center of importance, appears upon the nether edge of its field, 110 miles distant. So that within a circuit of 200 miles sweep it is the city regnant, the center of commerce, paramount and supreme.

COMMERCIAL ENTERPRISE.

The larger cities of the country all, of course, intrench upon this infield of Knoxville for business; but it has grown steadily while measuring its strength against them; and far outside these tributaries of its own, it is making new conquests of territory daily. Some of its larger jobbing houses sell goods as far from home as Baltimore, Md.; almost all that sell through drummers, meet the rivalry of Atlanta, Birmingham, Nashville, Louisville, and even Cincinnati and New Orleans. It is true that it has, with these same cities, reciprocal commercial relations; but where competition is involved, it displays as innate and forceful a spirit of enterprise as any of them.

Its railroad policy is a case in point, illustrating this enterprise. The $700,000 it has subscribed to four railroads, and the favor it has shown them generally, has been returned to it tenfold in business; and it has the benefit of its investments in these roads besides.

TEN YEARS' GAIN IN TRADE.

Of the $50,000,000 of annual trade—manufactures included—credited to Knoxville, $40,000,000 or 80 per cent, is the acquisition of the last ten or twelve years, the increment of business earned by its enterprise; for the Knoxville of 1880, with 10,000 inhabitants, could scarcely have claimed more than $10,000,000 of business a year. This increase of $40,000,000 of annual trade is 400 per cent over the year 1880; and of that $40,000,000, nearly the whole of the city's estimated $10,000,000 manufacturing production is new business, originated within these twelve years past.

Some say, to be sure, that the enterprise of the Knoxville community has been misdirected; distracted from legitimate industrial investments like manufacturing, for instance, which return from six perhaps, to twenty-five per cent, and turned into channels of real estate speculation where profits are frequently ten times that. But if this be true the trouble is one that corrects itself; in this business as in every other, the ebb invariably succeeds the rising tide—the waters immutably seek their level at last; and it must be confessed that $50,000,000 itself is a handsome sum total for this city to have reached.

SALES IN VARIOUS LINES.

Nearly every jobbing line known elsewhere contributes to make this grand aggregate. The grocery trade leads with $4,500,000 or $5,000,000 annual total; and if flour and provisions are included, a million and a half more. As a center for a great mining region, consuming foodstuffs and producing none, Knoxville has a particularly notable trade in provisions, flour, hay, grain and produce generally, liquors, etc.

The dry goods trade, including millinery and notions, comes next after groceries in volume. It aggregates probably $3,000,000 or $4,000,000. Boots and shoes, clothing, agricultural implements (usually allied with machinery and hardware), live stock, liquors, marble and coal, are lines in which the total sales here are a million dollars a year and upwards.

SOME LOCAL ESTIMATES.

Following is an estimate of the trade done by the jobbers of the city in the ordinary jobbing lines: Groceries and provisions, $6,500,000; dry goods, $4,000,000; hay, grain and produce, $2,000,000; hardware, implements, machinery, etc., $2,500,000; live stock (horses included), $1,525,000; boots, shoes and hats, $1,700,000; wholesale clothing, $1,500,000; marble, $1,000,000; wholesale liquors, $1,000,000; lumber, interior finish, etc., $1,000,000; drugs, $600,000; saddlery, $600,000; furniture and carpets, $500,000; house furnishings, $500,000; crockery, etc., $500,000; building and works of improvement, $1,500,000; iron manufactures, $500,000; retail business, $5,000,000.

Of flour, $500,000 worth is made in the city and, perhaps, $200,000 worth imported; the manufacturers of furniture produce $200,000 worth a year; and the manufacturers of saddlery employ 125 hands, and pay $75,000 a year to them in wages. The retail aggregate is large, because many of the establishments so engaged are jobbers, supplying, to a limited extent, the country people roundabout here.

The houses doing a wholesale business at Knoxville number something like 100. That figure includes coal and marble and lumber dealers, as well as one or two houses manufacturing and jobbing both; and also several that are wholesale and retail too. The number of houses exclusively wholesale is eighty. There are seven large wholesale grocery houses; five in grain, hay and produce; three in dry goods and notions; two in clothing, besides two others that are retailers also; two in boots and shoes, and two more retailing as well as jobbing; two in the hat trade; three in drugs; three in liquors; two in hardware and implements, and two in addition retailing; two in crockery; five in saddlery; two in furniture; four in the flour trade; nine in coal; fifteen in lumber and fifteen in marble.

The establishments retail exclusively, number a couple of hundred; strictly manufacturing, 225, of which classification we shall say more hereafter.

CREDIT OF THE COMMUNITY.

RESPECTING the credit and standing of this even hundred jobbing houses of Knoxville, we can only repeat the common report, that with drummers selling here, the rule is, that every Knoxville house is good. A failure, or even a suspension, is a rare event in this exceptionally prosperous center. Credits to the country trade are usually sixty days; and as a rule, these customers, who are prosperous themselves, are good pay.

One striking effect of the development of the resources of East Tennessee, and of the adjacent region, has been the rapid rise and growth of new towns, like Middlesborough, Ky., sixty-five miles distant, which, with the stimulus of English and other capital, is making remarkable strides of late; Harriman, Tenn., a railroad junction and center of the coal trade, fifty miles, and Lenoir City, Tenn., twenty-two miles.

Railroads, foreign capital, immigration, all contribute to solidify Knoxville in trade.

The opportunities for business adventure at Knoxville are still excellent. There is as yet no sign of a stay in its growth. The conditions might, indeed, be bettered in some particulars perhaps; but as a whole they are far more favorable than anywhere else in the South.

In this connection we may refer those interested in the subject, to the information given in a previous chapter—that upon real estate, as to rents, taxes, etc.

Let it be understood here, however, that the representations made herein are not in the nature of a plea for Knoxville. They are simply the facts as we, the compilers of this book, see them; with such conclusions, from grouping these facts, as would naturally arise to any intelligent man.

LEADING GROCERY HOUSES DESCRIBED.

IN the following sketches leading houses in the various lines are briefly described, beginning with the grocers and provision dealers, which, in aggregate sales, lead all the rest:

M. L. Ross & Co., wholesale grocers, candy manufacturers, and jobbers of tobacco and cigars, at 180 Gay street, have been established since 1878. The house is, however, seven years older than that; it was originally established in 1871 by the firm of Carpenter & Ross, the latter now senior member of the firm.

During the twenty years since its foundation, it has gradually expanded in resources and patronage along and apace with the trade center of Knoxville, and now has recognition, wherever the commercial influence of that city extends, as one of its foremost business concerns.

It has twenty employes here, and five men on the road selling for it to the trade of the field for which Knoxville is the commercial capital, viz.: East Tennessee, Eastern Kentucky, Southwestern Virginia, the Carolinas, Georgia and Alabama, almost as a whole. Its place of business here is a four-story house, 50 feet by 160, stocked throughout with all the staples of the grocery trade, to the value, usually, of

$50,000, and with many specialties besides. Its candy factory is on the third floor of the building. In it the firm manufactures plain, fancy, stick and candies of every sort known to the trade. Last year (1891,) its output was 250,000 pounds.

Mr. M. L. Ross, the head of the house, is a man of considerable note here. He is president of the Knoxville Chamber of Commerce, is vice-president and a director of the Mechanics' National Bank of this city, a director of the Knoxville Real Estate Co., and has other investments besides. He is a native of Anderson county, and has been a merchant pretty much all his life. His partner, Mr. S. B. Dow, is a native of New Hampshire. He came here shortly after the war ended, and was, until he went into this business in 1878, a real estate man here.

H. B. Carhart & Co., wholesale grocers, of 19 Jackson street, one of the largest, if not, indeed, the largest house of this line in East Tennessee, occupies its own premises, a large four-story and basement brick building, with marble trimmings, one of the most substantial in the business quarter of the city.

This building is stocked throughout with the staples of the trade and with many specialties besides. Among the latter, imported table delicacies and goods of that sort in great variety. The house is noted for and prides itself on its reputation for the high quality of its goods—a reputation acquired and carefully preserved during the fifteen years it has been established.

Mr. H. B. Carhart, head of the house, is a New Yorker. He has, however, been resident here since the house was established. He is president of the Third National Bank of Knoxville and is a director in a number of the local corporations.

Hazen & Lotspeich, wholesale grocers, of 206 Gay street, carry, usually, a $50,000 stock, as varied in assortment as that of any house here; have four men on the road selling for them, in Virginia, Kentucky, Tennessee, the Carolinas and Georgia, and do a business in sales of from $350,000 to $400,000 a year. They have been established now going on four years, and every year since the first, have experienced a rapid increase of trade over the one that preceded it. They have popularized themselves with the trade of Knoxville's field by enterprising, liberal and straightforward business methods, and they are recognized as a house of metropolitan characteristics and system.

The partners in the house, two in number, are experienced grocery merchants. Mr. R. S. Hazen, of the firm, has spent fifteen years of his life in this branch of trade, and his associate, Mr. J. O. Lotspeich, has been in it as long, and is also a man of practical knowledge of its details.

Mr. Hazen takes charge of office and financial concerns of the house; Mr. Lotspeich of the buying and sales.

The Knoxville Provision & Sugar Co. is a consolidation, effected January 1st last, of two of the most important mercantile concerns of the city, the Knoxville Provision Co. and the Knoxville Sugar Co., the object of which merger is to do the business of both at the expense of one. The combination was the more readily brought about by reason of the fact that the same parties practically were interested in the two. These parties are leading jobbing grocers of Knoxville.

Among the stockholders of the consolidated company are the following: H. B. Carhart & Co., W. B. Lockett & Co., M. L. Ross & Co., Shields Bros., Hazen & Lotspeich, Knaffl & Locke, Smith & Bondurant, and H. Coffin.

The officers elected recently are as follows: R. Knaffl, president; R. S. Hazen, vice-president; H. Coffin, secretary and treasurer, and H. C. Bondurant, general manager.

The business of the two companies aggregated, before their union, a million dollars a year. It embraced a trade in all the States tributary to Knoxville, and was done largely through the forty traveling representatives of the houses having membership in the two associations. This same plan will be followed for the reorganization, and a sufficient capital has been paid in for a larger business even, than has been done heretofore.

The Provision Company had been established five, and the Sugar Company one year, when the new company absorbed them. Both had been eminently successful. There is scarcely a shadow of doubt but that, under a more economical system, their successor will have greater prosperity even than they.

It will occupy the new building at 27 and 29 Jackson street, formerly occupied by the Provision Company. This building is of brick, three stories, substantially built, especially fitted for the storage and handling of provisions and sugars, and it adjoins the depot of the East Tennessee, Virginia & Georgia road.

Dick, Payne & Co., wholesale and retail grocers, of 30 Market Square, are successors to

Jim Anderson, established in 1880. They bought him out in 1887. They carry an extraordinary stock and do a correspondingly large

W. B. LOCKETT & CO., WHOLESALE GROCERS.

business. They have men on the road selling for them, and they cover as jobbers, pretty much all the trade territory of the city.

Four partners hold interests in this house, A. C. DICK, R. R. SWEPSON, R. S. PAYNE, and W. E. YEATMAN. Messrs. Swepson and Payne are not actively engaged in the management. They are capitalists of the city, devoted to numerous other affairs.

Messrs. Dick and Yeatman direct the business. The former is buyer for the house, and the latter the office and creditsman. Both have had lengthy experience of the trade.

Mr. Payne is president of the East Tennessee National bank, and is also of McTeers, Payne, Hood & Co., wholesale clothiers on Commerce street here. Mr. Swepson is president of the City Gas Co., is of Davis & Co., wholesale hats, and has many other interests here besides.

W. B. LOCKETT & Co., wholesale grocers, of 7 Jackson street, have recognition as a leading house of the State, everywhere in it. At the recent organization of the wholesale grocers of Tennessee, MR. W. B. LOCKETT, senior member of the firm, was chosen temporary chairman of that association.

It is an old house as well as a large one. It was founded in 1873, by the late W. B. Lockett and M. L. Ross, now president of the Knoxville Board of Trade. Mr. Lockett had been a planter of Mississippi, and an extensive merchant there and in New Orleans, before he came here. His house, Lockett & Lockett, was well and widely known. In 1882 Mr. Lockett withdrew from this partnership with Ross and established another in company with his sons, W. B., Jr., and Ed. The elder Lockett died in June, 1889, and another son, A. P., acquired an interest when he came of age, in 1890.

An old house directed by young heads like this one has these advantages: It has the resources, the reputation, the system founded upon experience, of age, coupled with the energy and spirit of youth. The sons raised under him, follow in the footsteps of the sire, but proceed at the pace set by the times. The house has grown wonderfully of late years. It has seven men on the road in Southwest Virginia, Eastern Kentucky and Tennessee, Western North Carolina, North Georgia and Alabama, and its sales now aggregate, approximately, $500,000 a year. It usually carries in stock fifty to sixty thousand dollars' worth of goods.

The brothers divide the responsibilities of management as follows: W. B. is general manager; Ed. directs the sales departments; A. P. the shipping and out of town business. W. B. is the representative of the house in other concerns also in which it has interests. He is a director of the Knoxville Sugar Co., the Knoxville Provision Co., and the Third National Bank, and is president of the Wholesale Grocers' Association of the city.

KAISER BROS., wholesale grocers and produce dealers, at 222 Gay street, were well known here from their previous business relations, when they began in their present line, in 1890. They are brothers, three in number. MR. H. O. KAISER was the "Co." of W. W. Scarborough & Co., commission-produce men, before that. MR. G. H. KAISER was book-keeper for Chapman, White, Lyons & Co., wholesale druggists, of this city, and MR. F. C. KAISER was with the East Tennessee, Virginia & Georgia road. Their business experience had not, therefore, been limited.

They have built up a trade that keeps four traveling men busy in Tennessee, Kentucky, Virginia and the Carolinas. In addition to groceries, they handle fruits and vegetables largely, in the season for them, and they make a specialty of the trade in canned goods and fancy groceries.

They are doing a first rate business, and their trade is growing every day.

BORCHES & CO., wholesale grocers of 32 Market Square, are successors to McNulty & Borches, who were themselves successors to McNulty, Lillard & Co., established in 1870. The house is, therefore, now, in its twenty-second year. It is a leading house as well as an old one. It occupies a three-story place, 30 by 150, stocked throughout with staples of the trade, destined eventually, to fill the orders sent the house from all parts of Tennessee, Kentucky, Virginia, North Carolina, Georgia and Alabama.

It has also a very fine local trade. Its specialties are fancy groceries, imported delicacies, tobacco and cigars.

MR. J. W. BORCHES, sole principal in the house at present, has lived here since 1880, and has been in this business twenty years. He has another grocery house here, a retail establishment at 11 Market Square. He is a director of the Mechanics' National Bank, and is one of the most prominent business men of Knoxville.

GAMMON & LA RUE, grocers, confectioners, tobacconists and dealers in fresh meat, at 142 Broad street, corner of Depot, do a wholesale business to some extent, with patrons in the towns adjacent to the city, but the bulk of their trade is with local consumers and with country people visiting the city to buy.

They carry a very large stock—one filling, in fact, a three-story place. They handle all the staples, and many fancy lines besides.

They have been established about seven years. Mr. Gammon has been in the grocery trade pretty much all his life, and Mr. La Rue also has a lengthy experience of it.

They have another house here also, corner of Holston and Broad streets.

J. M. DAILEY, JR., leading retail grocer of Knoxville, is established at 12 Market Square, East Side. He is successor to Caldwell & Selden, who began in the trade here twelve years ago, and he acquired from them, when he started for himself in August, 1890, a very considerable business. This he has increased largely by intelligent and enterprising management, so that his house compares favorably with many of the oldest here. Its sales aggregate $50,000 and upwards a year.

His place is large and roomy, his stock both extensive and select. He makes a specialty of the trade in table delicacies, shelf goods, and dried and canned fruits. He was cashier at the local freight office of the East Tennessee, Virginia & Georgia Railroad here before he embarked in business, and he has earned recognition, while established for himself, as one of the liveliest young merchants of East Tennessee.

The KNOXVILLE STOCK YARDS cover five acres of ground about a mile and a half to the west of the depot of the Knoxville, Cumberland Gap and Louisville, and East Tennessee, Virginia & Georgia roads, and has stall accommodations for 1,500 head of mixed stock, pens, ample water supply, feed barns, etc. It has side track connections with the roads running in here, and is a feeding station, as well as sales yard, for stock shipped over these roads

THE KNOXVILE STOCK YARDS.

destined for points along their lines in Knoxville's trade territory. It is, therefore, the resort of the drovers and dealers of all this part of the country, especially of the cattle-buyers, who furnish it with most of its business.

It is the only stock yards at Knoxville. It was established in 1890 by S. P. CONDON, a resident here for many years, formerly engaged in railroad contracting, and S. H. Davis. Having bought out the Davis interest, Mr. Condon has been sole proprietor, however, since November last.

A trade of about $50,000 in the aggregate was transacted here during the first year of the establishment of these yards, embracing dealings in cattle, hogs, sheep, horses and mules. The facilities afforded by this enterprise promise to increase largely the business of this kind done here.

Mr. Condon is the owner of the celebrated trotting stallion, "Baron Egbert." Terms for the service of the horse will be made known on application.

WHOLESALE LIQUOR DEALERS.

W. C. PERRY & Co., wholesale liquor dealers, of 244 Gay street, had sales last year aggregating $150,000, a figure ranking them with the largest concerns of their line doing business in Knoxville's trade territory. They have trade in Tennessee and Kentucky, Virginia, North Carolina, Georgia and Alabama, and do business in true metropolitan fashion with traveling men representing them on different routes.

They handle superior goods only—Kentucky and Tennessee bourbons, Pennsylvania and Maryland ryes, and imported wines and brandies. They are sole agents here also for the sale of Pabst's celebrated Milwaukee beer.

Mr. Perry, senior member of this firm, has been in the liquor trade here for twenty-one years. He was a salesman in it before he started on his own account in 1877. He has been a resident here since 1870; and having been successful in business has accumulated considerable property. He is considered among his associates a progressive and enterprising man.

His partner, MR. J. E. CAMPBELL, has also been a business man here for very many years. He was born near here, and he too, has property acquired by the successful prosecution of business.

J. F. HORNE & BRO., wholesale liquor dealers, of 37 Market Square, corner of Asylum street, have been established in that line here since 1869. They have two men on the road, and have trade as far away as Kansas and Illinois. They usually have a stock on hand of about 600 barrels of old whiskey, wines and other liquors, and they make a specialty of the trade in old North Carolina corn whiskeys and in "Old Poplar Log" whiskey—a brand well known throughout the State.

They began the manufacture of this brand here some twenty years ago.

J. F. and W. A. HORNE are principals in this house. They are brothers, natives of this city. Both own real estate here largely, and both have stock, to a considerable amount, in local enterprises. Both are members also of the wholesale grain firm of Horne, Goans & Co., Loudon, Tennessee.

The CRESCENT BREWING CO., of Aurora, Ind., has an agency here, a bottling works, and a storage house with refrigerating departments and facilities for the steaming of beer such as are enjoyed by no other brewing agency at Knoxville (or for that matter in East Tennessee), at 50 and 52 East Depot street. This agency covers East Tennessee, and a part of both Alabama and Kentucky, and is managed by MR. JOSEPH LIVSEY. He handles a business embracing sales of about 15,000 barrels of the company's superior product, or $90,000 worth a year. Most of this is sold in the shape of keg beer; but twenty-five barrels a day, or 250 dozen, is bottled. It is regarded as a most superior beverage wherever it has been introduced. The following are the brands handled by Mr. Livsey: "Pilsener," "Standard Lager," "Felsen Beer," and "Export Beer."

Mr. Livsey has been the company's agent here since 1889. The agency, however, was established several years before he came. He was with the Chr. Moerlein Brewing Company before he accepted his position here. Under his management the Crescent Company's business has increased largely, and the signs are that it will long continue so to do.

BROKERAGE AND COMMISSION.

R. K. GIBSON, general merchandise broker, with office in the handsome bank building at No. 248 Gay street, has been established in that line here since 1887. He is the representative of a number of the leading manufacturers, importers and jobbers in the country who sell to the exclusively wholesale grocery and provision trade, and he is doing a large and continuously increasing business.

He is sole agent here for the Spreckels Sugar Refining Co., of Philadelphia; the American Cereal Co., of Chicago; the Collier Shot Tower Works, of St. Louis; the American Starch Co., of Columbus, Ind.; Lopez, Dunbars Sons & Co., canners of Biloxi, Miss.; the Kentucky Flour Co., of Louisville; Cornwall & Bro., of Louisville; S. H. Conover, of Plymouth, Wis.; the Eagle Lye Works, Milwaukee, Wis.; the Pillsbury Flouring Mills, Minneapolis; the Midland Elevator Co., Kansas City, Mo.; the Clifton Salt Co., Clifton, W. Va.; the Western Paper Bag Co., Batavia, Ill.; Griffin & Skelley Co., of Riverside, Cal.; Bennett, Day & Co., of New York, and some other houses of like position in trade.

Mr. Gibson is a native of the city, and, therefore, thoroughly acquainted with its people and business concerns. He is a young man, discerning and energetic; and he counts his friends here by the score. No young man in Knoxville stands better than Mr. Gibson in the estimation of its business men.

E. S. McClung & Co., wholesale dealers in hay, grain, flour, feed and field seeds, have a large brick warehouse on Hardee street, running back to the tracks of the East Tennessee, Virginia & Georgia Railroad, and an office at 218 Gay street. Their telephone numbers are 285 and 186.

This house was established by its senior partner, Mr. McClung, in 1869. It is the oldest produce house of Knoxville, and it is the recipient of a very large share of the trade of its line in this market. It enjoys also an enviable reputation for reliability, fair dealing and liberality towards its customers. It carries always extensively the commodities of its trade, and sells largely to the adjacent towns and mining districts. Long ago a rule was established by its management which has been strictly observed; to buy nothing but the best of its kind.

In field seeds, one of its specialties, a particularly large trade has been upbuilt by it. It is a shipper of seeds to five or six different States; and the farmers of East Tennessee, Virginia, North and South Carolina, Georgia and Alabama, have a firm reliance in the freshness and quality of the goods of this sort handled by it, and look to the merchants that supply them to procure a stock from it. It is indeed, for this district of the country, the headquarters for field seeds.

A very large flour business is also done by this house. It handles the product of the Lexington, Kentucky, Roller Mills Co., of the Plant and Kehlor mills of St. Louis, and of the Pillsbury mills at Minneapolis, Minn., without any exception the largest and finest mills in the world. These flours are shipped to all parts of the world; they are of world-wide celebrity, and the acknowledged standard of quality everywhere.

Mr. McClung himself is buyer for his house. During a business experience extending over twenty years or more, he has supplied the trade of this part of the country to its entire satisfaction. He is the proprietor also of the Merchants' Transfer Co., a concern having the patronage of the principal merchants of Knoxville. Mr. H. W. Booth, the junior partner in the produce house, is a rising young merchant of the city. He takes charge of the warehouse, and gives an undivided attention to the filling and shipping of orders.

KNOXVILLE'S DRUG HOUSES.

Sanford, Chamberlain & Albers, wholesale and manufacturing druggists, of 172 Gay street, lead their line in that part of the country which, in the commercial sense, is tributary to Knoxville. They do a business, indeed, which, in any part of the land, would be considered more than respectable; a business that makes them fairly comparable with the larger houses in the leading cities, North or South.

They occupy a three-story building, 40 feet by 150, with double basement, the upper floor of which basement is used for the manufacture of extracts and proprietary medicines and for storage purposes, and the others for their stock, which is especially complete in such lines as drugs, druggists' sundries, patent medicines and proprietary articles, and ready-mixed and dry paints. They have six men on the road in Virginia and West Virginia, North Carolina, Georgia, Kentucky, Alabama and Tennessee, and they have twenty employes altogether.

This is the oldest as well as largest drug house here. It was founded in 1864, and the successful management of its affairs has made its proprietors rich in resources, which accumulation their enterprise has directed toward development of the mining, manufacturing and landed interests of Knoxville and its vicinity.

Mr. Sanford is vice-president of the East Tennessee National Bank of this city, president of the Knoxville Woolen Mills, the Lenoir City

Co., and the Knoxville & Ohio Railroad. Mr. Chamberlain is a director of the Knoxville Iron Co., and secretary and treasurer of the

W. W. WOODRUFF & CO., WHOLESALE HARDWARE.

Coal Creek Mining and Manufacturing Co. Mr. Albers is likewise interested in ventures of this character.

Mr. Sanford has been a resident of Knoxville since 1861; Messrs. Chamberlain and Albers for twenty-five years past. All three, notwithstanding their other interests, still manage to give the business of the house personal supervision in its several departments.

RODGERS, TEDFORD & CO., wholesale druggists, of 21 Jackson street, carry a stock that fills a house of four floors, each 50 by 200 feet, and have five men on the road in Virginia, Kentucky, Tennessee, the Carolinas, Georgia, Alabama and Mississippi. They handle all the staples of the drug trade, all the standard patent medicines and proprietary articles, all kinds of druggist's sundries and toilet articles, and are manufacturers also of extracts and perfumes.

This firm has four members, JAMES A. RODGERS, E. W. TEDFORD, B. L. SMITH, and H. C. BONDURANT. Messrs. Rodgers and Tedford established the business here in 1889. In March 1890, Messrs. Smith & Bondurant, well-known here as a wholesale grocery firm, and as principals in the Knoxville Provision Co., acquired an interest.

Management of the business is in the hands of Messrs. Rodgers and Tedford. Both are drug men of twenty years' experience. Mr. Rodgers directs the affairs of the house generally. Mr. Tedford looks after the laboratory.

WHOLESALE HARDWARE.

W. W. WOODRUFF & Co., wholesale dealers in and importers of hardware, farming implements, fire arms and ammunition, sash and blinds and saddlers' materials, at 176 and 178 Gay street, have been in that line of trade at Knoxville since 1865. They began as retailers only, with their field, like that of the city itself, circumscribed by its provincial situation and surroundings; but they have risen as a firm with the progress of Knoxville, to the rank not merely of one of its leading jobbing houses, but of one too, of the most notable in the South. They carry a stock usually, which would require six figures to represent at its full valuation; they have thirty employes, five of them traveling men, covering eight States, and their sales are upwards of $300,000 in the aggregate, a year.

Their standing in the trade is indicated by the fact that they have been entrusted with exclusive agencies for the following: Oliver Chilled Plows; Syracuse Hillside Plows; Webster Farm Wagons, Buggies and Spring Wagons; Dexter Corn Shellers; Excelsior Cider Mills; Black Diamond Tool Steel; Disston's Circular Saws; Dupont's Powder; Atlas Powder; Howe's Scales; Remington's Breech-Loading Shot Guns and Rifles; Parker's Breech-Loading Shot Guns; Winchester Repeating Rifles; Colt's Repeating Rifles, and Colt's Breech-Loading Shot Guns.

Their specialties are rubber belting, barb wire, straw cutters, sash, doors and blinds, builders' hardware and sole leather.

An engraving showing the front of their establishment accompanies this matter. This place, since the additions necessitated in 1890 by the growth of the business of the house, has twelve floors, each 25 by 150 feet, or a third of a mile altogether, of superficial floor space.

MESSRS. WOODRUFF and W. E. GIBBINS, the partners in the house, are among the best known, most substantial and most respected merchants of Knoxville. Mr. Woodruff is president of the Savings Building and Loan Association, of Knoxville, vice-president of the Knoxville Fire Insurance Co., director of the Knoxville Car Wheel Co., the Knoxville Ice Co., and Knoxville Real Estate Co., and is identified, also, with other enterprises here. He is conspicuous, also, for his energy and generosity in good works, and especially in those of his church, the First Baptist, for the building of which he contributed the handsome fund of $25,000. Mr. Gibbins, like Mr. Woodruff, is a Kentuckian, and a resident here since the war. He is vice-president of the Covenant Building and Loan Association, of this city, and is a stockholder of the Knoxville Real Estate Co., and has other investments besides.

CRUZE, BUFFAT & BUCKWELL, wholesale and retail dealers in hardware and builders' supplies and machinery, at 34 Market Square, occupy there a place of three floors, each 150 feet deep, and, besides, a large three-story warehouse, on Curry street, both of which are stocked throughout, at all times, with the staples of their line. They have their traveling men traversing the trade territory of Knoxville, and make a specialty of the sale of farming machinery, tools and builders' hardware.

They are sales agents for the Whitely mowers and reapers in East Tennessee, and for other standard products of the same sort; and they do an annual business of $125,000 or more.

This house was established in 1875 by James H. Cruze, senior member of the firm now. As at present organized, the firm dates from 1887. All three of the partners are natives of the city and have long been identified with the trade they are in. They were all formerly with the house of W. W. Woodruff & Co., a leading house of this same line, and Mr. Buckwell was with Sargent & Co., manufacturers of hardware, New York, for five years.

MR. CRUZE is general manager and financial man for the house; MR. BUFFAT is manager of the sales, and MR. BUCKWELL the buyer.

The GREER MACHINERY CO., one of the largest concerns of its line in the State, carries usually a $75,000 stock of agricultural implements, wagons, and general machinery, and does a business approximating $300,000 a year. It has fifteen representatives on the road, and has sales in every Southern State. Its trade extends, indeed, as far Southwest as the Mexican line.

It is an old house also; it originated before the war had closed at Maryville, a town near here, with J. Gray Smith, an Englishman, who, in consequence of the fact that he had no politics, was harassed during the troublous times of hostilities, by the partisans of both sides—North and South. In this strait he appealed to his friend, J. M. GREER, and thus Mr. Greer's interest in the house began.

That gentleman had been an active participant in the war, as a soldier of the Fifty-fourth Indiana regiment of the Federal army, and afterwards in the Third Tennessee Mounted Infantry, and after the war was an official of the United States. He was Provost Marshal at Maryville when he acquired the business of Smith. He was a revenue assessor later, and also a special agent of the Post Office department; but finally tiring of political preferments, he resigned his position and gave his entire time and attention to the business he had acquired.

Under his management it grew rapidly, and at various stages of its growth, some of the more efficient and zealous employes of the house were given an interest by Mr. Greer. These gentlemen are now managing officers of the company which was organized to succeed him in 1890.

Mr. Greer is general manager of its business; Mr. J. G. Duncan takes charge of the department of outside sales and men on the road; Mr. J. R. McDowell has general charge of the sales and stock, and Mr. O. Schmalzreid, secretary and treasurer, is, as his title implies, in charge of the office, books and credits business. Judge S. A. Rogers, of the Federal Circuit Court here, and Mr. H. H. Taylor, clerk of that tribunal, are also identified as directors with the company.

THE GREER MACHINERY COMPANY'S WARE HOUSE.

The salesrooms and offices of this company are on Jackson street, opposite the freight depot of the East Tennessee, Virginia & Georgia road,

An engraving of it accompanies this matter. And besides these premises they maintain a warehouse on Hudson street for storage of surplus stock, having nearly as much capacity as the Jackson street house.

To illustrate the extent of the business of the house, a recent order given it may be instanced. This order was for ice machinery and it amounted to $16,000. This is a larger order than was ever received before by any jobbing house in this city.

SHETTERLY & TIPTON, dealers in stoves and ranges, tinware and house furnishing goods, at 66 Union street, are but lately established (only since May, '91), yet they have a good trade, both city and country, already—as much, perhaps, as any concern of the kind in this place. Mr. Shetterly is, however, it is but fair to remark, "an old hand" at the business. He has been in it for twenty years or more here.

They do a general tin roofing and cornice business, and handle house furnishings in very great variety. They make all their own tinware and have some ten to fifteen persons at work in their shop, which is located on the second floor of their place. This shop is thoroughly equipped with tools and machinery of

SHETTERLY & TIPTON'S PLACE.

the latest pattern for cornice, tin and other metal work. Some of the finest jobs of roofing, guttering, spouting, etc., done here lately have been executed by this firm, among others, the following: Mr. S. M. Dow's (of M. L. Ross & Co.), and Judge Engersoll's fine residences in West Knoxville, and several others.

Their business, in short, is increasing daily. They occupy the place of business shown in the cut on this page, a place affording them ample room for enlargement. It has 7,400 feet of flooring.

Mr. Shetterly is the inside and credits man of the firm, Mr. Tipton manager of their outside business.

PHILO B. SHEPARD, SR., manufacturers' agent for agricultural implements and machinery, fire department supplies, type-writers and type-writer supplies, etc., of 158 Gay street, has been established in that line here about four years on his own account, and has been in the trade pretty much all his life. He was with H. G. Mead & Co., a notable house here, before he started for himself, and is credited with much of its uncommon success.

His agency for agricultural machinery covers chiefly, East Tennessee; for fire supplies, the entire South. He is manager also for East Tennessee, of the Eastern branch of the TENNESSEE PHONOGRAPH CO. His sales all told, will aggregate $50,000 a year, and this aggregate is rapidly increasing.

He handles, among other things, saw-mill machinery, brick-making machines, wood-working machinery of all kinds, iron and felt roofing, street cars, fire engines and fire apparatus of all kinds.

SHEPARD & MANNING, plumbers and dealers in plumbing supplies, at 158 Gay street, have the most complete establishment of the kind at Knoxville. They are fitted up to do both a wholesale and retail business in pipe and machine supplies, brass goods, chandeliers and all that sort of thing, and to take contracts, large and small, for plumbing and steam fitting of all sorts. Estimates for this class of work will be furnished on application. They occupy a three-story place, 25 by 258 feet, the exterior of which is shown in an engraving accompanying this matter.

Mr. Philo B. Shepard, Jr., of this firm, has had several years' experience of the machine supplies business. This department will be managed by him. Mr. Manning was formerly superintendent of Thacker & Co.'s works at Philadelphia, one of the largest concerns making gas fixtures and brass goods in the land.

This firm owns State rights for RIFE'S IMPROVED HYDRAULIC RAM, the very latest and best device for elevating water automatically for household purposes, irrigation, railroad tanks, mills, etc. These State rights cover both sale of the machine, and territory for the same.

A large number of these water elevating machines have already been put down in Knoxville, and they are all giving unqualified satisfaction, largely because, being absolutely automatic in action, they require so little attention. A pamphlet containing testimonials to this effect will be mailed to any address upon application.

The house is also sole local agent for the sale of the SPRINGFIELD GAS MACHINE, designed especially for furnishing gas to suburban and country homes that have no city gas works accessible.

ALLIED LINES.

R. VAN GILDER & CO., wholesale and retail dealers in leather, window glass, mirror plates, shoe findings, etc, at 195 Gay street, is the representative firm of the city in this line of business. Their trade extends into the States of North Carolina, Virginia, Kentucky and Georgia, as well as throughout all of the East Tennessee territory of the city. Their stock is complete in all the lines enumerated above, and particular attention is given to the careful filling of all orders, solicited or voluntary, entrusted them.

This characteristic is fully appreciated by their customers, and general satisfaction on the part of the trade results from their honest endeavors to please.

Merchants, therefore, can be assured that their interests in trade will be carefully attended to when committed to this wide-awake, thorough-going firm. Their reputation for fair dealing and for the quality of their goods (always the equivalent of the money paid—the lowest priced at market rates)—is as well known as their name; and this fact is fully appreciated by their business friends.

ROGERS VAN GILDER, managing member of the firm, is the son of his associate in the partnership, JNO. S. VAN GILDER, who is intimately identified with the leading enterprises of the city, as president of the Merchants' Bank, of the Knoxville Leather Co., and the Tazewell Turnpike Co., and largely also by interests in real estate.

BEECH BROS. & CO., sanitary heating and ventilating engineers, with office at 26 Deaderick Building, are young, but remarkably energetic and successful business men, five years resident here. There are three of these brothers associated under the firm name, PAUL W., LUKE P. and JOHN M. BEECH.

SHEPARD & MANNING, PLUMBERS' SUPPLIES.

As ventilating and heating engineers, they make a specialty of the BENNETT & PECK HEATING AND VENTILATING CO.'s apparatus for warming, system of continuous ventilation, and dry closets for school houses especially, and public buildings generally. This Bennett & Peck Co.'s apparatus for warming and system of ventilation and dry closets, is to-day conceded to be many years in advance of anything of the sort on the American market, and in every respect, the most desirable and satisfactory. It is so perfect in operation that the air in any school building can be entirely changed every fifteen minutes continuously throughout the entire day and term, thereby rendering the school room as healthful and pleasant during the winter as the balmy outdoor breezes of spring.

This system is in use in the leading schools and institutions of learning in the Northeast and West, as well as in many in the South; and is being rapidly adopted wherever introduced.

Beech Bros. & Co., as agents for the manufacturers, furnish this system for schools and public buildings, churches, court houses, jails, res-

THOMAS KANE & CO.'S FACTORY, AT CHICAGO.
Beech Bros. & Co., Agents, Knoxville.

idences, and all classes of buildings requiring modern heating and ventilating apparatus. They will promptly supply full and complete information, upon request, to building committees of all kinds, as well as individuals, relative to this system of heating and ventilating, together with the most convincing proofs of its superiority; and, where the case will warrant, will bear all railroad and traveling expenses of committees desiring to see the apparatus and system in practical operation. Building committees will, therefore, do well to consult this firm of heating and ventilating engineers as soon as their architect's plans for building are accepted.

Beech Bros. & Co. also repair, remodel and remove old heating systems not now in satisfactory operation, guaranteeing, in all their work, the highest results attainable in the art; the complete and satisfactory operation of all their work, in fact, or no pay.

Beech Bros. & Co. are also general Southern agents for the well-known manufacturing firm of THOMAS KANE & COMPANY, of Chicago, the most extensive manufacturers of school, church and opera house furniture in this country. The extensive works of this firm are shown on the page opposite this. The cut will give some idea of the facilities of this concern for turning out a full line of these goods.

Thomas Kane & Co. are the oldest concern in this business in America, and their products are in use in every State in the Union. And none are more generally praised; in fact, every one interested in the school, church or opera house (and their name is literally legion), using the furniture of this firm, is enthusiastic in endorsement of it. Beech Bros. & Co. are enabled, by arrangements with their principals, to furnish the Thos. Kane school, church, court house, opera house, post office, and bank furniture at the lowest prices ever touched in this line for first-class goods, and building committees, and purchasing agents, and school boards will find it pays to investigate these goods and prices before purchasing elsewhere. Not only will they find the goods and prices entirely satisfactory in every respect, but Beech Bros. & Co. are enabled to offer the most liberal inducements in the way of terms and contracts for payment.

They will promptly send a representative to meet any building or purchasing committee, furnish printed catalogues and full information of all kinds, relating to their business, with dispatch, upon application. And no contract is too large for them to undertake and fill "on time" to the satisfaction of all parties concerned.

The KNOXVILLE SUPPLY CO., dealers in sewer pipe, terra cotta material, cement, plaster, building paper, lath, hair, etc., at 71 to 75 Hardee street, is the largest concern here of the kind. It has the largest and most varied stock, and is in receipt of the building materials dealt in by it direct from the manufacturers in this country, or from the importers of the seaports. It is agent for the ROYAL CLAY MANUFACTURING CO., Uhrichsville, Ohio, the

KNOXVILLE SUPPLY CO.'S WAREHOUSE AND YARDS.

largest manufacturers of sewer pipe, terra cotta, and all fire clay products in the United States, for RICKETSON'S MORTAR COLORS, and for the TENNESSEE ADAMANT COMPANY, of Nashville.

It was incorporated last year (1891), with $5,000 capital, and the following officers: A. Y. REID, president; GEO. P. CHANDLER, secretary and treasurer. Mr. Reid is secretary and treasurer of the Ervin Lime Co. of Cincinnati, and is vice-president and a large stockholder also of the Royal Clay Manufacturing Co. just mentioned. He is a resident of Ohio. Mr. Chandler was formerly of the firm of Chandler Bros., in the coal and building materials trade in Xenia, Ohio, but came here in the spring of 1891 especially to establish the business of his company.

This company has trade in all the States that look to Knoxville for supplies. It will quote its prices on application, and will guarantee them as low as those of any competitor.

CARRIAGES, HARNESS, IRON COMMISSION.

T. C. ELDRIDGE, 103 Gay street, maintains there the largest carriage repository in Knoxville. He is, in fact, the only exclusive dealer in light vehicles in the city. He has been established about twenty years, and has trade not here merely, but throughout Tennessee, Kentucky, Virginia, and North Carolina. He has been successful in this line, and has interests also in other affairs here, as for instance, the Knoxville Savings & Development Co., of which he is a director. He also owns considerable real estate here.

He is sales agent for the Clark carriages made in Cincinnati, for the Buckeye carriages made at Columbus, Ohio, and for the Stratton Jump-seat carriage made at Buffalo, N. Y.; and he usually has about fifty fine carriages of these and other fashionable makes in stock.

T. J. PEED & Co., wholesale and retail dealers in harness and saddlery of every description, at 226 Gay street, cover, with traveling men, all the States of Knoxville's trade territory. They are manufacturers, are importers of English goods of their line, and have been entrusted with the sale in their field of numerous fine American and English harness specialties.

They carry an exceedingly large and very varied stock—one filling a place of four stories, each 40 by 150 feet. They have forty hands employed in their manufacturing department.

This house was established about two years ago. MR. PEED, senior member of the firm, was with O'Connor, the oldest house of this line here, for twelve years, and for four years with Butt, Williams & Co., another large saddlery house, before he started for himself. His house is a strong competitor of both these concerns now.

He is a director of the Knoxville Savings Bank and is interested in other enterprises here. His partner is MR. W. N. WREN. Mr. Wren manages the mechanical departments of the house.

H. VICTOR HART, commission merchant for the sale of iron and steel, grain and flour, at 124 Gay street, does an exceptionally large business. He controls sale of the product of a number of Tennessee, Kentucky and Alabama furnaces, and of flouring mills whose joint capacity is 4,000 barrels a day. His sales will aggregate easily $300,000 a year. Incidentally he handles Western and Tennessee grain, railroad and general machine supplies, coke and fire brick, etc.

He represents as sales agent here the following notable concerns: Carnegie Bros. & Co., of Pittsburgh, Pa., manufacturers of steel and iron. The Pennsylvania Steel Co., of Steelton, Pa., steel and iron; the Cambria Iron Co., of Philadelphia and Johnstown, Pa., steel and iron manufacturers also, and other Northern establishments of the same general class. Also the Citico Furnace Co., of Chattanooga and Rockwood, Tenn.

With his facilities for the sale of flour, he controls considerable of the trade in that staple in this market, which may be said to include all the territory south of the Ohio. During the three or four years he has been established here he has displayed business ability of an uncommon order, and his business has grown almost every day.

His sales are made direct in all parts of Knoxville's tributaries, and even outside the district of country in which the influence of the city as a trade center prevails.

STABLES; HORSE STOCK.

P. A. ROBERTS' livery, feed and sale stable, of 398 Broad street, is one of the largest at Knoxville. It is three stories, with basement, 48 feet by 135, and has accommodations for seventy head of horses. He bought the ground it occupies and built the place himself. And he owns considerable other property here besides.

Mr. Roberts keeps about forty head of fine saddle and driving horses for hire, and has as stylish turn-outs as there are in the city.

He does considerable trading in horses and mules, and has always stock on hand for sale. He has been in the trade for twenty years or more; in this city for the last fifteen.

BELL & McCAMPBELL's livery, feed and sale stables, 67 and 69 Cumberland street, were established in 1865, and are therefore, the oldest stables in Knoxville. They are the largest also. They have accommodations for fifty head of horses, including boarders, with corresponding room for vehicles, and have as stylish rigs for hire as the country anywhere affords.

Messrs. Bell and McCampbell are both breeders themselves. Each has a farm not far from the city, on which stock is raised. The livery business is, however, their principal employment.

McKinney & Carpenter's "Knoxville Palace Stables," 25 to 35 Commerce street, are headquarters here for the drovers and horsemen generally. They have accommodations for 200 head of horses and mules, and they have the finest livery turn-outs in the city. They feed, on an average, fifty teams a day for their customers.

They also do quite a sales business in work and driving horses, both for a commission and on the account of the proprietors themselves.

These are the best equipped stables also in the way of carriage service for weddings, funerals, etc. They have one special turn-out which is drawn by white Arabian mares, and is used for nothing but wedding parties.

Mr. McKinney, the senior partner, is an old stockman of this part of the country himself. He established the business about four years ago. His partner, Mr. F. A. Carpenter, is a prominent business man here. He is a son of D. A. Carpenter, who is president of the Knoxville Fire Insurance Co., of the Powell Station Brick Co., and the Central Market Real Estate Co., and interested largely also in other important enterprises here. Mr. Carpenter has held an interest in the stable for a couple of years. Both parties give its business personal supervision.

They propose to erect, this year, a new four-story stable of brick, with stone-trimmed front, and provided with all modern improvements and appointments. They intend to have an establishment that will vie with anything North or South in the matter of style and conveniences.

DRY GOODS, NOTIONS, MILLINERY, ETC.

Cowan, McClung & Co., wholesale dry goods, notions, and boots and shoes, 160, 162 and 164 Gay street, is a house of no common order. It has trade outside the ordinary tributaries of the city; it is an old house; a solid one; and, in its development and prosperity, a type of the best commercial concerns of the South.

It was founded in 1835 by Cowan & Dickinson. It has thirty-five or forty employes, in its various sales and office departments, and for its trade in seven States, Tennessee, Kentucky, Virginia, North Carolina, Georgia, Alabama and Mississippi, maintains a staff of several trusty traveling men.

Its place of business is a five-story block, 85 by 175 feet, itself an indication, in its external proportions, of the extensive business transacted within. These premises are appointed throughout with every facility and improvement known to the trade. They disclose, in their arrangement, the order and system which has been evolved from nearly sixty years' experience.

The firm, as at present constituted, was organized in 1859. The partners in it are Perez Dickinson, J. D. Cowan, C. J. McClung, F. H. McClung, Matt. McClung, J. L. Thomas and R. M. Rhea. Mr. Dickinson, senior member of the firm, is a native of Massachusetts, but has lived here upwards of a half a century. The other members of the firm are Tennesseeans and life-long residents of the city. They all bear an equal share of the responsibilities of management, each having his department. That of Mr. Matt. McClung is the credits department.

Maxwell & Co.'s dry goods and millinery house, at 141 Gay street, it has often been said by persons who have traveled, is "just like one of the great New York retail stores." The story of this establishment might be told briefly after this fashion:

In 1879 H. J. Owens came to Knoxville and opened a dry goods store. After ten years of successful business and the practice of rigid economy he acquired a modest competency and retired by selling out his business to Maxwell & Co.

Up to that time modern retail methods had not been introduced, or applied at all, in Knoxville, and Messrs. Maxwell & Co. wisely proceeded to make use of them. Contracts for advertising were made by them with the local daily papers, for a page daily in each, and it was soon evident that the business usances of the city were to be practically revolutionized.

Mr. Owens had enjoyed the patronage of what is known as the "finest trade," but was a believer in high profits. The new firm bought a finer class of goods even than he had carried, but sold everything upon close margins.

The natural, logical, to-be-expected result followed.

Any day now you may see in this store, perhaps, five hundred buyers; and it looks, in truth, during a special sale, "like one of the great New York houses."

Maxwell & Co. are specialists in the dress goods, millinery, hosiery, linens and kid gloves trade, and in every article used by ladies' and children. And bonnets and dresses made at Maxwell's are the standard of excellence throughout East Tennessee. The house is known, far and wide, for its straightforward characteristics and performance of its every promise.

DANIEL & BOSTWICK, DRY GOODS.

DANIEL & BOSTWICK, wholesale and retail dealers in dry goods, notions, boots and shoes, etc., at 155 Gay street, have been established in that line here for but two years. They had both, however, been in the trade before that with the large and well-known house of John Keely, of Atlanta, Ga. Mr. Daniel was buyer for that concern, and Mr. Bostwick was its financial manager for many years. Their experience of the trade is, therefore, anything but limited.

This is the leading department house of Knoxville. It is modeled after the large houses of the same sort in other cities, like Macy's, in New York; Marshall Field's, in Chicago; Shillito's, in Cincinnati, and Barr's, in St. Louis. It has a buyer permanently located in New York, and its stock is renewed at regular intervals, so that it is always fresh and seasonable.

Its departments are the following: 1. Dress goods; 2. White goods; 3. Domestics; 4. Ginghams and calicoes; 5. Notions; 6. Hosiery and underwear; 7. Furnishing goods; 8. Shoes.

Among other standard goods handled by it the following may be mentioned: "Diamond" shirts, made in Baltimore; Blacker & Gerstle's Cincinnati shoes for ladies, and Hough & Ford's Rochester makes; also Williams, Kneeland & Co.'s, and Blanchard's (Lynn, Mass.), men's shoes. Dress goods and cloaks are a specialty with it.

It has a thoroughly systematized mail order department for its country patronage.

It has usually a stock displayed worth $45,000.

Its annual business, measured by the sales of the year 1891, is not far short of $100,000. And both its business and fame grow daily.

MESTER, NEWCOMER & PAULUS, dealers in dry goods, fancy goods and millinery, at 167 Gay street, were in the retail dry goods business in Pittsburgh, Pa., before they came here in March, '88, to establish business in that line at Knoxville. They are, therefore, men of long experience in the line they follow.

They took from the start, a leading position among the houses of their line here, and they have had an uninterrupted season of success since. They occupy a place 25 by 150, and three stories, with all its departments thoroughly stocked with the various lines they

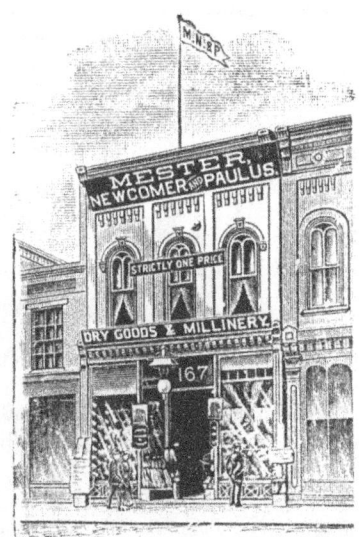

MESTER, NEWCOMER & PAULUS, DRY GOODS HOUSE.

handle; they employ twenty-four clerks and they do a business, in Knoxville and its vicinity, of $100,000 in sales and upwards, a year.

Their specialty is the sale of dry goods, fancy goods, millinery, upholstery, gents' furnishings, cloaks, books, stationery, etc.

MEEK & ANDES, importers of, and dealers in dry goods, notions, millinery and fancy goods, at 145 Gay street, occupy a handsome structure of three stories, and carry the most varied, if not the largest stock of the sort, in Knoxville. They are dealers exclusively in goods for ladies and children, and are importers on their own account, of kid gloves, laces, embroideries and novelties. They have fifty employes, and besides their local patronage, have a very large mail order business in all parts of the State. They do business, in short, in true metropolitan fashion.

This is the largest retail dry goods house of the city. It was established in 1886. Its principals, James K. Meek and Geo. Andes, are dry goods men of life-long experience. As a firm they are notable for the success they have had in upbuilding a house of the first order in a comparatively short time.

This house has its own millinery and dress making departments, and those branches of the trade are its specialties.

B. H. SPRANKLE & STOUFFER, is also a leading Knoxville house.

Mr. B. H. Sprankle, the senior member of the firm, is one of the youngest business men of the city. His career in Knoxville has been a succession of rapid advances. He is originally from Altoona, Pa.; he was in the clothing business there with his father, who still carries on an extensive business in that city. Not content however, in this circumscribed field, he looked abroad for a wider one, and upon due consideration opened up a large clothing house in Newark, Ohio. He enjoyed a large and remunerative business in that city for two years; still, he was not entirely satisfied. He saw the march of Southern development, and grasped at once the fact that the vast mineral section of Tennessee was of necessity, sure to become a scene of prosperity, flourishing through the evolution of its diversified industries.

So four years ago he opened up a large establishment in the three-story building at 113 Gay street, and has continued therein with a steadily increasing business. His stock consists of mens' and boys' clothing, gents' furnishings, boots, shoes, hats, and an extensive wholesale and retail wall paper department. He has by far the largest and best stock of wall paper in the city. His business amounts to something like $50,000 a year, and for honest dealings with the people that patronize it, no house stands higher than his.

He also deals extensively in real estate. He has laid out several additions to the city of Knoxville, and is a large owner of city and suburban property. He has also numerous mineral and timber tracts throughout East Tennessee. He owns, at the present time, several large and choice tracts of coal and timber land.

He is public-spirited, and has identified himself with the material concerns of the city, by aiding directly, enterprises looking to its improvement with his influence and money and the gift of free manufacturing sites. He is president of the East Tennessee Canning & Preserving Co., established a few miles west of the city, along the East Tennessee, Virginia & Georgia Railroad, and in company with others is exerting himself to develop that section of country beyond West Knoxville, which section promises a rapid growth in the near future. He and his associates have secured a 75-foot right of way for four miles, and have given that district early prospects of rapid transit, so that soon this will prove to be one of the most valuable tracts of residence suburban property.

By industry, close attention to business, a clear judgment and strict integrity Mr. Sprankle has advanced his fortunes rapidly, and is now looked upon as one of the progressive as well as solid men of Knoxville; the men who will advance its interest in every possible way.

Mr. Stouffer, the junior member of the firm, is an estimable young man and sure to succeed.

J. E. LUTZ & Co., dealers in fine shoes, hats, caps, trunks, valises and umbrellas, at 153 Gay street, are successors to S. C. Dismukes & Co., established in 1880. MR. J. E. LUTZ, head of the house, has been a resident here for twenty years. He was formerly in the dry goods trade with Alvin Barton, and was with the Dismukes house before he succeeded it in 1882. His partner, MR. C. G. SCHWEICKERD, is also an old resident here, well known as formerly with the Southern Express Co., and at present Alderman from the Third Ward of the city. He is the owner of valuable property here, and so also is Mr. Lutz; and the latter is a director besides of the Third National Bank.

They do a big business, not here in Knoxville alone, but in all the States for which it is a market place. They carry a very fine stock and make a specialty of superior goods.

POWERS, LITTLE & CO., wholesale dealers in clothing and gents' furnishings, at 208 and 210 Gay street, are successors to Powers, Little & McCormick, established in 1883. They bought that firm out in the month of January, 1891.

POWERS, LITTLE & CO., WHOLESALE CLOTHING.

They have six men on the road in this State and Kentucky, North Carolina, Georgia and West Virginia. They are, in brief, one of the largest houses of the kind in the South.

The partners in this house are three in number. REV. J. P. POWERS, pastor of the North Knoxville Baptist Church; M. S. LITTLE, who was a partner in the original firm, their predecessors, and MRS. M. D. POWERS, the widow of S. T. Powers, formerly a merchant here. Mr. Little is buyer for the house and looks out for the stock. Mr. Powers is office and credits man and manager of the finances.

MCTEERS, PAYNE, HOOD & CO., wholesale dealers in clothing, at the corner of State and Commerce streets, is a consolidation of two houses, effected in 1885, which were the two leading houses of the trade here then. This union made an establishment which, in resources and business, is practically beyond local rivalry, and which is enabled to go outside the trade territory proper of the city and compete with leading concerns of other cities on their own ground. This it does, not infrequently, but every day.

It has fifteen traveling men traversing all the South Atlantic and Middle Southern States, and sales of a million dollars and upwards a year. In the matter of stock carried, facilities for the business, patronage and enterprise, it is, in short, a type of the foremost houses to the south of Baltimore city.

Its goods are manufactured for it by the principal clothing factories of the North, and are also bought in the large markets of the country. Its stock is as varied as any carried in the land, its methods liberal and its whole system thoroughly metropolitan and modern.

It occupies a building here which was built by and for it at an expense of $50,000.

It has five principals—J. T. MCTEER, R. S. PAYNE, C. E. MCTEER, W. M. HOOD, and R. N. HOOD. The McTeers were of the old house of J. T. McTeer & Co., and Mr. Payne and the Messrs. Hood, of Payne, Burger & Hood. These were the two houses whose consolidation made the establishment as it is.

Mr. J. T. McTeer has been actively identified with the clothing trade of the South for twenty-five years. He began in it just after the war, at Baltimore, as a wholesale dealer. In 1876 he came here, and has followed the business at Knoxville continuously since. Mr. C. E. McTeer is his brother, and has been associated with him for twelve years past. Mr. W. M. Hood has also had many years experience of the business. These three are the managing partners. Mr. Payne is president of the East Tennessee National Bank, one of the principal banks of the city, and the duties of that office and other concerns in which he is interested, prevent his participation in the direction of the house. It is so, likewise, with Mr. R. N. Hood. He is president of the Third National Bank, and also of the Knoxville & Augusta Railroad, and he is a leading lawyer of the city besides.

R. WALTERS' SONS & CO., 174 Gay street, are a branch of the large Baltimore clothing house of R. Walters' Sons, and the house here is the only one of the city handling goods of its own manufacture. It is the occupant of a four-story place, and it makes therein an extensive, varied and fine display of its stock of men's, youths' and boys' clothing. It has eight men on the road in Southwest Virginia, Eastern Kentucky and Tennessee, the Carolinas, Georgia, Alabama and Mississippi.

MR. G. R. WALTERS is general manager of it. He came here when the branch was established, as Southern distributing agency for R. Walters' Sons.

EDINGTON, GRONER & FLENNIKEN, dealers in boots, shoes, hats and umbrellas, at 20 Market Square, is a leading house of that line here, four years established, and enjoying a trade in the State and those adjoining it, as well as Knoxville itself. It carries a very large and very complete stock and makes a specialty of medium and fine goods.

Four partners have an interest in the business, R. H. EDINGTON, J. C. and H. B. GRONER, and W. P. FLENNIKEN. Messrs. Edington and the Groners are members of the firm of EDINGTON, GRONER & Co., stone contractors here, and are chiefly engaged in that line, so that management of the business devolves on Mr. Flenniken, who has been following this line here, about all his life.

Mr. Edington is president of the Knoxville Canning Co., and is chairman of the Board of the Turnpike Commission of the county. He is also a large real estate owner. Mr. J. C. Groner is also financially identified with important local enterprises. Mr. H. B. Groner is one of the owners of the Beaver Creek Nursery, and is the "Co." of the stone contracting firm of Edington, Groner & Co.

HUDDLESTON & SMITH, 223 Gay street, do a large business in several lines, chiefly boots and shoes, hats and caps, valises, umbrellas, etc.

They make a specialty of fine shoes for both men's and ladies' wear, and have the largest trade at Knoxville in that line.

Their business is not, however, confined to the city. They have a large mail order trade, with patrons in Virginia, North Carolina, East Tennessee and Kentucky. They handle the productions of leading shoe manufacturers, North and West—goods which are well known to the trade, and are sales agents here for them. They also have the sole agency here for the Dunlap hat.

The business of the house was established by Huddleston, Carr & Co., in 1885. Huddleston, Smith & Co. succeeded that firm in 1889, and Huddleston & Smith succeeded them in turn in 1891. Mr. L. Huddleston was formerly one of the well known clothing firm of Huddleston, Smith & Little. He does not participate actively in the management of the house. Mr. Smith is general manager. The other members of the firm were traveling for a leading wholesale grocery house here before they went into the shoe business.

CALLAWAY & BROWN, dealers in shoes, hats, caps and umbrellas, at 157 Gay street, have trade throughout East Tennessee and in the adjacent parts of Kentucky, North Carolina and Georgia, as well as in the city. They make a specialty of the following goods, for which they are sales agents: Youman's stiff hats, Krippendorf, Dittmann & Co.'s and Edwin C. Burt & Co.'s fine ladies' shoes, and Lilly, Brackett & Co.'s men's and boys' fine shoes. These goods have no superior in this market.

Both partners in the house have had long experience of the trade they are in. They have been associated in it about four years and are well, widely and favorably known. They do an extensive mail order business in all of Knoxville's trade territory. Correspondence receives prompt attention at their hands, and goods and prices are guaranteed by them.

CULLEN & NEWMAN, importers of and wholesale dealers in china, glassware, lamps, fancy goods, plated ware, etc., at 182 and 184 Gay street, are the oldest and largest concern of that kind in the city. They have been established over twenty years, and they occupy a large double-front four-story and basement block situated on the main street of the city.

This building is 50 feet front and 155 feet deep, and is stocked throughout with all the staples of their line of trade, and with many specialties besides.

An engraving, showing its external appearance, accompanies this matter. In it they

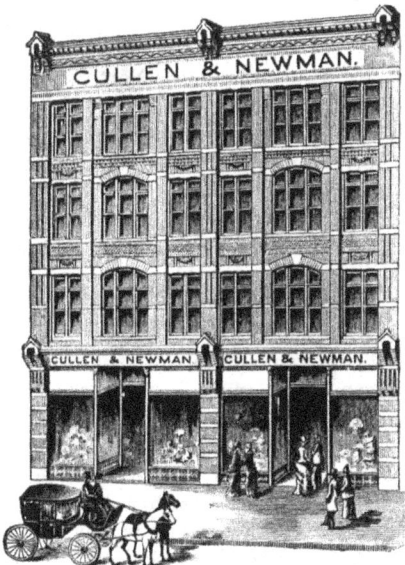

CULLEN & NEWMAN, WHOLESALE CROCKERY.

have twenty-seven persons employed besides their ten traveling salesmen, who traverse all the dozen States of the South, namely, Virginia, the Carolinas, Georgia, Florida, Kentucky, Tennessee, Alabama, Mississippi, Louisiana, Arkansas and Texas. They carry a stock at all times sufficient to meet any demand, and their annual sales are larger than those of any competing Southern house.

They are sole proprietors also of DR. ROC'S LIVER, RHEUMATIC AND NEURALGIC CURE, a standard remedy, sale of which makes a department of their business, of itself.

MR. CURTIS CULLEN, senior member of this firm, came to Knoxville from Richmond, Va. (of which city he is a native), twenty-two years ago. He is president of the Knoxville and Fountain City Land Co's., and of the Fountain Head Suburban Railway Co. Mr. CHAS. S. NEWMAN, of the firm, is also a Virginian by birth, and a twenty-year resident here, and, like his partner, a man of solid resources acquired by the successful prosecution of business affairs.

OGDEN BROS. & Co., wholesale and retail booksellers and stationers, and printers, binders, and blank-book makers, at 160 Gay street, carry a stock, and have facilities for manufacture in their line, equal to those of the best concerns of the kind in the Southern country. They occupy a place 25 by 200 feet and three stories. Their various lines of goods are usually of the value of $50,000; they are thoroughly equipped with presses, and other mechanical devices for fine work. They employ forty persons, three of them traveling salesmen, and they have trade in Kentucky and Tennessee, Virginia, North Carolina, Georgia and Alabama.

They do a large amount of railroad and commercial printing for patrons in all these States; theirs is the only jobbing book and stationery house in Knoxville's trade territory, as well as here; and they have a number of specialties (like the making of rubber stamps, for instance), which constitute distinct departments of their business.

They have been established since 1870, and have grown from small beginnings as their field extended. They are incorporated with $50,000 capital and the following officers: S. R. OGDEN, president; J. T. OGDEN, vice-president; C. H. OGDEN, secretary. The Ogdens are brothers, resident here for over twenty years, and experienced in the business for a lifetime.

Mr. C. H. Ogden, of this company, is proprietor also of the KNOXVILLE PAPER BOX FACTORY, at 173 State street.

HENSELL & ARMSTRONG, stationers and booksellers, of 151 Gay street, are a prominent firm of that trade here. They are successors to Hensell, Bogart & Gaut, an old and well known house. They do a general stationery business, and handle everything found in a first class house of this sort, including fine stationery and writing materials, and all the works of the standard authors, as well as light literature, periodicals, etc.

They also carry a very complete line of pictures in crayon, pastel and etchings, portraits, etc., and a full line of leather goods, such as cuff and collar boxes, cigar and tobacco cases, gentlemen's and ladies' pocket-books, purses, etc. Both members of the firm are socially prominent, by reason of their connection with fraternal and other organizations here, and both are esteemed for the qualities of good-fellowship as well as those of business and trade.

The MCARTHUR MUSIC HOUSE, of 143 Gay street, the foremost house of its line in East Tennessee, and a house rapidly extending its field over a wider territory than that usually considered tributary to Knoxville, has for its head one of the most wide-awake, forward and intelligent business men of the city, MR. FREDERICK E. MCARTHUR; director of the Chamber of Commerce of Knoxville; delegate, in 1889, from that body to the National Assembly of Boards of Trade, at Louisville; member of the Masonic Order, the Elks and other social and fraternal organizations; patron of music, as much for the sake of the art itself, as for business reasons; still, comparatively speaking, a young man, but one of ripe experience in his chosen walk, illustrating his breadth of view by liberal but judicious expenditure for advertising purposes—to sum up, an active, public-spirited and progressive man, imbued with the spirit of the times.

All this may seem a fulsome strain of praise but it is the meed accorded him by his fellow-citizens of Knoxville, who have known him, man and boy, since he came here first in 1871, at the age of 16. For he is, like many other notable residents, although thoroughly identified in spirit and sentiment with the community, not a "native and to the manor born." He was born in Wisconsin, but the best part of his life has been passed in the South. He has married here, and has family as well as property attachments binding him to Knoxville.

So much for the principal; now for the house and business. Mr. McArthur's connection with the music trade began in the eighties. He was at first advertising man for a Savannah house, and afterward its manager. On one of his visits to this city he was struck with its growth, and he thereupon resigned his employment in Savannah and established himself here. That was in 1889.

He began modestly, with sales of about 10 pianos and organs a month; now he averages 60 instruments in the same time. He has had strong competition from houses of this and other cities, in the same line, but he has borne the palm from them all. Advertising has been a most effective weapon in his hands—figuratively speaking, the sword and javelin—in these contests with powerful and resourceful

formances a success, and he has determined to utilize the large hall over his salesrooms for similar entertainments in the future.

Mr. McArthur sells chiefly of pianos, GEO. STECK & CO.'s, made in New York; the New Scale KIMBALL, and JAMES M. STARR & CO.'s, manufactured in Richmond, Ind.; and the organs of FARRAND & VOTEY, Detroit, and KIMBALL, Chicago; but he handles also other standard makes. These, however, are his best, those he recommends and warrants. He sells both for cash and on easy terms; if for cash, with freight paid.

Accompanying this matter are illustrations showing the interior and exterior appearances of this establishment.

INTERIOR AND EXTERIOR OF THE McARTHUR MUSIC HOUSE.

rivals. One house was driven from the field by him; another taken captive and its business incorporated with his.

Advertising freely is one only of his methods; another is his periodical trip North to examine for himself the latest improvements in the instruments he handles. Twice a year he goes North to buy, and inform himself of the condition of the trade.

Still another plan of his, and as we have said, with not altogether a mercenary motive, is to encourage liberally all forms of musical cultivation. He has interested himself in bringing out native talent, vocal and instrumental, and lent his aid to make musical per-

SCHEITLIN & CLARK, wholesale and retail dealers in musical instruments, and merchandise, and sheet music, at 143 Gay street, are successors to Marshall & Co., established in 1870, and, as the oldest dealers in their line here, have a very handsome business in this and all the neighboring States. They make a specialty of standard and classic sheet music and books, and the smaller musical instruments, such as the "Benary" professional guitars and banjos, and imported guitars and violins.

MR. CLARK, of the firm, was with Marshall & Co., their predecessors. MR. SCHEITLIN came here four or five years ago from Minneapolis, and this is his first business venture in Knoxville.

The RICHMOND PIANO CO., of which W. H. HARRELL is manager and principal, has sales and warerooms in the Harris Building, 320 Gay street, near the East Tennessee, Virginia & Georgia passenger depot. It carries there a full line of Bradbury and Behr Bros. pianos, and Packard and United States organs. It has

MCCRARY & BRANSON, PHOTOGRAPHERS' SUPPLIES.

been established here only since January 1st last, but it is already doing a very good business.

In connection with this business, Mr. Harrell is also engaged as the general agent for East Tennessee of the "Adjustable Automatic Lamp Bracket." Information concerning this device will be furnished by him, and illustrated catalogues sent out by mail on application.

MCCRARY & BRANSON, photographers and dealers in picture frames, mouldings, and artists' and photographers' supplies, at 130 Gay street, occupy there the handsome new and modern building shown in the engraving accompanying this matter. It is of three stories, 25 by 150 feet, and is occupied entirely by this firm.

They are the leading photographers of the city, and as such, have appointments and facilities to do the very finest portrait work, not merely with the camera, but in oil, pastel or water colors. They have artists employed for this purpose the year round, and as fine instruments and accessories as can be procured.

As dealers in frames and supplies, they have a trade extending well over the field for which Knoxville is trade center, viz., Tennessee, Kentucky, Virginia, the two Carolinas, Georgia, Alabama and Mississippi.

The principals in the business, MESSRS. F. B. MCCRARY and LLOYD BRANSON, have been established in partnership since 1877. They are expert artists and designers, as well as photographers themselves. Their photographic work has elicited the highest praise at the annual convention (which is also a competitive exhibition) of the photographers of the country, held usually in one or other of the large cities. And Mr. Branson is a designer of exceptional ability, known as such throughout the country at large, and a master with the brush as well. His pictures have a place in the New York galleries alongside the best work done.

The DAVIS SEWING MACHINE COMPANY, of Dayton, Ohio, which operates the largest factory of the kind in the West in that city, maintains one of its numerous branch distributing agencies at Knoxville, with Mr. JULIUS E. MARTIN, in charge. He is allotted, for trade territory, the district of East Tennessee, and he has ten sub-agencies under his direction.

He has been established at Knoxville in this business since the early part of 1890, and has been doing a better business than any sewing machine agent here. He has fifteen clerks and salesmen under him here, and has been making sales at the rate of 800 machines a year, with prospects of a better business hereafter even than that.

He carries a stock, usually, at his place, corner of Third avenue and Crozier streets, of

50 to 100 machines, and besides these, a line of sewing machine attachments and sundries. He will exchange new machines for old for a

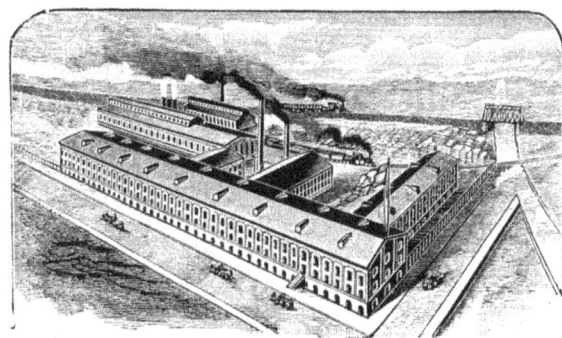

DAVIS SEWING MACHINE WORKS, AT DAYTON, OHIO.
J. E. Martin, Agent at Knoxville.

consideration, and can sell his machines in competition with any concern of the kind here.

The Davis machine factory at Dayton, covers some five acres of ground. It employs fully 100 hands, and its capacity is about 400 machines a day. The special merit of the Davis is, that it is the most simply constructed machine made, that it has vertical feed, and does all kinds of work without basting. In the trade it is called the Davis Vibrating Vertical Feed Sewing Machine.

Mr. Martin has been in the sewing machine business for many years. He has been very successful in it. He is a director of the Knox County Savings Bank, and a stockholder in other local enterprises.

J. M. HUGHES, dealer in sewing machines and supplies, at 98 Gay street, makes a specialty of trade in the "Standard" and "Household" machines, which are the favorites now, and of repairing. He carries a stock of attachments for all the ordinary makes and has expert workmen and teachers employed.

He sells on the installment plan, and exchanges old for new machines, with a fair sum to boot. He runs two wagons in Knoxville and its vicinity, and employs four salesmen.

S. W. GRAVES, wholesale and retail dealer in furniture, carpets, curtains, shades, etc., at 108 and 110 Gay street, has been established in that line here since 1886. He has been a merchant and business man of the city in this and other lines, for the past seventeen years. He was formerly in the harness business as one of the firm of S. W. Graves & Co. He has been successful, and besides this establishment has interests in others. He is a stockholder and vice-president of the Stephenson-Getaz Manufacturing Co., leading manufacturers of furniture and interior finish here.

As a furniture and carpet dealer, he carries a large and varied stock, embracing both fancy and plain parlor, bedroom, and kitchen furniture, desks, book-cases, etc. His lines of carpets, curtains, etc., are of especial variety. He does business in all the States embraced in Knoxville's trade territory and has sales of $150,000 and upwards a year.

Mr. Graves is also the leading dealer here in fine mantels of wood, metal and marble, and in tile fixtures; and in this line,

S. W. GRAVES' CARPET AND FURNITURE HOUSE.

it can be said safely, that he stands at the head of Knoxville's dealers, and, perhaps, rivals any in the South.

KNOXVILLE AS A MANUFACTURING PLACE.

HEN the raw material, which Nature has so prodigally piled up in Knoxville's environment of East Tennessee, Virginia, Kentucky and the Carolinas, shall have been even fairly utilized for manufactures by it, Knoxville must, unquestionably, become one of the great producing centers of the land. And the signs are that this prediction will be fulfilled ere very many years have passed.

A beginning, only, has been made in this direction; but, with 225 manufacturing establishments, representing an aggregate of $10,000,000 production a year, it would seem a pretty fair start. Some of these 225 concerns are of more than ordinary importance—the great marble works, and interior finish factories, already described herein, for instance; and there are other works uncommonly large also—a cotton mill, a woolen mill, the railroad shops, a rail mill, and a flour mill among them.

SOME LARGE CONCERNS.

The great bulk of the city's production must be credited to about twenty-five of these concerns of the first order, most of which have been established and have prospered, by reason of the unusual plenitude of raw material for them, which is this favored city's endowment, as lumber, for example, marble, iron, cotton, wool, grain and coal, provided by the adjacent or contiguous country. The other 200 are concerns that have their origin in local necessities. They are brick yards, lime kilns, shoe factories, trunk factories, shirt factories, machine shops, wagon works, stove works, plumbing shops, ice works, soap works, cornice works, broom factories, printing houses, book binderies, bakeries, candy works, laundries, and that sort of thing. Some of them—the more important—are noticed at length, and in detail, further on in this chapter.

SPECIAL INDUSTRIES OF THE CITY.

This class of 25 that are most conspicuous, to which we have just referred, includes the four large marble finishing works described in the chapter on the city's characteristic trade; and also the seven mills producing lumber, building material of wood, and fine interior finish. It comprises also the railroad shops of the East Tennessee, Virginia & Georgia road, at present employing 500 hands, and in process of enlargement so as to have room for 1000 or more; the Knoxville Iron Works, which produces rail and bar iron; the Knoxville Car Wheel Company, whose name indicates its line of business; the Southern Car Works, which also has its purpose disclosed in its title; the big spoke and handle factory; three pretty fair sized furniture factories; the Knoxville City Flouring Mills of 700 barrels daily capacity; the Knoxville Brewery, and the two institutions, that perhaps merit special mention: the Knoxville Woolen Mills, and the Brookside Cotton Mills.

THE COTTON AND WOOLEN MILLS.

The Knoxville Woolen Mills have an equipment of 600 looms, and it is said, the largest production of Kentucky jeans and doeskins, which are its specialties, of any concern of the kind in the country, viz.: $1,000,000 worth annually. They employ 600 hands; they cost, the machinery included, $475,000, and $500,000 of local capital is embarked in them; for this is emphatically a Knoxville enterprise, founded in 1877, upbuilt and carried to a successful conclusion by Knoxville parties with Knoxville money.

The Brookside Cotton Mills are not so extensive a project; but considering the fact that Knoxville is not immediately in a cotton district, they also disclose its business enterprise. They have been established about six years. A capital of $125,000 has been put into them by the proprietary company, and they have been equipped with 176 looms, and 5,312 spindles. They employ 125 hands, and produce 200,000 yards of product a month, which is, approximately, a business of $175,000 a year.

ESTIMATED TOTALS.

The capital embarked in manufactures at Knoxville all told, is in the neighborhood of $3,750,000. More than 5,000 of the city's population get a livelihood in shops and factories.

At least $1,500,000 a year is paid this number in wages, and over $5,000,000 worth of raw material is consumed in such establishments here.

There is a prospect that these figures will be doubled, or even trebled in the next ten years. Such an increase is not without its parallel, in places far less favorably situated than Knoxville is. Let us see, then, what the opening is for manufacturing business in this Knoxville field.

MANUFACTURING OPPORTUNITIES.

A MANUFACTURING center concretes upon a foundation whose components are these: 1. Raw material abundantly available; 2. An ample, cheap and tractable labor supply; 3. An extensive and unlimited market; 4. Comprehensive transportation facilities; 5. A plentiful fuel supply. And, incidentally, the favors of financial accommodation, convenient and low-priced sites or rentals, a sufficient and satisfactory water supply and freedom from onerous charges, like taxes, licenses, etc.

Knoxville enjoys advantages in "all and every," as the law phrase has it, of these particulars. It has behind it a forest domain of woods that have an especial manufacturing value, in view of the diminished and constantly diminishing timber supply of this country, a domain of poplar, and other furniture material, of hard woods and tanning bark the most extensive in the States. Here are the opportunities, at the distributing point for these materials, for manufacture of cooperage, of woodenware, of furniture and wagons, for all which there is constant demand, the world over as well as here.

It has, as once we have remarked already, and need not, therefore, emphasize here, at command, in the sense of commerce, a storehouse, a magazine, pre-eminently, of minerals of economic importance; iron ore with limestone and coal in juxtaposition, the materials for the metal of commerce, and for steel, which is fast displacing it; copper, zinc, soapstone, porcelain clays, and other constituents of chinaware, brick clays, marbles, and innumerable other of the inorganic elements of the Earth.

A DIGRESSION AS TO LEATHER.

IT has, of farming staples available, grains, fruits and hides. In the last named material, in conjunction with the tan bark of its forests, the basis for tanneries—only one of which, the KNOXVILLE LEATHER CO.'s, it has yet—and for manufactures of leather goods of every sort. This Knoxville Leather Co.'s establishment, by the way, is a large one. It follows the old fashion of tanning in bark liquor, and uses water power, and its capacity is 250 finished hides a week, which number it renders into sole, collar, harness, upper and skirting leathers that are of excellent repute for finish and quality in the leather goods trade.

The tan bark of East Tennessee, its oak bark especially, is shipped largely to Europe, where it is considered superior to the native growth of those parts. And the abundance of it in the Southern Appalachians can be measured, perhaps, by the fact that Knoxville is soon to have an establishment which, by a new process, will make from it an extract or tannic acid, prepared ready for use by the trade.

LABOR, TRANSPORTATION, ETC.

As for labor, Knoxville has a population one-fifth or more of the colored race, unskilled mechanically, but stalwart and governable. It has a steady influx also of laborers, skilled and unskilled, drawn to it by the promise of employment it holds out, by its growth.

For transportation conveniences, there is the East Tennessee, Virginia & Georgia, a system ramifying the South; and along with this other roads whose facilities and connections give it a horizon practically unbounded for trade. All which a preceding chapter unfolds.

For market, there is the city itself, the growing towns tributary, the States over which it queens, the country, in fine, at large. The entire district in which it holds sway as a trade center is in process of development, settlement, enrichment; and in this respect of field, the city is a star in a firmament, boundless and infinite—not a mollusk in a shell.

COAL AND INCIDENTALS.

FOR fuel, no city on the footstool takes precedence of it. There is a superabundant store of it as near as 16 miles—unlimited quantities certainly, 30 to 60—of coal that can be laid down at the factory door, at $1.25 a ton.

And as to the incidentals of water supply, money matters, building sites, taxes, licenses, insurance and all that, we have already expatiated upon these. A reperusal however of what has been said in the preceding chapters upon these topics, may perhaps refresh the interested reader thereupon.

In all those miscellaneous lines that arise from local necessities, and that thrive by their custom trade, like the manufacture of tinware and cornice, wire work, foundering in brass and iron, electrical devices, shoe making, grocers' specialties and all that, Knoxville affords as promising a field as any city in the land. These, however, in an atmosphere of prosperity like its, will spontaneously grow. The larger and more important projects—the great fabrics mills, furnaces, etc., for which it has also unequalled oppportunities, are usually assisted, if not actually accouched, without. One such scheme there is in embryo at present, the construction of a steel plant to operate with a late process, by which the metal shall be produced direct from the valley ores.

IRON WORKS OF THE CITY.

The KNOXVILLE IRON CO. was incorporated in 1868 and has been engaged continuously since in the mining of coal in East Tennessee, and the manufacture of bar and channel iron, fish plates, and light T rail, etc., for which they get their material from the Chattanooga and other East Tennessee furnaces.

Their principal business is the mining of coal and the manufacture of bar iron and small rails. Their works here have special importance, in connection with the topics discussed in this work, as the only establishment of the kind at Knoxville.

First and last the company has invested in these works something like $250,000. Their equipment consists of a puddling mill of seven single, and three double furnaces (equal to thirteen in all), and a rolling mill of twenty-five tons daily capacity. This mill consumes 20,000 tons of coal a year. It furnishes a livelihood to some 200 residents of the city. It is situated at the junction of the East Tennessee, Virginia & Georgia, and the Knoxville & Augusta railroads here, so that it has ample transportation facilities. Its annual output of finished material is 6,000 tons, valued in round numbers at more than $250,000.

The coal mines of the company are at Coal creek and Briceville, about thirty miles from the city. The coal produced is the well-known Coal Creek variety, suitable for both steam and domestic purposes. The company employs three hundred men at these mines, and produces in the neighborhood of 200,000 tons annually.

The coal and iron products of this company find a ready market in this State, Virginia, North Carolina, Georgia, Alabama and Louisiana. New Orleans is largely supplied with bar iron by these works.

This company was organized in 1868. It began business with $150,000 subscribed capital. This has been increased since to $300,000 paid up. Those who organized it are principals in it still. These gentlemen are, O. A. BROWN, president; COL. E. J. SANFORD, of Sanford, Chamberlain & Albers, wholesale druggists of Knoxville, vice-president; T. I. STEPHENSON, secretary. The general manager of the mill is Mr. J. J. REBMAN.

Mr. Brown has been connected with this enterprise, as we have intimated, almost from its inception. He was secretary and treasurer, then vice-president, and finally, last year, became president and general manager. The company's business has been largely developed by his industry and ability. The secretary, Mr. Stephenson, has also been many years with the company—since 1879 in fact.

The city office of this company is at 162 Asylum street.

The SOUTHERN CAR WORKS at Knoxville, situated about a mile west of the central depot, is one of the most substantial establishments of the kind in the Southern country. It covers, including its yards and side track, over eleven acres of ground. It affords a livelihood to 150 hands, and represents an investment in buildings, machinery, and stock, etc., of about $150,000.

It is run chiefly on freight and mining cars, new work mostly, ordered of it by the various roads of the South. The East Tennessee, Virginia & Georgia has, however, been heretofore its largest and best customer. Last year it turned out one lot of 670 cars for this road and its auxiliary, the Knoxville & Ohio Railroad.

The capacity of these works is equivalent to a production of six or eight new cars a day, running on new work alone. They have no special advantage over competitors more than this, that they have earned an enviable reputation for honest work and fair dealing, and are regarded one of the best managed among the many business concerns of Knoxville.

This company has $100,000 capital paid up, and a considerable surplus. G. W. COLWELL, its president, is a capitalist and lumberman of the State of Michigan. He is one of the firm of Colwell, McGregor & Co., general merchandisers, of Harrisville, in that State, which place is his home. R. Z. ROBERTS, vice-president and general manager, is president also of the Stephenson-Getaz Manufacturing Co., of Knoxville, the largest here in the line of interior finish, mantels, etc. He is also vice-president of the East Tennessee Marble Co. here, and is interested in other important concerns, besides. He is a Pennsylvanian, but has been resident here for about twelve years.

L. A. MADDEN, secretary and treasurer of the company, came here from New York City about two years ago, especially to direct its office affairs and financial disbursements.

D. A. GETAZ, superintendent, is also a principal in and general manager of the Stephenson-Getaz Co., already mentioned.

The directors of the company are these officers, and E. J. SANFORD, of Sanford, Chamberlain & Albers, wholesale druggists here, president also of the Knoxville Woolen Mills and the Knoxville & Ohio Railroad, and R. L. LOTT, of Harrisville, Mich.

The KNOXVILLE CAR WHEEL CO., of 120 Jacksboro street, has works there covering about two acres of ground. These works employ about 200 hands, and have an output equal to 35 tons of wheels a day and 20 tons of other castings. They have shipping facilities by means of their side track to the Knoxville & Ohio Railroad, to all parts of the land, and they have for customers all the steam railroad systems of the South, and besides these, many mining companies, street railroad lines, etc. Their annual business will aggregate $500,000 a year.

The company has $200,000 capital paid in. It has two men on the road in the South taking orders for it. Its specialties are chilled wheels, soft castings, light forgings, marble and dump cars, machine repair work, derricks and horse powers, and it handles incidentally, shafting, gearing, bolts and other engine supplies.

These works were established in 1872, by parties not now interested in them, and were re-organized in 1881 by the present principals: C. H. BROWN, formerly also of the East Tennessee Bank, president; W. P. WASHBURN, of Washburn & Templeton, lawyers, vice-president; D. A. CARPENTER, president of the Knoxville Fire Insurance Co., and of the Knoxville Brick Co. also, secretary and treasurer. Associated with these gentlemen in the management, though not actively identified with it, are the following: W. W. WOODRUFF, wholesale hardware dealer on Gay street, and M. L. ROSS, president of the Knoxville Chamber of Commerce.

The cut on this page is a representation of these works.

This company has recently acquired also, by lease, for a long term, the plant of the KNOXVILLE FOUNDRY & MACHINE CO. on Hardee street, which is one of the best

KNOXVILLE CAR WHEEL WORKS.

equipped shops in this section. This acquisition increases their manufacturing capacity fully seventy-five per cent. The additional works embrace blacksmith, machine and woodworking departments, and incidentally, a very large collection of valuable patterns.

DEMPSTER'S MACHINE SHOP, 12 Main street, is fully equipped for the manufacture of stationary and portable engines, steam pumps, rock drills and channelers, saw and planing mill machinery, etc., and especially for repairs on that sort of work, which is its specialty. A great deal of work is done by it for the country adjacent to Knoxville—first-class work, guaranteed by it, and performed at prices exceedingly moderate.

MR. JAMES DEMPSTER, proprietor of this shop, is an expert machinist himself. He has been

DEMPSTER'S MACHINE SHOP.

in the business, man and boy, twenty-five years, and all work entrusted him is executed under his personal supervision.

He is a native of Perth, Scotland, and served an apprenticeship there, after the thoroughgoing fashion of the old country, for five full years, thus obtaining a most thorough, practical and fundamental knowledge of general machine work. From Perth he went to Glasgow, the greatest of all centers of his trade, and there put in nine years at his business. Then he went to the East Indies, where he worked for three years, and from there came here six years ago.

The CLARK FOUNDRY & MACHINE CO., has works at the corner of Hardee and Hume streets here, employing 60 hands, and turning out about 10 tons of finished work a day, for a trade extending over this and the States adjacent to it. It has nearly all the work of the East Tennessee, Virginia & Georgia's Knoxville division, some 300 miles long, and does besides a vast amount of architectural and other house work, and general castings, like sash weights, grate bars, etc.

H. W. CLARK, proprietor of this establishment, has been in the business here since 1882. He has been in it altogether about twenty-four years. His establishment is thoroughly equipped with devices for the business, and its trade is growing every day.

The ENTERPRISE MACHINE WORKS, 66 to 76 Chamberlain street, were established about seven or eight years ago, by Richards & Guinn.

MR. D. C. RICHARDS, of that firm, is now proprietor of them.

This is one of the most completely appointed works of the kind here for machine repair work, which is its specialty. Saw mill and marble machinery is largely made and repaired by it. Considerable general new work is also done by it, and a specialty is made of hoisting and light engines.

Mr. Richards has been a resident here since 1869. He is one of the directors of the East Tennessee Coal Co., and of the Workingmen's Building and Loan Association of Knoxville.

FAIR, DAY & DEKLYNE, foundrymen and pattern makers, of Jacksboro street, and the line of the Knoxville & Ohio Railroad, are successors to Fair & Day, established in 1890. MR. DEKLYNE has been a member of the firm about a year. They employ about fifteen or twenty hands, and have a cupola of about four tons daily capacity. They run chiefly on house work, machine castings and hardware findings. Fronts and grates are a specialty with them; that and sash weight work, a vast amount of which is done by them for the local builders and for out-of-town contractors.

These works occupy about an acre and a half at Second Creek, from which stream they get their water supply. They use the native Tennessee iron largely and they have experienced a 25 per cent increase of business yearly since they began.

The proprietors commenced business on a very small scale. In the beginning their place was but 40 feet square. Their trade has grown so, however, that they have not only been compelled to enlarge their premises, but have lately found their power insufficient. So they have given an order for a large engine to be made in Cincinnati to run their works.

They have been making a good many Scates furnaces for the firm controlling that device, and also turning out mantel fronts and grates largely. They are making preparations now to produce enamelled and other fine work of this last named sort.

Mr. Day manages the mechanical department of the business, Mr. Fair the office and finances, and Mr. DeKlyne assists generally.

capacity which are all giving perfect satisfaction. The parties for whom they were built are Mr. Savage's references.

Mr. Savage will build buhr mills also and supply all the accoutrements for mills of any sort. He will act as heretofore, as sales agent for the James Leffel water wheels and engines, the Erie City Engine Works, the Cordesman Machine Company, Bodmus "Old Reliable" bolting cloth, and for other manufacturers of wood-working and wheat-cleaning and marble and lumber milling machinery.

H. O. Nelsen, manufacturer of iron fencing of all kinds, on the track of the Maryville railroad, near Asylum street, was formerly located at the "Valley Forge" further in town, but has lately moved to his present place to

H. O. NELSEN'S IRON FENCE FACTORY.

W. J. Savage, millwright and mill furnisher and dealer in machinery and mill supplies, at 34 Tulip street, is the largest in that line here. He has a large wood-working and machine shop and is prepared to estimate on or undertake mill construction of any sort. He handles mill supplies very largely, also metals and heavy hardware, and has customers for these wares in all of Knoxville's tributaries.

He has been established since 1885, the year he first located here, and is successor to the Knoxville Supply and Machine Co., which has been making a specialty of the building of roller flour mills and of which he was a principal, and this business he will continue. That company built last year in East Tennessee seven roller mills of 15 to 200 barrels daily

secure larger and better quarters. He has fitted up the new place with the latest machinery and appliances for the business, and with fifteen or twenty hands usually employed, has a capacity of about 60,000 feet a year.

He makes fencing of all sorts, from the cheapest to the costliest, and is a shipper of it to all parts of the South. He is an expert mechanic himself, and a very clever designer. He has been in the business here since 1873, and was in it in other places before that from his youth. He sends out, through the mails, an illustrated catalogue and price list, and will furnish estimates when desired. His work may be seen here on most of the first-class residences of the city, among them C. M. McClung's, E. J. Sanford's, and others.

FRANK H. POST, manufacturer of wagons, buggies, etc., at 186 to 192 Crozier street, is successor to his father, who established himself in this line here some twenty-one years ago.

His is the largest carriage shop here. Mr. Post has about thirty hands employed, chiefly on fine light ordered work, and has capacity equal to manufacture, in the course of a year, of something like 500 jobs. He has orders for these coming to him from all the States in Knoxville's trade territory.

Mr. Post is manufacturer of the popular POST FARM WAGON, known everywhere hereabouts as the best made for the climate, wear and tear and general conditions affecting vehicles in this part of the country. He sells about 500 of these every season.

He is a native of the North, but was raised here. He is substantially "fixed," as the saying is, is a director of the Farmers' & Traders' Bank, the Mechanics' Building & Loan Association, and has other interests besides.

SHERIDAN & QUINCY, manufacturers of carriages and wagons, have a repository on Jackson street, near the Central Depot, and shops on State street employing twenty-five hands, who, with machinery to aid them, turn out several hundred jobs of all kinds a year, mostly made on orders, and chiefly light farm and spring wagons, trucks and city delivery wagons. They have trade in this part of Tennessee, and their name is familiar also, as manufacturers of first-class work, in all the neighboring parts of Kentucky, Virginia and North Carolina. They also do considerable jobbing and repair work for local patrons.

They are the makers of the DIXIE farm wagon, and this is their leading specialty.

They have been established now about seven years. The partners are both expert workmen, bred to the trade in that greatest of all centers for it, Rochester, N. Y. Mr. Sheridan manages the wood and iron-working departments, and Mr. Quincy the paint shop. The latter is an expert in the line of fancy and decorative work, and considered generally one of the best ornamental painters in the State. Fine sign and banner work is done by this shop also to a considerable extent.

The KNOXVILLE BRICK CO., which has offices in the city at 148 Gay street, has works employing 150 hands at Powell's station, about eight miles out, which have a capacity equal to production of 120,000 bricks a day, running full.

This company is capitalized for $100,000, and is the largest manufacturer of brick here, if not also in the South. Its products, all kinds of hard paving and building brick, ornamental brick, pressed front brick, and fire clay and terra cotta work for buildings, are shipped from the works into all parts of Tennessee, Virginia, Kentucky, Georgia and the Carolinas.

D. A. CARPENTER, president of this company, is president also of the Knoxville Fire Insurance Co., and is interested in other local enterprises of importance. W. H. FIZER, vice-president, secretary and treasurer, is well and widely known, as formerly in the iron trade in Alabama before this company was organized. The directors of the company are men prominent in business affairs here: C. E. Lucky, attorney at law; W. H. Simmonds, vice-president of the State National Bank; R. M. Rhea, of Cowan, McClung & Co., wholesale dry goods, and Messrs. Carpenter and Fizer.

The KNOXVILLE STONEWARE, SEWER PIPE & TILE CO., which has works in the Northeastern end of the city, on the line of the East Tennessee, Virginia & Georgia road, and an office at the corner of Union and Prince streets, was organized in 1890. It has 20 employes making hollow brick, sidewalk and paving brick, farmer's drain tile, vitrified sewer pipe, and fine stoneware, and is a shipper of these products to all parts of Virginia, Kentucky, Tennessee, North Carolina and Georgia. It has fine clay beds where its factory is located, and an ample quantity of raw material at hand to meet the demands of its trade.

The directors of this company are W. M. SWEANEY, C. A. ROSENBECK, E. D. CRAMER, and A. ZOLLER, all four of whom came here from Ohio especially to go into this business at Knoxville, with W. H. STEWARD, likewise one of the founders of the business, who is secretary and treasurer of the company. The company has $30,000 capital, and about that much invested in its works and plant.

CARTER & TUTT, pavers and roofers, of 88 Hardee street, do the principal business of that kind at Knoxville, and have few real competitors even in East Tennessee. They began business here in 1888, and were the first to introduce here, to any extent, the tar concrete pavement which is their specialty. They have laid a vast amount of it here and at other places, for sidewalk, cellar flooring, etc., among other jobs the following: The cellar work of both the houses of C. M. McClung & Co.; all the work of the Southern Express Co. here;

all that has been done by the University of Tennessee; numerous jobs in private residences here, and carriage drives, sidewalks, etc., besides, all which work has given perfect satisfaction; and they are now doing a vast amount of sidewalk work for Newport, Tenn.

They have done also a great deal of felt and tar roofing.

Mr. Payton Carter of this firm, is also of the Payton Carter Brick Works of Knoxville. He directs the office business of the firm, and Mr. Tutt supervises their workmen, and attends to other outside details.

R. W. Owens, slate roofer, of 154 West Depot street, does nearly all that sort of business here, and has a big business besides in other parts. The following work executed by him is an indication of what his aggregate is: Of residences here, he has slated W. C. Fulcher's; J. C. Woodard's, in the suburb of Fountain City; Metler's on Central avenue pike; Wm. Caswell's and Col. R. R. Swepson's, on Fourth avenue; and others as conspicuous for their beauty and costliness.

Of public buildings here, the following: The new Y. M. C. A. and Science Hall buildings, at the University of Tennessee, and many of the larger edifices, like churches, schools, etc.

Of work out of town, the Corson-Newman College at Mosse Creek, Tenn., two school buildings at Johnson City, Tenn., the Pace residence at Raleigh, N. C., railroad work for the East Tennessee, Virginia & Georgia road at Atlanta, Macon, Selma, Tuscumbia and other cities on the line, and at Bridgeport, Ala., a big job on the pipe works.

Last year his contracts, all told, aggregated between $40,000 and $50,000. He employs about a dozen hands steadily.

Mr. Owens mastered the trade in Wales, where he was born. He has been in the business, as a quarryman in Pennsylvania, and as a roofer and dealer in slates at Utica, N. Y., and Canton, Ohio, as well as here.

W. H. Alexander, contractor for house moving and raising, and incidentally for heavy hauling and the reconstruction of buildings, at 92 West Park street, has followed that line here for over twenty years. He does most of that sort of work here and considerable besides in the country. He has all the necessary equipment for raising and moving, including heavy timbers, rollers, blocks, jacks, etc., and has about twenty-five hands employed when trade is brisk.

In the course of business here he has performed, successfully, some remarkable feats of moving and raising, including structures requiring very great care, and among them the largest jobs of the kind ever undertaken in this part of the country. He has handled, also, some very heavy safes. Those in the Post Office here, the largest in the city, were set up by him.

He is a carpenter by trade himself, and he supervises personally the execution of all contracts entered into by him.

Hacker & Co., house, sign and decorative painters, of 150 Gay street, do the greater part of the fine work of that sort executed here, and are the most notable firm in the business in East Tennessee. Among other contract work of their's, remarkable for its quality and cost, the following jobs may be cited: The interior and exterior of Maj. Swepson's mansion here, which cost $20,000; the $125,000 residence of Maj. E. C. Camp; the ornamentation of the new Post Office of the city; the exterior and interior work of the Lamar House, and the new University building, a very large job.

Fine interior decoration and sign writing, indeed, are their specialties. They employ usually, about 50 hands, and are open to engagement for work to be done in any part of Knoxville's trade territory, whether, in Tennessee, Virginia, Kentucky, the Carolinas, or Georgia.

The partners in this firm are uncle and nephew. Mr. Isaac N. Hacker, senior member of the firm, is a Confederate veteran. He established himself here after the "late unpleasantness," and has built up both trade and reputation since. The junior member, Mr. Bruce Hacker, is a native of East Tennessee, and is a clever workman of this line himself.

Schaad & Rotach, 101 Kennedy street, are manufacturers of extra fine work in the furniture line, established since 1885, and with a State trade and reputation. Their factory is large, fully equipped with machinery, and they have the advantage of situation in a great market for fine cabinet woods, oak, poplar, walnut, etc. They are expert workmen themselves and they supervise personally construction of all turned out of their place.

They have designed and constructed special work as follows:

Bank fixtures for the Mechanics' National Bank; the Farmers' and Traders' Bank, and the Central Savings Bank; drug store fixtures for Mr. Rosenthal, corner Gay and Depot streets, and for Mr. Caulkins at Central Market. And they will furnish estimates for this class of work whenever desired.

HOOKER, LITTLEFIELD & STEERE, MANUFACTURING CONFECTIONERS.

Mr. Schaad has been employed in fine furniture factories here and in Boston, Mass., Cincinnati, O., and Atlanta, Ga., all his life, and the mechanical affairs of the firm are directed by him. Mr. Rotach has had a business experience including a long term of service with the Southern Express Co., and he is the office man of the firm.

HOOKER, LITTLEFIELD & STEERE, manufacturing confectioners, and jobbers of roasted coffees, teas and spices, No. 262 Gay street, do business not only in the trade territory proper of Knoxville, but cover nearly the entire South, including Texas and Florida.

They have four men on the road selling their popular brands of candies and other goods, and in their factory give employment to forty people.

They occupy a building of six floors, each 25 by 150, which building is equipped throughout with a most complete steam plant for the manufacture of candies, and the roasting of coffees. They have facilities for a daily output of 4,000 pounds of roasted coffees, and 7,000 pounds of candies.

This is the most notable concern in their line of trade here, and they are the largest manufacturers of the finer class of chocolates and bonbons in the South. They are well known to the trade by these specialties (fine chocolates and bonbons), which for style, finish and delicious eating qualities, are not surpassed by any manufactured in this country.

This firm has been established about three years. Five partners have an interest in the house, J. A. Anderson, I. H. Anderson, E. E. Hooker, H. E. Littlefield, and A. H. Steere. Mr. J. A. Anderson has been prominent in business circles for the last fifteen years. Previous to embarking in this partnership, the Messrs. Anderson were engaged in the coffee roasting business. They take no active part in the management of the business. Mr. Hooker directs the coffee, tea and spice department; and the candy department is managed by Mr. Littlefield. Mr. Steere is the principal traveling man, and is on the road nearly all the time.

PETER KERN, wholesale and retail dealer in and manufacturer of confectionery, corner of Market Square and Union street, was the last mayor of Knoxville, elected to that office in January, 1890, to hold for a term of two years; in which respect it may be said of him, without undue flattery, that he has served his con-

PETER KERN'S WHOLESALE CONFECTIONERY.

stituency faithfully, zealously and satisfactorily. He is a native of Germany, but has lived here so long that all his interests, social and business, are centered in this city of his adoption, of which he has been continuously a resident and merchant since he established this house in 1864.

He occupies, for business purposes, the handsome and modern structure shown in the engraving accompanying this matter, a place of three floors and basement, each 50 by 120 feet in area, and is the owner of it. The second floor of this establishment is fitted up and used as ice cream parlors and restaurant, and this is the largest and finest of these resorts in Knoxville.

The first floor is the salesroom, and on the other floors he runs the largest candy factory and cake bakery also, in this part of the country. He has it equipped with steam machinery and employs twenty-eight skilled workmen and salesmen in it. His specialties are supplies of ice cream, cakes, etc., for balls and parties, and candies made from the best, most wholesome and purest materials. He handles, also, extensively foreign fruits and fireworks.

He supplies a jobbing trade over the whole Tennessee, Kentucky, Virginia, Carolina and Georgia trade territory of the city, and having been established for several years, does a leading, if not the largest business of that kind of any house here.

SWAN BROS., bakers and confectioners, of 341 and 343 Broad street—the junction of that thoroughfare with Central avenue—do, in all probability, the largest city trade of any concern in their line here, and they are about making preparations to extend their business and do an outside and jobbing trade as well.

They came here from Chicago, where they had followed the business also, and established themselves here six years ago. In the meantime they have won reputation as the most expert bakers and confectioners in East Tennessee. They have always on hand a stock of fresh candies and cakes of all sorts, holiday and fancy goods. They make a specialty of bread and fine cakes.

A cut of their place illustrates this matter. They have a stall, also, for the sale of their stock in the public market.

MR. CHAS. H. SWAN, the elder of the two, manages the store and bakery; MR. GEO. P. SWAN, the other brother, all their outside business.

The TRIO MILLS, corner of Crozier and Clinch streets, have a full process roller equipment of 100 barrels daily capacity, and a buhr equipment also. They are run on both flour and meal, and are shippers of their product direct to all the parts of Kentucky, North Carolina, Georgia and Tennessee, adjacent to this city.

Their principal brands are the following: Of flour, "Silver Leaf," "Choice" and "Famous;" of meal, bolted and rough, made by the old-fashioned buhr process, and this meal is their specialty.

The local trade of these mills is also very large.

SWAN BROS., CITY BAKERY.

They were established in 1878 by Scott, Dempster & Co. SCOTT BROS. & Co. acquired them in the spring of '91, and they are still operated by that firm, the members of which are Messrs. F. A. R. Scott and his sons, J. A. and D. D. The elder Scott has been in the milling business here ever since the war, and has been very successful in it. He is president also of the Central Savings Bank of this city, and secretary and treasurer of the Knoxville Leather Co. Mr. J. A. Scott is a director of the Savings Bank. He manages the mechanical affairs of the mills, and his brother, D. D., the office.

The CRYSTAL ICE CO., which has works in North Knoxville, and is a shipper of its superior product throughout all East Tennessee, as well as a source of local supply, was organized in 1887, by Knoxville capitalists, who have invested about $40,000 in its plant and equipment. It has an output of about 65,000 pounds a day, or 9,750 tons a year, and is operated upon the absorption plan. Its machinery is of the Columbus Iron Works pattern. Its water is derived from the noted Moses spring, which furnishes a supply unsurpassed for purity anywhere in these parts.

G. M. HARRELL, president of this company, is proprietor also of the Knoxville Transfer Co. H. W. LYNN, secretary and manager, is also president of the East Tennessee Fire Insurance Co. He was formerly local freight agent for the East Tennessee, Virginia & Georgia road, and has been a resident here for the past twenty-five years.

The office of this company is at 144 Gay street, with the East Tennessee Fire Insurance Co.

The KNOXVILLE BREWING Co., corner of McGhee and Chamberlin streets, occupies there a site fronting 250 feet on Chamberlin, 150 on McGhee, with an "L" extending 200 feet along the latter thoroughfare. This whole area is covered with the buildings of the company—a four-story brick, comprising, besides the brewery proper, malt and bottling departments, and refrigerator cellars, stables, etc., necessary for an establishment complete in itself.

This brewery was established in 1886, and was fitted up then with as comprehensive an equipment as there is in the land. It has refrigerating apparatus of the latest sort. It is a buyer of the finest malt and hops, both in this country and Germany, and it produces, with a force of 30 employes and a head brewer of long experience, 25,000 barrels annually, of as prime a beverage as there is sold anywhere, North or South. It is certainly the best beer made in this State, or for that matter in Knoxville's trade territory of Virginia, the Carolinas, Kentucky and Tennessee.

The company that operates this brewery has $60,000 capital. A. BINDEWALD is its president, and W. MEYER, vice-president. They were in

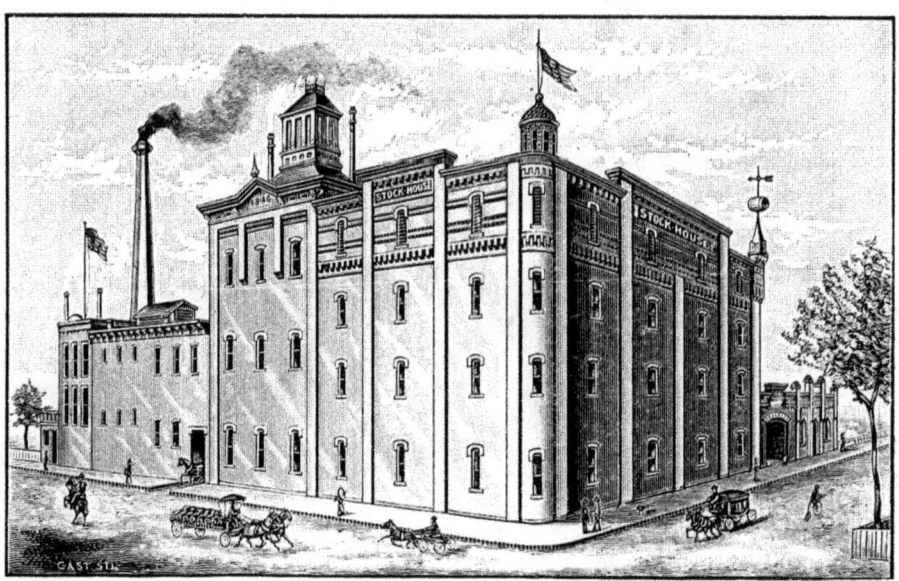

KNOXVILLE BREWERY.

the business at Louisville before they came here; have been in it indeed, pretty much all their lives.

The KNOXVILLE TOBACCO Co., of 439 Crozier street, is the only tobacco factory in the city, and is one of the largest making plug and smoking tobaccos, which are its specialties, in the South. It was established in 1889, and has already attained an important position in the trade of Tennessee, Georgia, Alabama and Mississippi, in which States it has four men on the road selling for it.

It has a factory equipped with the very latest devices for the business, and in this factory has about 50 hands at work. Its products are about fourteen different brands, and as many grades of plug and smoking tobaccos, all made from the best North Carolina and Virginia leaf.

Its leading brands are as follows: "Charity," "Peach Mountain," "Managers' Choice," "Bay Horse," "Orange Leaf," "North Carolina Chew," and "Virginia Leaf," chewing plug brands, and "Red Rose" and "Crown" specialties in smoking tobacco.

W. C. McCoy, J. A. Hensley and S. G. Haynes are proprietors of this business. They established it, and have built up the trade it enjoys. Mr. McCoy has lived here for thirty years or more. He was formerly in the gents' furnishings business here. Mr. Hensley was a wholesale grocer of Knoxville from the time he came here, in 1871, until he went into this line.

He has charge of the manufacturing departments, and Mr. McCoy has general supervision of affairs. Mr. Haynes, the other partner, acquired his interest in June, 1891. He is engaged, most of his time, on the road in the interests of the house. He was formerly with the East Tennessee, Virginia & Georgia Railroad for a number of years.

The jobbers of Knoxville's trade territory, should bear in mind that it is the best of policy to patronize a home industry, especially so when the goods are warranted to be equal in quality and lower priced than any competitors, in the same field.

J. R. Smith & Co., manufacturers of cigars, at 11 Market Square, west side, are the leading concern of their line in the field which we have described as Knoxville's trade territory, embracing Southwest Virginia, Eastern Kentucky and Tennessee, Western, North and South Carolina and Georgia. They do business however, over a much more extensive scope of country even than this. They have customers in Alabama and Mississippi on the one hand, and as far away as the District of Columbia, New York, Boston, Connecticut and Vermont on the other, and also in Texas, Washington and Dakota.

They employ usually 25 hands in the factory, and have a product of about 1,000,000 cigars a year. These they sell, through their drummers mostly, at prices ranging from $22 a thousand to $65, according to quality. Their leading brands are well known and highly esteemed throughout the district supplied from Knoxville. These brands are the following: "Spanish Cavalier," "La Doncella" and "La Senorita," ten cent goods, and "Pride of America," "Planters' Delight," and "Aldonna," five cent specialties. They also make special brands to order for all sections of the country.

This factory was established by J. R. Smith, senior proprietor of it, in 1886. He had been in the business before that for seventeen years, at Lynchburg, Va. His partner, Mr. Ben Hurxthal, Jr., is a New Yorker, formerly connected with the Aultman & Taylor Threshing Machine Co., at Mansfield, Ohio. He came here in 1889, and has since been identified with Mr. Smith in the management of the business. He supervises the office details, while Mr. Smith has charge of the manufacturing departments.

The Knoxville Cigar Co., of 233 Gay street, has for its principals Harry and Louis Levy, brothers well-known here as substantial, shrewd and enterprising business men. They began business as cigar manufacturers here about six years ago, in a moderate way, but now have one of the largest concerns of the kind in the State. They occupy two upper floors of a large building in the heart of the town, and besides twelve or fifteen skilled men at work in their factory, have two men on the road in the South selling for them.

Their output is about 1,000,000 cigars a year of the following brands: "Bouquet," "Imported," "Commercial," "Orr," "Our Trade," "Flirtation," "Pair of Queens," "Our Babies," "Con Gracia," "La Flor De Rica," "Out of Sight," and "Blue Tag."

Of these their ten-cent brands are the "Bouquet," "Imported," "La Flor De Rica," and "Orr," all of which brands are far superior to the average goods of the same price in this market. The "Imported" is conceded as good as anything in the world. Their five-cent brands are the others mentioned. This firm also makes a specialty of getting up private brands to order for patrons in all parts of the country, even those so far distant as Philadelphia, Penn., and Indian Territory, and north up into Michigan.

C. L. Larew, printer, of 8 Asylum street, has been established in business here about three years. He is a native of the city, and an expert craftsman of the "art preservative of all arts" himself. His specialty is job printing, and he has as fine type and appointments as there are in the city. He does work for all parts of the trade territory of the city, and he carries a stock of commercial stationery sufficiently large to fill orders promptly. Artistic and ornamental work is his specialty.

S. B. NEWMAN & CO., book and job printers, of 186 Gay street, employ about fifty persons, and do the largest printing business at Knoxville. They have a very complete equipment of type and presses, and their own bindery, and they carry a considerable stock of commercial stationery besides. They have trade in six States, Virginia and Kentucky, Tennessee, the two Carolinas and Georgia.

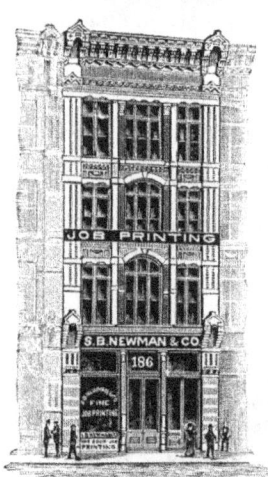

S. B. NEWMAN & CO.'S PRINTING HOUSE.

MR. NEWMAN established the business of the house about twelve years ago. He began in modest fashion, and finding his patronage rapidly increasing, took in Mr. W. S. TEALL as partner, in 1885. In 1889 their Union street establishment (in which they were then located), became too small; and they, therefore, moved to the situation they occupy now, which premises had been specially prepared for them.

A cut of their place accompanies this matter.

The KNOXVILLE PAPER BOX FACTORY, 173 State street, is owned and operated by C. H. Ogden, secretary also of OGDEN BROS. PRINTING Co. here, a leading house of the book, stationery and printing trades at Knoxville. He established the box factory in 1884 in a small way, but has built up a business employing (with steam power) twenty hands.

The drug, shoe, millinery, dry goods and confectionery trades of Knoxville's field are largely supplied with the paper boxes they use by this factory. It is the only factory here of the kind, and the only one of any note in the district of country for which this city is the center. It has all the latest facilities for manufacture; its capacity is about 5,000 boxes of all kinds daily, and its product is a very superior article.

GEO. HEAVEN, sheet metal worker and manufacturer of cornices, etc., at 346 North Crozier street, is a practical man in all branches of the trade. He was formerly foreman in the cornice department of De Pue, Cruze & Co., which position he filled for six years. They were the leading firm of the city at that time. During this period he supervised some of the best work of the sort executed in the city, viz. The Court House, First Baptist Church, and others. And, upon their dissolution, seeing an opening he took advantage of it and started for himself, and, within the past four years, has succeeded in building a reputation and business second to none of the kind, not only in Knoxville, but throughout East Tennessee, North Carolina, Kentucky and other Southern States. He is now doing in this city some very handsome work; that of the St. John's Church, East Tennessee Female Institute, and other fine buildings, deserve special mention. He has a complete and modern outfit, six hands employed, and every facility for doing jobs of any size promptly and well.

BAYLESS, KING & CRUZE, of 183 and 185 Gay street, are manufacturers of and dealers in stoves, ranges, tinware, house furnishing goods, oil tanks, transportation cans, cornice, roofing, sheet metal work, etc. They carry a large and complete stock, have about thirty-five employes, and do a business in Tennessee and adjoining states of more than $100,000 annually.

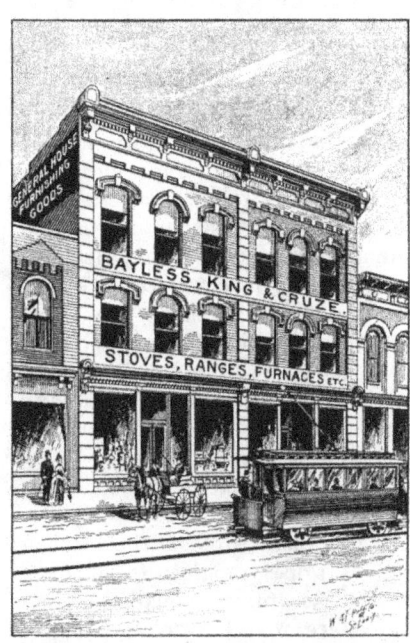

BAYLESS, KING & CRUZE, STOVES, TINWARE, ETC.

This firm manufactures tinware, oil tanks, jacket cans, etc., largely, and makes a specialty of job work, iron and tin roofing, galvanized iron cornices, finials, window caps, chimney caps, etc.; for this work, employing a large force of experienced and skilled workmen.

A special feature is also made of oil, gas and gasoline stoves, for cooking and heating, and of refrigerators, freezers, etc. The house has sole agencies in these special lines for the largest manufacturers in the country, and thus can supply the trade at factory prices.

This firm succeeded the D. B. Bayless Stove Co., established in 1883. Dr. Bayless, a principal in it, is a leading physician of the city and enjoys a large practice. He is identified also with several other institutions in the city in a financial sense.

Mr. King was formerly engaged in the wholesale saddlery business here, but abandoned it in 1889 for the line in which he is now engaged. He has charge of affairs as general manager.

Mr. Cruze has been identified with the stove business longer, probably, than any other person in the city. His experience extends through a period of over 30 years, and he stands particularly high in the business.

This firm is the occupant of the large three-story and basement building shown in the engraving, which accompanies this sketch. It is located at Nos. 183 and 185 Gay street, one of the very best locations in the city for its business, and it affords nearly thirty thousand square feet of floor space.

THE NATIONAL GARMENT CUTTER and *Voice of Fashion*, is another of Knoxville's institutions. It was established here the first of April, 1887. The office was opened in May, at 257 Gay street, where it remained until August 1st, 1891. It was then removed to the property shown in the accompanying cut, situated at the corner of Gay street and Fifth avenue, extending along Fifth avenue to Williams street, making it a really imposing concern.

This company has its main office, factory and publishing house in Chicago, with Southern headquarters in Knoxville. It manufactures and sells a "system" by which anyone may learn to cut all manner and styles of clothing. The company is also doing an immense and really serviceable business in the way of teaching pupils in this useful art, as well as teaching dressmaking upon scientific principles.

They have also here one of the finest equipped dressmaking establishments in the South; one rivaling those even of the Eastern cities to such an extent as to get them orders from New York, Philadelphia, and other large places; while at the same time their patronage extends over much of the South outside of Tennessee.

THE NATIONAL GARMENT CUTTER COMPANY'S ESTABLISHMENT.

In addition to this work, the company is sending out large forces of agents into all parts of the United States to present these specialties. The business is carried on upon a large scale, and is thus giving remunerative employment to thousands of people.

The Knoxville work is under the personal direction of the company's general manager, J. K. DORAN.

Mr. Doran is an East Tennesseean, who has been in active business in different States for many years, and has been eminently successful. He is ably seconded by a large corps of assistants from various parts of the Union, people who have been selected on account of their special ability in the lines in which they are employed.

It will be seen from the foregoing account, that this is an institution with many local, as well as national features.

The NATIONAL MANUFACTURING CO. is a new Knoxville project, backed by some of its most enterprising and substantial business men. It has been chartered to take hold of inventions, to introduce those that have merit, to establish a regular agents' supply house for such as it handles, and to manufacture such as promise to be profitable. The design is to manufacture, indeed, whenever practicable and

NATIONAL MANUFACTURING COMPANY'S OFFICES.

supply the trade through agencies or the jobbers.

To inventors, the advantages thus to be derived are obvious; and it would be supererogatory in this connection to recount them. To those seeking an investment, the plan of the new company presents an opportunity rarely so much as afforded. Here is a chance for the stockholder to obtain the profits of the inventor, the dealer and manufacturer compounded; a better investment than real estate, or any other. And to persons seeking employment it affords an equal share of advantage.

Knoxville, with its industries unborn, but its prodigiously resourceful surroundings, with a future pregnant with infinite possibilities, needs just such an aid to development of its destiny as a productive center. An institution of this sort is worth to it a dozen pursuing the methods of Boards of Trade, and the project will, doubtless, be appreciated by the public-spirited citizens of the city. Indeed, the names of those interested show that it has been already.

J. W. BORCHES, a successful merchant and property owner, is president of the company; M. W. RULE, editor of the *Knoxville Journal*, vice-president; JAMES GILLILAND, of the National Garment Cutter Co., secretary; EDGAR J. PRATT, real estate agent, treasurer, and JAS. K. DORAN, manager of the business of the National Garment Cutter Co. here, is to be general manager. The directors are these gentlemen and other prosperous and responsible business men of the city.

The KNOXVILLE STEAM LAUNDRY, 295 Broad street, operated by E. H. DE PUE, is the largest and best equipped laundry in East Tennessee. It has a full complement of A. M. Dolph laundering machinery, and has twenty employes. Work is done by it for customers throughout the country, as well as in the city, and in its specialty, the cleaning of lace goods, etc., it has no real competitor.

It was established about six years ago by Mr. De Pue. He has made a success of it, and has acquired property and other resources here by means of it.

KNAFFL BROS., photographers, of 144½ Gay street, are natives of Nashville, but were raised here, and brought up to the business they follow in this city. They have been established since 1884, and have made themselves a reputation by the quality of their work, especially of photographs in crayon and pastel, and other sorts requiring exceptional skill. They have been very successful and have acquired realty and other interests here also.

Their specialty is fine photographs and picture frames.

THE STATE OF TENNESSEE.

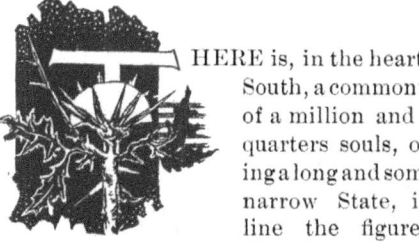HERE is, in the heart of the South, a commonwealth of a million and three-quarters souls, occupying a long and somewhat narrow State, in outline the figure of a rhomboid, stretching from the lowlands of the Mississippi river on the west to the rugged peaks of the Appalachian chain on the east, upon and above the line of the thirty-fifth parallel.

This commonwealth is an old one; in its history more than one great personage of the nation figures. Its people subsist by agriculture, mining, commerce, manufactures; and are alive, like their brethren of the Southern group of States, to the prospect unfolded it by utilization of its vast natural resources, which are similar in kind, and scarcely inferior either in quality or extent, to those that have concreted the Keystone State of the Union, the great State of Pennsylvania.

OTHER CHARACTERISTICS.

This central and fruitful State of the South lies in the border land between the temperate and sub-tropic zones; it is blest, therefore, as a whole, with a climate of mellower mean than either of these. From its infinite variety of surface and soil it derives that ample measure of enrichment which comes from diversified production; it rejoices, indeed, in a superabundance of cotton, corn, tobacco, wheat, fine stock, hard woods, iron, coal, marble—all the staples, nearly, in fact, of the field, the forest and the mine. Three noble and navigable rivers traverse it, draining it, fructifying it, affording it avenues of transportation. It sustains four large cities, seats of its industries, of eighty-five thousand, sixty-five thousand, forty thousand and thirty thousand inhabitants respectively. And its enterprise is burdened with a lighter load of the backward negro race than there is in any of the other old slave States.

PAST AND PRESENT CONTRASTED.

This commonwealth, this State, is Tennessee, the fame of which, only a few years ago—scarcely more than a generation—in many of the pursuits that now give it prestige, was not greatly extended.

To its cousins at the North, many of whom are now identified with its interests by investment, its praises were sounded chiefly in negro melodies; it was of note mostly for its corn stills, its thoroughbreds, its baronies of cotton and planting gentry. Its great cities of to-day, Memphis, the first of inland cotton markets; Nashville, a commercial, manufacturing and educational, as well as political capital; Knoxville, steadily rising in importance, as an industrial center; Chattanooga, a lesser Pittsburgh, were towns, river landings, mere villages.

It had, indeed, contributed its quota of characters illustrious in the service of the State; heroic figures like Jackson, or with a touch also of the romantic, like Houston of San Jacinto and Crockett of the Alamo; stately, like Benton; respectable, rising a little above mediocrity, like Polk and Johnson. But while these as individuals were largely instrumental in the molding of our prodigious empery of the West and Southwest, it had small part of itself in that tremendous material development which has made us powerful and glorious among the nations of earth. It was rich in the resources that are attractions for enterprise, that support large populations and that aggrandize communities; yet, measured by the progress of the States of the West, its growth was slow. With its bowels gorged with inestimable wealth of iron and coal, its advancement was restricted mainly to the furtherance of agriculture, by a social system which (though in less degree than in its neighbors of the South) was discouraging to free labor, and to a forward spirit generally.

THE CHANGE THROUGH WAR.

ALL this now, happily for the State, is changed; and all this now, except for the contrast it affords of the present with the past, it would be unnecessary and unprofitable to recall. What was good in the *ancien regime* we have no occasion to remark; the social graces it engendered, the ancestral pride, the chivalrous spirit—these are matters for the consideration of the historian, the essayist, the writers of tales and romance; and the issues of politics that were involved in the change that came over this State, are hardly subjects here for cold discussion.

The transition came through war, a terrible corrective, but in this case not altogether an unmitigated affliction. The old order of things was burned out, rooted out with fire and sword, amid the thunders of artillery and the smoke of ravaged fields and pillaged cities. It gave way for the new, which rose, in the serenity of peace, like the dawn over the hill

MOCCASIN BEND, TENNESSEE RIVER, FROM LOOKOUT MOUNTAIN, NEAR CHATTANOOGA.

tops of the State, ushering in the morning of regeneration, the era of restoration for Tennessee.

THE STATE RE-ESTABLISHED.

THE same forces that struck the shackles from the slave, burst the bonds that held the dominant race in the restraints of a system which was picturesque, patriarchal, hightoned, perhaps, but repugnant to the spirit of the age. The scales fell from the eyes, that, blinded by a delusive prosperity saw, but hardly heeded, the treasures under foot, the ledges of marble and iron, the layers upon layers of coal, and besides these the affluence of forest resource, from all which, and from the manufactures that have originated in them, the later prosperity of the State has largely proceeded.

In the evolution of new industries, the old however, have not been neglected; those of the soil have been prosecuted with vigor, and the agricultural yield of the State is now greater than in the palmy days before the war, to which we have referred. The wealth of the State has been especially augmented in the period covered by the census reports of 1890.

THE STATE OF TENNESSEE.

It is a matter of regret to the compilers of this work that the statistics showing its advancement in that period are not yet available; that its progress must be guaged by other information, and must be stated, if at all, in general terms.

THE STORY OF TENNESSEE.

A WORD first as to its history. It was the earliest of the States West of the Alleghanies settled by persons of British blood. Its pioneers found, however, a few French traders already on the ground, for one of whom, Timothy Demonbreun, a street in its capital has been named. In the original colony, which migrated from North Carolina before the Revolution, the Scotch-Irish stock of that province predominated, and to this hardy breed and their issue the country is indebted, not merely for the founding of the State, but for the decisive victory of New Orleans, in which battle, under the orders of Jackson, they bore the brunt of the fight. The white inhabitants to-day are largely of this derivation; a matter of interest in connection with the fact, that the State has a remarkably small percentage of people of foreign birth.

Tennessee, at first, was merely a county of North Carolina. In 1790, by cession of that State, it became a part of the "Southwest Territory." Its present name, signifying in the Indian tongue, the "River of the Big Bend," was given it upon its admission to the Union in 1796.

It seceded May 6, 1861, but for a part of the time during the war, two governments were maintained in it, upheld respectively, by the opposing North and South. While that war lasted it was almost continuously a theater of conflict. The battles of Shiloh or Pittsburgh Landing, in which the Confederate general Albert Sidney Johnston was killed, of Island No. 10, Chattanooga and Lookout Mountain (the Battle among the Clouds), Murfreesboro, Stone River and Nashville, were fought upon its soil. It was readmitted to the Union in July, 1866.

This is the story, in a nutshell, of the State of Tennessee.

AN ARRAY SIMPLY OF FACT.

LIMITATIONS of time, space, and purpose, prevent more than the merest allusion in this chapter, to many matters of general interest, perhaps, concerning Tennessee. Our sketch of the State is intended simply to direct attention to some of the more salient features of its progress, present condition and resources; a marshalling of various facts with something of order and arrangement, is all, therefore, attempted hereinafter.

THE STATE HOUSE OF TENNESSEE, NASHVILLE.

Tennessee is naturally divided, by its conformation, into three districts, and it is customary among its people to consider it a State

The tax valuation of the lands of the State in 1890 was $167,000,000, or about $6.50 average an acre, which does not, certainly, seem exces-

"THE HERMITAGE," NEAR NASHVILLE, TENN.
Showing Jackson's original cabin home, and on the right his tomb.

of three distinct parts: East Tennessee, the mountain country, abounding in coal, iron, marbles and timber, with many charming, productive valleys along the two great rivers, the Tennessee and Cumberland, and their tributaries; Middle Tennessee, a plateau region, embracing the rich valley of the Cumberland, over which Nashville is regnant; and West Tennessee, comprising the bluff lands and bottoms of the region between the Tennessee river and the Mississippi.

The total area of the State is 42,050 square miles, or 27,000,000 acres, that is, just about the size of Virginia, a little smaller than Pennsylvania, and slightly larger than Ohio. Notwithstanding the mountainous character of its eastern side, only four and one-half per cent of the State is considered absolutely unproductive.

Of its total area, 41½ per cent, or 10,825,000 acres, is woodland, covered largely with timber of commercial value. The lands susceptible of tilth at present are estimated 65 per cent of the whole, and of the total area, 37.2 per cent (over 8,000,000 acres) is cultivated, not quite four per cent of it in grass.

sive, for the crop, that year, of its eight millions and odd acres under cultivation was estimated worth $96,000,000, equal to $12 an acre average.

TENNESSEE FARM PRODUCTS.

THE average cotton crop of the State is 212,000 bales, valued at $10,500,000; the average wheat crop, 9,500,000 bushels, worth about the same as the cotton; the average corn crop, 47,000,000 bushels, worth $22,500,000; the average oat crop, 8,129,000 bushels, $3,100,000; the average tobacco crop, 31,500,000 pounds, $2,250,000. These are the staples of the State, but hay, potatoes, fruits, peanuts, broom corn and other produce, are grown also largely.

Potatoes and other early vegetables and berries are largely sent North from Nashville. The berry crop of West Tennessee, last year, was worth $1,000,000 to the growers, and the potatoes shipped from three counties of Middle Tennessee fetched $200,000. The peanut crop of the State is valued ordinarily at $600,000.

The live stock of all kinds on farms in Tennessee is valued at over $55,000,000 in the aggregate; the horses, 290,000 in number, are considered worth $22,000,000; the 190,000 mules, $15,307,500; the 817,614 head of cattle, $11,252,000; 430,000 sheep, $835,000; and 2,000,000 hogs, $5,900,000.

The State is of note as a breeding place for stock. Choice strains of cattle, sheep, hogs and horses were introduced years ago, and special attention has been given to the raising of fine horses and mules. A leading industry in some parts of the State is the maturing of young mules bought in other parts. Columbia, Maury county, is one of these maturing places. The thoroughbred cross in the Tennessee mule makes him extensively in demand.

The neighborhood of Nashville is famous for its nurseries of racing horses.

MINERAL WEALTH OF THE STATE.

TENNESSEE is one of the richest of the States in iron ore and coal; and of marble, is the principal source of the domestic supply of the Union. In 1890, 300,000 tons of pig iron were produced in the State, 250,000 tons more than in 1880, and 65,000 more than the whole South in 1872. Besides the vast field of the eastern parts of the State, there is a western iron belt covering fifteen counties nearly, and having an area of 100 miles by 50. Nashville is centrally situated with respect to this belt, and has two furnaces operating upon the product of its mines. The ore is a brown hematite, very free from sulphur and well adapted to steel making.

Iron was mined in this field so long ago as 1790. The late Montgomery Bell, of Nashville, furnished cannon balls made from its ores for the defense of New Orleans in 1814.

Tennessee's advantage in the manufacture of iron lies in the proximity of the materials for it, the iron and coal and limestone employed in the work of the furnaces. The manufacture of basic steel has been made a success at Chattanooga, at a cost less than in the North, and approximating the expense for it in Europe.

Tennessee ranks fifth of the States in production of coal, with nearly 2,000,000 tons mined in 1890, an increase over 1880 of 1,400,000 tons. As a coke producer, it is fourth.

OTHER MANUFACTURES.

THE timber of the State is largely hardwood, such as is used in the making of wagons, furniture and fine interior house finish. Excellent poplar, a wood greatly in demand for furniture manufacture, is especially abundant in the State.

Tennessee had, at last accounts, 442 saw mills, 29 shingle mills, 169 planing mills, 12 stave mills and 32 sash and blind factories.

HOME AND TOMB OF PRESIDENT POLK, NASHVILLE, TENN.

Sixty logging railroads and 21 dry kilns were counted as auxiliaries of these concerns. The daily capacity in feet of these mills was 5,400,-

STATUE OF JACKSON.
Capitol Grounds, Nashville, Tenn.

000, and the value of their product $10,800,000 a year.

Tennessee had 16 cotton mills in 1880; it now has 35 with 116,783 spindles. Besides the advantage these mills have in the price of raw cotton bought at their doors, they pay 25 per cent less wages than in the North, and have 10 to 20 per cent more product per loom; so that some of them are enabled to declare 20 to 40 per cent dividends as against 6 to 10 in New England. This statement we present on the authority of the Boston, Mass., *Commercial Bulletin*.

It has 379 distilleries, producing $5,000,000 of product annually.

VARIOUS MATTERS.

TENNESSEE had 1,843 miles of railroad in 1880; now it has 2,901, operated chiefly by three organizations, the Nashville, Chattanooga & St. Louis, the Louisville & Nashville, and East Tennessee, Virginia & Georgia road, heretofore described.

Tennessee has 151 banks with a capital of $16,168,400 and deposits of $36,227,492.

Tennessee has a population, by the census of 1890, of 1,763,723 persons. At the rate of increase shown since the last census was taken, in 1900 it should have 2,034,454. It has 38 denizens to the square mile, and at Pennsylvania's percentage in this particular (a State of similar characteristics and not a whit richer), could sustain, easily, over 5,000,000. It has, like all the South, a very large birth rate, something like 38, as compared with New Hampshire's 19; so that its natural increase is double the amount of the Granite State.

Its four principal cities, Nashville, Memphis, Chattanooga and Knoxville, have increased in population, as a group, during the last ten years, 84 per cent. Nashville has, by the last census taken, 76,309 inhabitants; Memphis, 65,486; Chattanooga, 29,109, and Knoxville, 21,181.

The taxable values of Tennessee are nearly $350,000,000, an increase of $25,000,000 in one year and $125,000,000 in four. The revenue of the State is about $1,875,000 a year. The largest expenditure of the State is for public schools. It is estimated that the State and the various counties and cities expend over $2,000,000 a year for free education. Like the other Southern States it is remarkably liberal in this regard.

The State University at Knoxville has 275 free scholarships. The chapter of this work on the schools of KNOXVILLE, indicates sufficiently, however, the educational facilities of one, at least of the Tennessee cities, without further remark.

Other State institutions maintained, are a school for the blind, at Nashville, and three insane asylums, one in each of the three divisions of the State of which we have heretofore spoken.

RESOURCES OF EAST TENNESSEE.

AFTER a hundred years and over, of settlement and cultivation in its generalty, the superior agricultural possibilities of the VALLEY OF EAST TENNESSEE, may be said to be pretty thoroughly demonstrated. This region never strictly accorded, even in the palmy days before the war, with the sub-tropic South in its life, sentiment or material characteristics. It was not a cotton district; the slave-holding methods of planting were not distinctive of it; and its social phases were modified much thereby. It was like West Virginia and some parts of Kentucky in farming way; a province by itself, of small farmers mostly, and of products like the temperate North. Time and the development of other and richer resources than those of its fields, have made some changes in it; but these are its agricultural features yet.

There are no lands open to pre-emption left in this part of the country; but by reason of the fact that much of it is still unconditioned—in its very first estate—there is a great quantity of new land available to the immigrant. It has one advantage over the Great West—which, like a vast loadstone, draws so many home-seekers to it—it is easily and quickly accessible from the great seats of population. It is but twelve hours run or so from Cincinnati, twenty-four from Chicago, and twenty-six from New York to Knoxville, its center. The prices of unimproved lands hereabouts are moderate; improved lands and places near the towns and cities of the valley, have, as a matter of course, a value corresponding with similar ground in other parts.

The agricultural advantages of the Valley of East Tennessee are these:

1. A top soil of mineral constituents—the disintegrated rock, largely, of the mountains; somewhat thin, but rich and lasting. 2. Abundance of water in the drainage of the mountains. 3. A mild and even climate. 4. A market growing by reason of the incoming population. 5. Pretty fair transportation facilities now, and these in process of extension and enlargement.

In the luxuriance of the timber growth and the native grasses of the valley, is evidence of the fertility of its soil. The streams are numerous; some of them, the affluents of the larger rivers like the Tennessee, of quite a volume. A hundred degrees is exceptional summer weather; sixteen above, the coldest known in the vicinity of Knoxville. The altitude, combined with the protective agency of the mountains, is a great regulator of the atmospheric conditions. The prevailing winds are from the South and Southwest, where there is any exposure at all; rains usually come from the Gulf, which has a perceptible climatic influence even that far inland. The annual rainfall is fifty-two inches, or thereabouts.

Wheat and oats are the staple crops; some tobacco is raised; much fine fruit of the hardier varieties, small fruits especially; truck pays near the larger settlements; dairying is a business of increasing proportions. The valley is remarkable for the variety and thriftiness of its native forage; the woods of the mountains even, are excellent stock ranges. In the neighborhood of Knoxville there is fine stock breeding, particularly of cattle.

The valley is not exactly a champaign, dead-level, prairie like; it is rather a vast oval trough, hollowed out of the mountains, open at either end, and with its longer axis extending northeast and southwest. Its surface is, generally speaking, rolling; it is in fact, a succession of minor vales forming one great valley. On the hillsides and ridges, as well as in the bottoms, the lands are productive. With its physical conformation, its climate, soils, cool waters, natural pastures, and situation on the border of the sunlands of the South, it is especially adapted for this dairying industry, which can hardly be successfully prosecuted in the lower alluvial South.

COAL IN THE VALLEY.

COAL was discovered in the Valley of East Tennessee about forty years ago. It first began to be utilized largely, when the railroad was completed from Knoxville to the Coal Creek fields twenty-five years ago. The arrival of the first carload of it in there, was hailed there as an event, a disclosure of new destiny for the city; which, indeed, in conjunction with the marble and other mineral and timber development of this section it verily has been.

There are three fields in the valley tributary to Knoxville, Coal Creek, Poplar Creek and Jellico, the last opened up in '84. Another field practically in the valley, though not in the State, is that at Middlesborough, Ky., which

NATIONAL CEMETERY, KNOXVILLE, TENN.

SUNSET ROCK, LOOKOUT MOUNTAIN.
Line of the Nashville, Chattanooga & St. Louis Railway.

city has lately been united with Knoxville by the new K., C. G. & L. railroad. The coal in all these districts is bituminous; it is of fine quality, both for domestic and steam purposes; the Jellico especially so. Nothing has yet been done to test thoroughly its coking qualities, but experts in the business say that it has the proper constituents, and that when the demand arises, a process will doubtless be presented to make use of it for coke.

As the Coal Creek field was developed it was discovered, by those interested as miners and shippers of its product, that a wide expanse of the Union, south, southeast and southwest of the city could be relied on to furnish a market for this coal, and this fact greatly stimulated coal mining enterprises hereabouts. Knoxville enjoys peculiar advantages as a market for these coals. The coal fields are at the southeastern extremity of the Cumberland range, the western boundary of the valley, and are the southern finale of the coal formation in these mountains; so that Knoxville must, in all probability, command the trade of the country to the south and southeast, as far as the ocean, wherein no coal is found, for all time.

Knoxville handles now, as the trade phrase is, a million tons a year. It consumes 125,000 tons of this total itself. The Jellico field is important, not merely as a cheap fuel supply for it, but for a large part of the South. The coal from this field is laid down in Knoxville at $1.35 a ton, and in Atlanta, Chattanooga and other Southern centers, the haul considered, at approximately as cheap a rate. There are 100,000 acres of coal lands in this Jellico field alone, and 15 workable veins. The supply is therefore, to all intents and purposes, simply inexhaustible.

METALIFEROUS WEALTH.

IRON ores, copper, lead, zinc, mica, and even gold and silver are all components of the crust of the valley and its mountain barriers, and are all mined for in these parts. Iron is especially prevalent; and although at present, owing to the state of trade in pig, it is not especially sought; it has here an uncommon value because much of it is particularly adapted for the making of steel.

Utilization of these valley ores for that purpose, it is agreed, must come soon. Knoxville has advantages over Birmingham and the other Southern iron centers in the quality of its ores available, and its nearness to the Pocahontas and other coking coals, and in the saving it can make in the item of transportation—a favor it did not enjoy till of late. It has no furnace yet; but a steel plant project is under way and likely to be realized. The rest will follow; for indeed, there is room and reason for many. At present the nearest furnace to it in the valley is at Harriman, on the

Queen & Crescent and East Tennessee roads, 40 miles distant.

According to a census bulletin lately issued, there was in the State of Tennessee in 1890, 19 furnaces producing 290,747 tons of pig, or not quite 4 per cent of the whole American product. This was a gain in ten years of 507 per cent. And most of this gain is the progress made in this industry in East Tennessee.

So much for manufacture; now as to the material in a state of nature. Hematite or red ores abound in the valley. They vein, as we have said once before in this work, the very streets of Knoxville. There is a vast store of limonite or brown hematite in the Smokies—on their northern side chiefly, just without the valley, and of specular ore and manganese adjacent to that. The great Cranberry magnetic lead, of Mitchell County, North Carolina, trends, it is said toward, and approaches nearly to Knoxville. And in the valley hard by, and in the mountains that face these containing the ores of which we are speaking, is the coal and the limestone to convert it all easily and cheaply into the merchantable metal. The finest car-wheel stock of the world is the ore of this valley.

TENNESSEE MARBLES.

The marble, like the coal business of East Tennessee, is of comparatively recent development. It began at the northern end of the valley and extended thence southward to Knoxville, which is now the great center of the trade because the largest deposits and most quarries are in this county, Knox, a name that defines, in the technic of the trade, a certain kind and quality of marble. The Tennessee marbles are at once the most beautiful and durable of the variegated sorts. They are free from iron and sulphur, and do not stain. The following classification, incomplete though it is, illustrates their diversity of colors: white, gray, blue, pink, brown, green, chocolate, claret; white with pink blush; white and red variegated; black and red variegated; chocolate and white variegated; green, black and red variegated, and fossil figured.

The proportions the trade has attained in this one county alone are indicated in the following figures: Rough marble sold at Knoxville daily, $1,200 to $1,500 worth; rough and dressed both, $3,000 to $5,000 worth; shipments by rail last year (1891), about 30,000 tons. These shipments embraced business with all parts of the land between Montreal and Mexico, New York and San Francisco.

Tennessee marbles have been used in construction of the capitol at Washington, of the New York State House, the post offices at Chicago, Indianapolis, Memphis, and other large places, and it is largely in demand for all the finer architecture of the American cities. In quantity the supply of it is apparently as exhaustless in the valley as that of coal.

THE TIMBER SUPPLY.

Except in the cultivated parts of the valley, there is a primeval forest covering a circuit of more than a hundred miles from Knoxville on every hand. The Tennessee river and its confluents, the Holston and French Broad, and the streams that are the headwaters of these, drain a territory of 6,000,000 acres, the most of which is densely clothed with valuable timber. This great forest apparels the Cumberland and Smoky mountains and the Blue Ridge again beyond, from base to crest. It extends, in fact, outside the valley and its bounds, into Kentucky and Virginia to the north and northeast, the Carolinas to the east and Georgia southeast. It is accessible by means of numerous streams, and by rail in large part as well.

ANTE-BELLUM RESIDENCE TYPE, TENNESSEE.

It begins already to pour a steady stream of wealth into Knoxville as trade center for all these parts, which has a boom in the Tennessee just above the town, several saw mills on the river bank, and a number of large factories, as we have seen, turning out building finish, furniture and cabinet work.

The timber of this forest is of infinite variety. In the higher altitudes of this region the woods are evergreens, pine for the most part, and hemlock, spruce and fir. Lower down on the slopes of the mountains, and on the ridges in the valley, it is poplar, cherry or mountain mahogany, maple, elm, beech, birch, gum, ash, oak, sycamore, basswood, sassafras, holly, persimmon, and other species literally too numerous to mention. There are seventeen varieties of oak alone—abundance of it everywhere along with the ash and hickory, for carriage woods. There is no end of building and furniture material; and of hemlock and oak bark, enough here to run all the tanneries of New England for many a generation.

Much, indeed most, of this timber is of unexcelled quality. The truth is, this great forest forms one of the last remaining sources of a hardwood supply for the Union, and is certainly the greatest of all in the matter of poplar. Here there is poplar of prodigious dimensions; trees, 100 to 125 feet high, 6 to 24 feet in girth, 50 to 80 feet to the first branch, yielding, with so many trees of Falstaffian circumference, a very much larger than usual percentage of high grade lumber. Enormous chestnut and oak there is here too, hickories and ashes, stalwart and clean cut against their background of tall pines, in the sheltered coves at the foot of the mountains, and the rich bottoms of the rivers.

Lumbering is, however, still in its infancy here; but the signs all point to a great transition. The lumbermen of the depleted North and Northwest are coming in here; building logging and other railroads, sawmills, booms along the streams, buying up lands, which, when they shall have cleared them, will still be valuable for mineral prospects as well as for planting. Such lands are worth $2.50 to $5 an acre. They will yield 5,000 to 15,000 feet of timber to the acre; at a cost to log them of $2 to $5, milling not included.

THE COUNTY OF KNOX.

Knox county in which Knoxville is, is the richest as well as most populous county of East Tennessee. It is the third in these particulars in the State. Shelby, in which Memphis is, and Davidson, where Nashville sits, only, outrank it. It is central with respect to this Eastern side of the State comprising the great valley, and has an area of 473 square miles, or 302,500 acres. It is a rolling country, about two-fifths wooded, but not however with timber trees to any extent. About three-fifths is cultivable, and nearly half of it is under cultivation.

The Holston, French Broad, Little Tennessee, Great Tennessee and innumerable creeks water it. The Holston and French Broad unite to form the Tennessee a little above its county seat, which is Knoxville. It has no swamp lands, and its climate, like that of such highland vales generally, is very salubrious. The iron ores that abound in it, along the French Broad and the Holston, have not received any great share of attention; chiefly because its capital and enterprise is absorbed in the quarrying of marbles in that very locality, a business already largely developed and easier of achievement.

It has increased remarkably in population in the last ten years, by 20,453 persons in fact, or 53 per cent; but this increase is that of its city, Knoxville. Farming settlers are not coming in especially fast. The advancement in its agriculture is chiefly the result of the growing demands of its urban population for certain of its staples, and of the effort of its gentlemen farmers, resident in the city, who affect much the breeding of fine herds. It has wide stretches of grazing land; yet there is little stockbreeding, considering what there might be, (only 5,190 horses and 30,525 cattle are taxed,) and the tendency is rather toward dairying than anything else; somewhat too it may be remarked to truck and fruits.

The assessed valuations of Knox county are $20,394,000, two-thirds of that for the city of Knoxville. The debt of the county is but $265,000; it was contracted principally for a court house which has been built in Knoxville, for bridges, and to encourage railroads. The tax rate for all purposes is $1.40 on the hundred, the 15 cents above the city rate of $1.25 for highways. The roads, however, are not in the best of condition, the turnpikes excepted that enter the city.

The annual expense of the county government is perhaps $75,000; of that $15,000 for the roads; on the whole, like the debt, with a population of some 65,000, a very moderate charge on the taxpayers. Growing crops are not assessed in Tennessee. There is no exemption for the homestead, but farmers are allowed $1,000 of personal property untaxed.

General Index.

A
	PAGE.
Abrams, Harvey, building contractor	47
Aldermen of Knoxville proper	15
Alexander, W. H., contractor for house moving and heavy hauling	107
Architects of the city	44—46
Art, letters, song and drama	29, 30

B
Banks of the city	58, 59
Barber, Geo. F. & Co., architects and publishers the "Cottage Souvenir, No. 2,"	45
Bauman Bros., architects	44
Bayless, King & Cruze, stoves and house furnishings and manufacturers tinware	112
Beech Bros., heating and ventilating apparatus, school furniture, etc.	87, 89
Bell & McCampbell, stables	90
Borches & Co., wholesale grocers	81
Building contractors of Knoxville	46—48
Building materials trade of Knoxville	75

C
Callahan, Geo. W. & Bros., marble and stone contractors	68, 69
Callaway & Brown, shoes, hats, etc.	95
Camp, E. C., capitalist and president the Coal Creek Coal Co	8, 72
Carhart, H. B. & Co., wholesale grocers	79
Carpenter, J. P., coal and brick	72, 73
Carter & Tutt, pavers and roofers	106
Central Guarantee Life Association of Knoxville, Newcomb F. Thompson, president and manager	62
Characteristic trade of Knoxville	65—76
City government	15, 20
Clark Foundry & Machine Co., H. W. Clark	104
Climate and public health	15
Coal Creek Coal Co., E. C. Camp, president	72
Coal supply for manufacturers	70, 101
Cole & Pratt, real estate	33
Comfort & Spilman, attorneys	42
Condon, S. P., proprietor the Knoxville Stock Yards	81, 82
Cooley Bros., building contractors	47
Cooper, W. R., Grand Secretary U. O. Golden Cross	63
Cotton and woolen mills of the city	100
Covenant Building and Loan Association, the	35
Cowan, McClung & Co., wholesale dry goods	20, 91
Crescent Brewing Co., of Aurora, Ind.; Jos. Livsey, Knoxville agent	82
Crozer, W. C., civil and mining engineer	39
Cruze, Buffat & Buckwell, wholesale hardware	85
Crystal Ice Co., the	109, 110
Cullen & Newman, wholesale crockery	95

D
	PAGE.
Dailey, J. M., Jr., grocer	81
Daniel & Bostwick, dry goods	92
Davis Sewing Machine Co., the, J. E. Martin, agent	98, 99
Dawes Bros., insurance	61
Dempster's Machine Shop, James Dempster	104
De Pue, E. H., The Knoxville Steam Laundry	114
Dick, Payne & Co., wholesale grocers	79, 80
Doran, J. K., Manager the National Garment Cutter Co.	113
Dun, R. G. & Co.'s Mercantile Agency, Henry Fenton, Knoxville manager	64

E
Edington, Groner & Flenniken, shoes, hats, etc.	95
Egan's cafe and restaurant	24
Eldridge, T. C., carriage repository	90
East Tennessee Coal Co., the	71
East Tennessee Coal & Iron Co	74
East Tennessee Stone & Marble Co., the	69, 70
East Tennessee Telephone Co., the, A. P. Harrison, Knoxville manager	19
East Tennessee, Virginia & Georgia R. R. System	50
Enterprise Machine Works, D. C. Richards	104
Evans, W. H. & Son, Marble Works, J. E. Willard, Superintendent	68

F
Fair, Day & DeKlyne, foundrymen	104
Fenton, Henry, Knoxville manager R. G. Dun & Co.'s Mercantile Agency	64
Fowler & Fowler, attorneys	43
Fountain Head Railroad, the	21

G
Galyon & Selden Co., the, planing mills and building contractors	46, 47
Gammon & LaRue, grocers	81
Gibson, R. K., merchandise broker	82
Gill, R. Z., architect	46
Godfrey, T. S., marble quarries	66, 67
Grainger, E., coal dealer	75
Gratz, Lewis A., mayor of North Knoxville	19
Graves, S. W., wholesale and retail furniture	99
Greer Machinery Co., the	85

H
Hacker & Co., house and sign painting	107
Harrell's Transfer, G. W. Harrell proprietor	56
Harrell, W. H., agent the Richmond Piano Co	98
Harrison, A. P., manager East Tennessee Telephone Co	19
Hart, H. Victor, flour and iron commission	90
Hazen & Lotspeich, wholesale grocers	79
Heaven, Geo., sheet metal worker	112

INDEX.

	PAGE.
Hensell & Armstrong, stationers and booksellers	96
Hickman & McSpadden, insurance	62
Homestead Investment Co., the	34
Hooker, Littlefield & Steere, manufacturing confectioners	108
Horne, J. F. & Bro., wholesale liquors	82
Hotels of the city	22—25
Hotel Hattie, the, John C. Flanders proprietor	22
Hotel Knox, the, Chas. McNabb proprietor	23
Howe, Alfred G., attorney	43
Huddleston & Smith, boots, shoes, etc.	95
Hughes, J. M., sewing machines	99

I

Ingersoll & Peyton, attorneys	40
Institutions of Knoxville	12
Insurance agents of the city	60—64
Insurance business of Knoxville	59—64
Iron works of Knoxville	102

J

Jellico Coal Mining Co.	74

K

Kaiser Bros., wholesale produce and groceries	80
Kansas City, Fort Scott & Memphis, and Memphis & Birmingham lines	56
Kern, Peter, ex-mayor and wholesale confectioner	108
King, E. P., insurance	60
Knaffl Bros., photographers	114
Knoke, L. P., Knoxville manager The Sun Life Insurance Co. of Louisville	63
Knoxville Belt R. R.	56
Knoxville Brewing Co., the	111
Knoxville Brick Co. (manufacturers), the	106
Knoxville Business College, the, J. T. Johnson, proprietor	28
Knoxville Car Wheel Works and Knoxville Foundry & Machine Co.	103
Knoxville Cigar Co., Levy Bros.	111
Knoxville's coal trade	70—75
Knoxville, Cumberland Gap & Louisville R. R.	55
Knoxville Electric Light & Power Co., the	20
Knoxville Electric Railway Co., the	20
Knoxville's enterprise	3, 4, 11
Knoxville Fire Insurance Co., the	61
Knoxville in finance	58—64
Knoxville Iron Co., the	102
Knoxville's jobbing trade	77, 78
Knoxville's manufactures	100—114
Knoxville "Palace Stables," the, McKinney & Carpenter, proprietors	91
Knoxville Paper Box Factory, C. H. Ogden, proprietor	112
Knoxville Provision & Sugar Co., the	79
Knoxville Southern R. R.	49
Knoxville Steam Laundry, E. H. DePue	114
Knoxville Stock Yards, the, S. P. Condon, proprietor	81, 82
Knoxville Stoneware, Sewer Pipe & Tile Co.	106
Knoxville Supply Co., the, sewer pipe and building material	89
Knoxville, the Trade Center	49
Knoxville Tobacco Co., the	110
Knoxville & Augusta R. R.	49

L

	PAGE.
Lamar House, the, Mrs. Laura Whitehead & Co., proprietors; Arthur Thompson, manager	24
Larew, C. L., printer	111
Lawyers of Knoxville	40—43
Levy Bros., Knoxville Cigar Co	111
Livsey, Jos., agent Crescent Brewing Co. of Aurora, Ind	82
Local insurance companies	61—64
Lockett, W. B. & Co., wholesale grocers	80
Lucky & Sanford, attorneys	42
Lumber Trade of Knoxville	75
Lutz, J. E. & Co., shoes and hats	16, 93

M

Manufacturing Opportunities	101
Marble Dealers of Knoxville	65—70
Marble Trade of Knoxville	65
Marietta & North Georgia Railway, & Knoxville Southern	52
Martin, J. E., agent for the Davis Sewing Machine Co., of Dayton, Ohio	98, 99
Maxwell & Co., dry goods	91
McArthur Music House, the	96, 97
McCampbell, G. S. W., attorney	43
McClung, E. S., commission merchant and proprietor of the Merchants' Transfer	57, 83
McCrary & Branson, photographers and photographers' Supplies	98
McIlwaine, C. R., attorney	43
McKinney & Carpenter, "Knoxville Palace Stables."	91
McMullen & VanDeventer, insurance and real estate	60
McTeers, Payne, Hood & Co., wholesale clothing	94
Mechanics' National Bank	58
Meek, J. M., capitalist and dealer in real estate	37
Meek & Andes, dry goods	93
Merchants' Transfer, the, E. S. McClung, proprietor	57
Mester, Newcomer & Paulus, dry goods	92
Miners and Shippers of Coal established at Knoxville	70—75
Mingo Mountain Coal & Coke Co	71

N

National Garment Cutter Co., the, J. K. Doran, manager	113
National Manufacturing Co., the, patent rights	114
Nelsen, H. O., manufacturer iron fencing	105
Nelson, D. R., attorney	42
Newman, S. B. & Co., printers	112
Newspapers of Knoxville	29
North Knoxville described	18

O

Osborne & Miller, attorneys	43
Ogden Bros. & Co., booksellers and printers	96
Owens, R. W., slate roofer	107

P

Palace Hotel, J. C. Flanders & Son, proprietors	23
Peed, T. J. & Co., harness and saddlery	90
Perry, W. C. & Co., wholesale liquors	82
Phœnix Marble Co., the	69
Places of resort	22
Police and fire service	16
Post, Frank H., manufacturer of wagons	106
Powers, Little & Co., wholesale clothing	94
Public improvements, sewerage, and street work	17

INDEX.

Q
	PAGE.
Queen City Coal Co.	74

R
Railroads of Knoxville............................9, 49, 57
Railroads projected from and to Knoxville............... 56
Real estate agents of the city.....................33—40
Real estate and building improvements at Knoxville.....................................31, 43
Richards, D. C., the Enterprise Machine Works......... 104
Richmond Piano Co., the, W. H. Harrell, agent........... 98
Roberts, P. A., stables................................ 90
Rodgers, Tedford & Co., wholesale drugs............... 84
Rosedale Land & Improvement Co....................... 37
Ross, J. Ed., block marble............................ 66
Ross, John M., dealer in rough Tennessee marbles..... 67
Ross, M. L. & Co., wholesale grocers.................. 78

S
Sanford, Chamberlain & Albers, wholesale drugs........ 83
Savage, W. J., millwright and mill furnisher.......... 105
Saxton & Co., exporters of lumber..................... 76
Saylor & Moore, attorneys............................. 43
Schaad & Rotach, manufacturers fine furniture......... 107
Scharringhaus, E. H., real estate agent, The Home Building & Loan Association, and North Knoxville Lot & Building Co..........................33, 34
Scheitlen & Clark, musical instruments................ 97
Schools of the city................................24—29
Schuermann, L. W., pension agent and insurance man... 63
Scott Bros. & Co., The Trio Mills..................... 109
Shaver, W. H., attorney............................... 43
Shepard, Philo B., Sr., manufacturers' agent for machinery, etc. 86
Shepard & Manning, plumbers' supplies (see also back cover)..86, 87
Sheridan & Quincy, manufacturers wagons............... 106
Shetterly & Tipton, stoves and house furnishings...... 86
Simmonds, W. H. & Co., insurance...................... 60
Simmonds & Henderson, real estate; The West End Land Co., and Riverside Improvement Co........... 38
Situation and surroundings of Knoxville............5—13
Smith, J. R. & Co., manufacturers cigars.............. 111
Sprankle, B. H., real estate.......................... 93
Sprankle, B. H., & Stouffer, clothing, furnishings, etc.. 93
Social conditions................................12, 30
Southern Building & Loan Association.................. 36
Southern Car Works, the............................... 102
Southern Monument Co., the............................ 70
Standard Coal & Coke Co............................... 74
State National Bank................................... 59
Steele & McMillan, real estate and insurance.......... 62
Stephenson-Getaz Manufacturing Co., manufacturers of fine interior finish.............................. 75
Street lights, public conveniences.................... 19
Street railroads...................................19-22
Suburban developmental projects....................... 31
Sullins, C. C. & Co., coal dealers.................... 75
Sun Life Insurance Co. of Louisville, L. F. Knoke, manager.. 63
Swan Bros., bakers and confectioners.................. 109

T
Taxes, revenue, debt.................................. 15
Taylor, Henry H., attorney............................ 42
Tennessee Coal Mining Co.............................. 73
Tennessee Medical College............................. 25
Tennessee Producers' Marble Co........................ 65
Tennessee river boats................................. 56
Thompson, M. E., mayor of Knoxville proper............ 14
Thompson, N. F., manager and president the Central Guarantee Life Association......................... 62
Three Knoxvilles, the................................. 14
Torrance, James R., architect......................... 44
Trio Flour Mills, the, Scott Bros. & Co............... 109

U
United Order of the Golden Cross, the, W. R. Cooper, grand secretary.................................... 63
University of Tennessee............................... 25
University School of Knoxville, the, Baker & Himel, principals... 27

V
Valley of East Tennessee.............................. 5
Van Gilder, R. & Co., wholesale leather, glass, etc... 87

W
Walters, R. Walters' Sons & Co., wholesale clothing... 94
Waring, Chas., surveyor, engineer and abstractor...... 39
Washburn, Templeton, Pickle & Turner, attorneys...... 40
Water supply.. 16
Welcker & Gaut, attorneys............................. 42
West Knoxville described.............................. 18
Wetzell, H. B. & Co., timber and mineral lands........ 38
Willard, J. E., superintendent W. H. Evans & Son's marble works....................................... 68
Wilson, Joe M. & Co., real estate..................... 38
Woodruff, W. W. & Co., wholesale hardware and implements... 84

Y
Young's College of Shorthand, A. E. Broyles, proprietor... 28

INDEX, TENNESSEE TOPICS.

	PAGE.
Appalachians of Tennessee	5, 6
Carriage and furniture woods in East Tennessee	75, 123
Character of the iron ores of East Tennessee	122
Climate of East Tennessee	120
Climate of the State	115
Coals in East Tennessee	121
Coal in Tennessee	5, 121
Copper, zinc, mica and other metallic wealth of the State	5, 123
Cumberland Range	5, 120
Dairying in East Tennessee	121, 124
Description of the State	115—124
Distilling in Tennessee	120
East Tennessee described	5, 120
Farming, mineral and timber lands in Tennessee, and dealers therein	33, 120
Financial condition of the State	118
Fine stock in Tennessee	119
Great Smoky mountains	5
Growth of the State in population, industries and wealth	115—124
History of the State	116
Incidental references	5, 31, 49, 65
Iron manufactures of Tennessee	118
Knox County in brief	124

	PAGE.
Lands near Knoxville	31
Live stock of the State	118
Lumber business of Tennessee	75, 118
Manufactures of the State	118
Marble in East Tennessee	65, 123
Mineral wealth of the State	5, 119
Mountaineers of East Tennessee	6, 120
Navigable waters of the State	115
Poplar in East Tennessee	123
Population of the State	120
Prices for timber lands in East Tennessee	124
Principal cities of the State	120
Productions of the State	115—124
Railroads of the State	120
Relative growth of the State	115—124
Relative size of the State	115—124
Resources of Tennessee	115—124
Scenery, East Tennessee	5, 6, 49
Schools of Tennessee	120
Social conditions of Tennessee	120
Staple crops of the State	118
State institutions	120
Statistical information	115—124
Tax valuations of Tennessee	118
Tennessee banks	120
Tennessee mules	119
Tennessee whiskey	120
Timber of Tennessee	123
Western iron belt of Tennessee	119

www.ingramcontent.com/pod-product-compliance
Lightning Source LLC
Chambersburg PA
CBHW080345170426
43194CB00014B/2691